MW01702580

Bewar

Free Bible Studies
207-616-8708/1565

THE

ANTICHRIST

666

Compiled by:
William Josiah Sutton

Edited by:
Roy Allan Anderson, D.D.

2005 EDITION
© COPYRIGHT 1980
W.F.G. Inc.
WITH SPECIAL ARRANGEMENTS WITH
SIM & SONS' PUBLISHING HOUSE
HENDERSON, NV

ALL RIGHTS RESERVED

PRINTED IN THE UNITED STATES OF AMERICA

BOOKS WRITTEN BY WILLIAM JOSIAH SUTTON:

Vol. I: *Beware It's Coming - The Antichrist 666*
Vol. II: *The New Age Movement and The Illuminati 666*
Vol. III: *The Real Truth About UFOs and The New World Order Connection*
Vol. IV: *Ancient Prophecies About Mysticism, Hollywood, and The Music Industry*
Vol. V: *Ancient Prophecies About The Dragon, The Beast, and The False Prophet*
Vol. VI: *The Great Apostasy of European and American Leaders: In Gog They Trust?*, Book I
Vol. VII: *In Gog They Trust?*, Book II

Contents

List of Illustrations

Acknowledgements

We would like to thank the British Museum, the Brooklyn Museum, the Victoria and Albert Museum, the Oriental Institute, the Religious News Service, and the Louvre, for supplying the photographs that have contributed to the credibility of this book immensely. Also we would like to thank the Macmillan Company, Loizeaux Brothers, Phoebus Publishing Company, BPC Publishing Limited, the Southern Publishing Association, the Pacific Press Publishing Association and the E. G. White Estate, for giving us permission to quote from their publications.

Further Study

1. *The Two Babylons,* by Alexander Hislop, Loizeaux Brothers, Neptune, N.J., 1916, 1943, 1959.
2. *The Golden Bough,* by Sir James George Frazer, The Macmillan Company, 1958.
3. *Adonis Attis Osiris,* by Sir James George Frazer, University Books, Inc., 1961.
4. *The Quest for Sumer,* by Leonard Cottrell, G. P. Putnam Sons, New York, 1965.
5. *Encyclopedia of World Mythology,* by Rex Warner, reproduced by arrangement with Phoebus Publishing Company, BPC Publishing Limited, 1970, 1971, 1975.
6. *Road to Nineveh,* by Norah Benjamin Kubie, Doubleday and Company, Inc., New York, 1964.
7. *Scandinavian Mythology,* by H. R. Ellis Davidson, The Hamlyn Publishing Group, Limited, New York, Sydney, Toronto, 1967, 1968.
8. *The Great Mother,* by Erich Neumann, Princeton University Press, Princeton, N.J., 1955, 1963.
9. *Indian Mythology,* by Veronica Ions, The Hamlyn Publishing Group, Limited, London, New York, Sydney, Toronto, 1969.
10. *Near East Mythology,* by John Gray, The Hamlyn Publishing Group, Limited, London, New York, Sydney, Toronto, 1969.
11. *Ancient Iraq,* by George Roux, The World Publishing Company, New York, 1964.
12. *Standard Dictionary of Fokelore Mythology and Legend,* Vol II, edited by Maria Leach, Funk & Wagnalls Company, New York, 1950.
13. *The Biblical World,* edited by Charles Pfeiffer, Published by Bonanza Book with arrangement of Baker House, 1966.
14. *New Larousse Encyclopedia of Mythology,* Introduced by Robert Graves, Larousse and Company, New York, 1968.
15. *The Masks of God: Occidental Mythology,* by Joseph Campbell, The Viking Press, Inc., New York, 1964-65.
16. Young's *Analytical Concordance to the Bible,* by Robert Young, LL.D, Wm. B. Eerdmans Publishing Company, Grand Rapids, Michigan, 1964, 1969, 1970, 1976.
17. *Mexico Mystique,* by Frank Waters, The Swallow Press, Chicago, Ill., 1975.
18. *The Aztecs,* by Fray Diego Duran, Introduced by Ignacio Bernal, Orion Press, New York, 1964.
19. *Man's Rise to Civilization,* by Peter Farb, E. P. Dutton and Company, New York, 1968.
20. *The World of the Aztecs,* by William H. Prescott, a Pierre Waleffe Book, Minerva, 1974.

21. *The Conquest of Mexico and the Conquest of Peru,* by William H. Prescott, The Modern Library, New York, 1936.
22. *Mexican and Central American Mythology,* by Irene Nicholson, The Hamlyn Group Limited, London, New York, Sydney, Toronto, 1969.
23. *A History of Greece,* by J. B. Bury, The Modern Library, New York, (no date).
24. *History of Rome to A.D. 565,* by Arthur E. R. Beak, William G. Sinnigen, The Macmillan Company, New York, 1965.
25. *The Oxford Dictionary of the Christian Church,* ed. by F. L. Cross, E. A. Livingstone, Oxford University Press, London, 1974.
26. *Vatican Council II,* General Editor Austin Flannery, O. P. Costello Publishing Company, Northport, New York, 1975.
27. *New Catholic Encyclopedia,* New York, McGraw Hill, New York, 1967.
28. *The Catholic Encyclopedia,* by Robert C. Broderick, Thomas Nelson, Inc., Publishers, Nashville, New York, 1975.
29. *The Wine of Roman Babylon,* by Mary E. Walsh, The Southern Publishing Association, Nashville, Tenn.
30. *The Roman Catholic Church,* by John L. McKenzie, S. F. Image Books by special arrangement with Holt, Rinehart and Winston, Inc., 1971.
31. *A New Catechism: Catholic Faith for Adults,* The Seabury Press, New York, N.Y., 1969.
32. *The Great Controversy,* by Ellen G. White, Pacific Press Publishing Association, Mountain View, California.
33. *Fox Book of Martyrs,* by John Fox, ed. by William Farbush, D.D., Holt, Rinehart, and Winston, New York, 1954.
34. *Consumer Beware,* by Beatrice Hunter, Touchstone, New York, 1971.
35. *Sugar Blues,* by William Duffy, Warner, New York, 1975.
36. *Preparation for the Final Crisis,* by Fernando Chaij, Pacific Press Publishing Association, Mountain View, California, 1966.
37. *Christ Among Us,* by Anthony Wilhelm, Paulist Press, New York, 1967, 1973, 1975.
38. *Italy,* by Herbert Kubly, Time, Inc., New York, 1861.
39. *Believers Unity, Organizational or Spiritual,* by Theodore H. Epp, The Good News Broadcasting Association, Inc., 1971.
40. *The Ecumenical Dream – One Big Church,* by Dr. Bruce Dunn, The Grace Worship Hour, Peoria, Illinois.
41. *The Vatican and its Role in World Affairs,* by Charles Pichon, Dutton, 1950.
42. *The World of the Vatican,* by Robert Neville, Harper and Row, New York and Evanston.
43. *Unfolding The Revelation,* by Roy A. Anderson, Pacific Press Publishing Association, 1953, 1961.
44. *The Prophetic Faith of Our Fathers,* by LeRoy Edwin Froom, Vol. II, III, Review and Herald, Washington, D.C., 1948.
45. *Prompta Bibliotheca,* Vol. 6, Art. "Papa" II, by Lucius Ferraris.

46. *The Papacy,* by Wladimir D. Ormesson, Hawthorne Books, Publishers, New York, 1959 Translated.
47. *Encyclopedia Americana,* Vol. 13, American Corps., 1979, p. 115.
48. *The Interpreter's Bible,* Nolan B. Harmon, Editor, Abingdon Press, 1957.
49. *Daniel and Revelation,* by Uriah Smith, Southern Publishing Association.
50. *The People's Almanac,* Bantam Books, 1978.
51. *Mythology of All Races,* Louis H. Gray, Ed., Cooper Square Publishers, 1964, p. 273.
52. *Encyclopedia of Religion and Ethics,* James Hastings, Ed., Vol. 12, Charles Scribner's Sons, N.Y., no date, p. 49.
53. *Encyclopedia Americana,* Vol. 20, American Corporation, 1980, p. 373.
54. *God's Graves and Scholar,* Ceram, Alfred A. Knopf, 1970, p. 306.
55. *Merit Students Encyclopedia,* Macmillan Educational Corporation, N.Y., 1980.

CHAPTER I

The Antichrist and His Mystery of Iniquity

From the time of our first parents, Satan has invented ways to turn man from the true worship of God, to the worship of created things, instead of the Creator. The Spirit of Satan, unlike the Spirit of God, is always at war with the Gospel of Christ, so are Christ's followers at war — "not against flesh and blood, but with principalities, against powers, against the rulers of the darkness of the world, against spiritual wickedness in high places." Ephesians 6:12.

Just as there is a Spirit of Christ in the world, so is there a Spirit of Antichrist. I John 4:3. Just as Christ prepared the world before His first Advent by the symbols in the ceremonial law of the Jews, which pointed to Him, so is the Antichrist preparing the world through human agents with false doctrines. But who is the Antichrist? God in His divine wisdom through prophecy and revelation, has given His servants understanding to know who this Antichrist was, is, and is to come.

The Father of Lies has invented paganism to counterfeit the pure teaching of the Gospel; and hide his falsehood under the cloak of Christianity. As in the True Faith, paganism had a promise of a Messiah; had a form of Baptism, Spiritual Rebirth, Confession of Sins, Communion, and the promise of Immortality. Where do we find this to be true, and where paganism started from? It had to start from the FIRST DESCENDANTS OF NOAH AFTER THE FLOOD, because his was the only family left on the face of the earth.

"AND EVERY LIVING SUBSTANCE WAS DESTROYED WHICH WAS UPON THE FACE OF THE GROUND, BOTH MAN, AND CATTLE, AND THE CREEPING THINGS, AND THE FOWL OF THE HEAVEN; AND THEY WERE DESTROYED FROM THE EARTH: AND NOAH ONLY REMAINED ALIVE, AND THEY THAT WERE WITH HIM IN THE ARK." Genesis 7:23.

Paganism was at its peak, along with the wickedness that came with it before the flood. "AND GOD LOOKED UPON THE EARTH, AND, BEHOLD, IT WAS CORRUPT; FOR ALL FLESH HAD CORRUPTED HIS WAY UPON THE EARTH. AND GOD SAID UNTO NOAH, THE END OF ALL FLESH IS COME BEFORE ME; FOR THE EARTH IS FILLED WITH VIOLENCE THROUGH THEM; AND, BEHOLD, I WILL DESTROY THEM WITH THE EARTH." Genesis 6:12, 13

Data from well-known scholars and recognized authorities on Mythology and Archaeology piece together how indeed it was from Babylon, as the Scriptures reveal, that all Idolatry had its origin and how all the gods of the Assyrians, Egyptians, Hindus, Greeks, Romans, and Mexicans, like the Babylonians, were derived from Astrology.* Thus all these ancient gods were but emanations of the one god, the Sun, the ruler of the zodiac. And, it will be shown later this number of doom, 666, was also derived from Astrology, with Satan as its inventor, and actually the god behind all the gods of paganism.

After the flood Noah's sons begot sons and daughters. The sons of Noah were Shem, Ham, and Japheth (Genesis 10:1). One of Noah's sons, Ham, had a son named Cush and Cush begot Nimrod (Genesis 10:6, 8). Nimrod was a mighty hunter, and was the first king to unite the inhabitants of the world after the Deluge into cities. Under Nimrod's supervision, the tower of Babel, in defiance to God, was built. It was Nimrod, the greatgrandson of Noah who was the original builder of the great cities of the ancient Babylonians and Assyrians (Genesis 10:10-12). The two capitals of Babylonia and Assyria were Babylon and Nineveh. These two cities, along with the other cities the first king of the world built, were believed by many to be just a legend. During the Dark Ages the Bible was kept from the ordinary people and they were taught to believe that only the priests could interpret it. In some places of the world the Bible was burned; and those who had in their possession a copy of the Scriptures, were tried as criminals. Satan, our great adversary, and the inventor of confusion tried to shut out all light from heaven. A flood of pagan superstitions, doctrines, and human theories began to take the place of the Bible. By the late seventeen and eighteen hundreds, many people were led to call the written accounts of the Creation; of Adam and Eve, the Deluge, Nimrod and the tower of Babel, and Abraham of Ur, found in the Bible, a myth.

Robert Fitzroy who was a Captain in the Royal Navy of Great Britain, for many years wanted to prove the literal truth of the Bible. In 1833, Captain Fitzroy embarked upon a voyage around the world to do this very thing. A passenger, on Captain Fitzroy's ship the H.M.S. Beagle, was Charles Darwin. Darwin as well as Fitzroy, at that time believed the written accounts of the book of Genesis could be proved in the natural sciences (God's Creation). However, Charles Darwin's father wanted him to become a minister and did not want Charles to pursue any course in life save being a minister. Charles Darwin, under the influence of his Uncle Josiah Wedgwood (of the china-making dynasty), felt the study of natural science (God's Creation), was an appropriate study for a minis-

---

* *Merit Students Encyclopedia,* Macmillan Educational Corporation, New York, 1980, p. 321.

ter. So the young Charles Darwin was permitted to embark upon Captain Fitzroy's ship, the H.M.S. Beagle, and he went as an unpaid naturalist. On the voyage, Charles Darwin, who in the beginning of the voyage was a defender of the Bible, became one of its chief enemies. Instead of seeking created things to show the literal truths of the Bible, he was led to apply evolutionary principles to geology, and, this evolutionary principle which he was introduced to by reading, (Lyell's Principles of Geology), led him also to believe that Lyell's Principles could be applied to animals.*

Thus this "Theory of Evolution" spread throughout the world as a huge tidal wave carrying on its crest infidelity, threatening to drown out the truths of the Genesis account of God's Creation. However, when the Theory of Evolution appeared to become man's standard of measuring truth about the history of the earth, the Lord who knows the end from the beginning, begot another science that would open the mouth of the earth and swallow the flood of all false sciences that try to disprove the credibility of the Bible. Satan's warfare against the Gospel is foretold in the twelfth chapter of Revelation:

"AND THE SERPENT CAST OUT OF HIS MOUTH WATER AS A FLOOD AFTER THE WOMAN, THAT HE MIGHT CAUSE HER TO BE CARRIED AWAY OF THE FLOOD. AND THE EARTH HELPED THE WOMAN, AND THE EARTH OPENED HER MOUTH, AND SWALLOWED UP THE FLOOD WHICH THE DRAGON CAST OUT OF HIS MOUTH." Revelation 12:15, 16.

While multitudes of people accepted and began to preach the Theory of Evolution, another science began to spring up out of the earth. It is called "ARCHAEOLOGY." In 1811, C. J. Rich made a survey in Babylon and visited two mounds thought to be Nineveh and Nimrud, where he copied inscriptions. In 1843-44, Paul Emile Botta uncovered the palace of Sargon II (WHOSE NAME APPEARS IN THE BOOK OF ISAIAH 20:1.) Botta uncovered a treasure of artifacts and inscriptions that were of great value to begin the science of Archaeology. In 1845-47, Austen Henry Layard, a pioneer British archaeologist, startled the world when he uncovered a mound in Iraq called by Arabs "Nimrud." Shortly after, excavations of the black obelisk of King Shalmaneser III, (WHOSE NAME ALSO APPEARS IN II KINGS 17:3; 18:9), was found. The inscriptions on the obelisk commemorated Shalmaneser's achievements in the first thirty-one years of his reign. In the second row of reliefs on the front of the obelisk is Jehu, the king of Israel kneeling before Shalmaneser. Jehu is pictured with his men carrying tribute, the inscription on the obelisk reads as follows:

---

* See *The People's Almanac,* pp. 411, 412, 1978.

"TRIBUTE OF JEHU, SON OF OMRI. I RECEIVED FROM HIM SILVER, GOLD, A GOLDEN BOWL, A GOLDEN VASE WITH POINTED BOTTOM, GOLDEN TUMBLERS, GOLDEN BUCKETS, TIN, A STAFF FOR A KING."[1]

Shalmaneser used the expression, "Son of Omri," in the sense of "Successor," because Jehu was not the son of Omri, Ahab was. Jehu ended the wicked Omri dynasty when Elijah the prophet, anointed Jehu the king of Israel. (I Kings 19:16).

During the excavations at Nimrud, a multitude of artifacts was uncovered from this mound which traced its ancient name to be Calah.[2] Calah is one of the cities Nimrod built in Genesis 10:11. About twenty-four miles north of Nimrud, Austen Layard uncovered another mound in Iraq called in the Arab tongue, "Kuyunjik." After excavating the mound, a palace was discovered. When earth and rubble were removed from the hallway of the palace, hundreds of small figures were found sculptured on the walls in realistic detail. Places were identified by the landscape, and people by their national costumes. On another part of the hallway was found a king supervising a block of stone on which a human-headed bull had been roughly chiseled, and it was being dragged to the foot of the palace. Above the head of the king was a short inscription in the wall. It reads as follows; "Sennacherib, king of Assyria, the great figures of bulls, which in the land of Bendad, were made for his royal palace at Nineveh, he transported thither."[3]

NINEVEH HAS BEEN FOUND WHICH NIMROD ALSO BUILT. (Genesis 10:11). — Two years later after the grand entrance to the palace had been uncovered, some long inscriptions were found. The inscriptions described the sixth-year reign of the Assyrian King Sennacherib. In these were Sennacherib's seige against Jerusalem. The events described in the inscriptions agreed with the events that took place in the fourteenth year of King Hezekiah, written in II Kings, the 18th chapter. The amount of silver Hezekiah paid in tribute to Sennacherib differs in Sennacherib's own inscriptions,[4] but the thirty talents of gold paid to the Assyrian king is the same as the Bible states in II Kings 18:13, 14:

"Now in the fourteenth year of Hezekiah did Sennacherib king of Assyria come up against all the fenced cities of Judah, and took them. And Hezekiah king of Judah sent to the king of Assyria to Lachish, saying, I have offended: return from me: that which thou puttest on me

---

[1] See *The Biblical World,* by Charles F. Pfeiffer, pp. 78, 79, 150, 339, 340.
[2] See *The Biblical World,* edited by Charles F. Pfeiffer, pp. 156, 157.
[3] See *Road to Nineveh,* by Nora Benjamin Kubie, pp. 242, 243.
[4] See *The Biblical World,* edited by Charles F. Pfeiffer, pp. 516, 517.

One of the Royal Standards of Ur found by Sir Leonard Woolley. Ur was believed by Bible critics to be just a mythical city for centuries. However, the Bible critics were hushed when in 1854, J. E. Taylor, who was employed by the British Museum to investigate some southern sites of Mesopotamia, unearthed some inscriptions from a mound. The inscriptions were deciphered, and among the inscriptions was the name of the mound, "UR." This was the homeland of Abraham (Genesis 15:7). Later Woolley for 12 years excavated the district and uncovered treasures and artifacts and knowledge about the people who lived there. His findings are compared to those of the Egyptians. Courtesy of the British Museum.

This is the prism found at Nineveh describing Sennacherib's campaign against Judah in 701 B.C. Sennacherib was the son of King Sargon II of Assyria. Sargon II died in 705 B.C., and Sennacherib took the throne. Courtesy of the British Museum.

will I bear. And the king of Assyria appointed unto Hezekiah king of Judah three hundred talents of silver and thirty talents of gold."

Eventually two palaces were uncovered at Kuyunjik that proved that Kuyunjik was indeed Nineveh, Nimrod's ancient capital of the Assyrians, that Bible Critics said for centuries was just a myth. The two palaces uncovered at Nineveh were of King Sennacherib and King Ashurbanipal. At Nineveh, Austen H. Layard and Hormuzd Rassam, uncovered over twenty-five thousand clay tablets in 1854 and 1855. They are known as the "Kuyunjik Collection," and they became the foundation of the science of Assyriology.

There were tablets of several kinds. One tablet was found that was sort of a dictionary of cuneiform symbols which were a key to understanding the rest of the tablets. Some of the tablets were deciphered to be an archive of Nineveh's history, royal decrees, temple offerings, lists of gods, medical practices, prescriptions for several hundred drugs, names of plants, chemical data, instructions for making glass and ceramic glazes, a catalogue of the stars (astrology), and an accurate track of time and dated events, in their history, from a fixed point.[5]

After a careful study of the tablets found by Layard and his successor, Hormuzd Rassam, Austen H. Layard said it was Ninus who appears to be the first god of Nineveh, and according to Layard, Nineveh's builder.* Now according to the pagan scribes and historians who wrote of the worship of this god-man of Nineveh, it is stated he had a wife named Semiramis. However, like as in Christianity, there is much disagreement found among archaeologists. Some archaeologists take the opinion of Sir H. Rawlinson who deciphered a text that said Sammu-ramat (Semiramis) existed during the time of Adad-Nirari III,** (9th century B.C.) and that she was believed to be the only Semiramis. However, Austen H. Layard, who found Nineveh, disagreed with Rawlinson, so do we. Although archaeology has not yet produced another Semiramis to this date, the proof that there was indeed another Semiramis from the post-flood era can be found in the ancient writings of classical literature. The ancients say she was alive at the time of the birth of Abraham, who was born 1996 B.C., according to Hebrew chronology.[6] This places her about fourteen generations before the birth of King David. From here we will let the reader form his own conclusions.

While searching the ruins at Nimrud, Austen H. Layard also uncovered a gigantic man-bull that symbolized the god-man Ninus, the first mortal to be deified. Many of these man-bull gods were discovered later in other parts of the old world, and it also has been traced that Ninus was

[5] See *Road To Nineveh,* by Norah B. Kubie.

[6] See *The Two Babylons,* by Alexander Hislop, pp. 5, 6, 22, 23.

* *Encyclopedia Americana,* Vol. 20, American Corporation, 1980, p. 373.

** *God's Graves and Scholar,* Ceram, Alfred A. Knopf, 1970, p. 306.

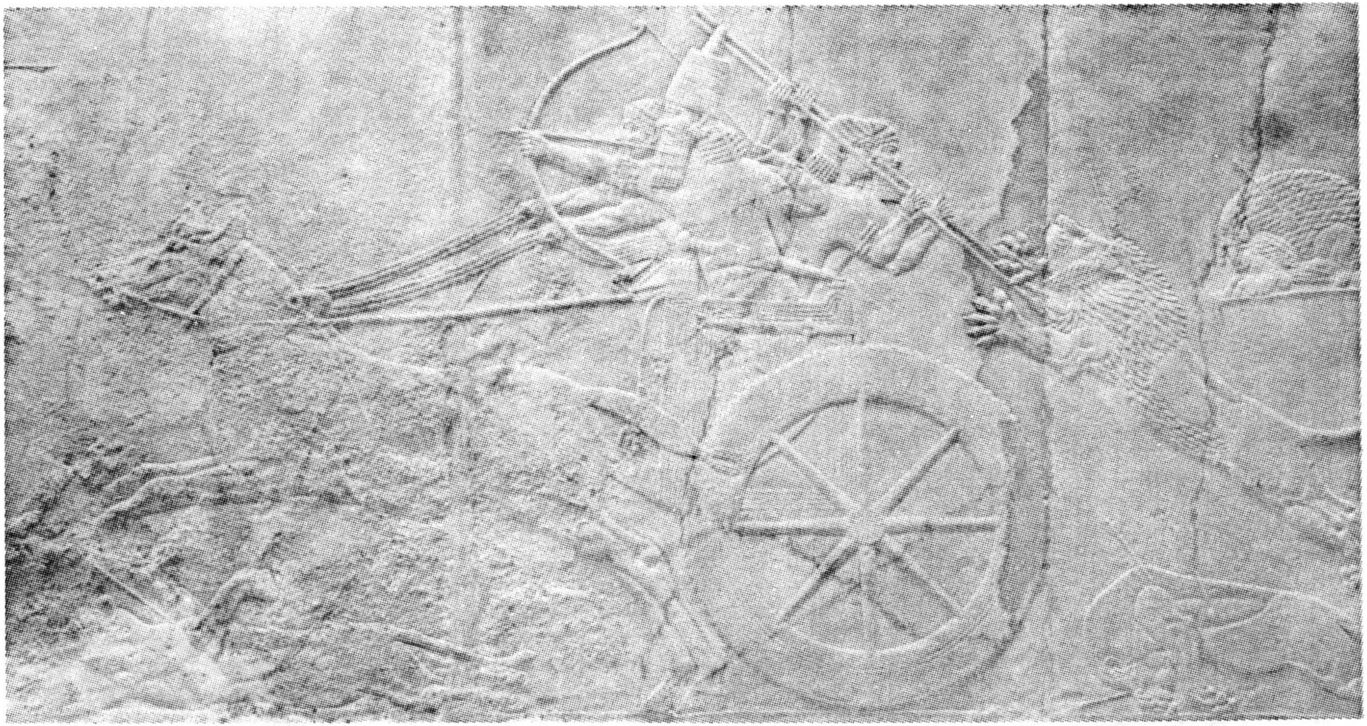

This is a relief of Ashurbanipal during a lion hunt. The Assyrian king was both scholar and soldier. Ashurbanipal created a large library by gathering and copying texts from royal archives and religious centers. In 1852-53, Hormuzd Rassam, one of the successors of Sir Henry Layard, excavator of Nineveh, came upon the remains of Ashurbanipal's library in the ruins of his royal palace and in the temple of Nabu, at Nineveh. Courtesy of the British Museum.

the legendary hero Hercules and also Gilgamesh, the ancient hero King of Uruk who built the ancient city. However, "Uruk," is the name the Arabs called the city of "GILGAMESH," however, a small tablet found there by William Loftus, was deciphered to be "ERECH," the second city Nimrod built after the flood.[7]

"AND THE BEGINNING OF HIS KINGDOM WAS BABEL, AND ERECH, AND ACCAD, AND CALNEH, IN THE LAND OF SHINAR." Genesis 10:10.

Alexander Hislop, a Bible scholar, spent painstaking years compiling data from inscriptions found by Layard, and a library full of the works from a multitude of ancient pagan scribes, and scholars of Mythology. Like a jigsaw puzzle, Hislop gathered pieces of historical data and placed the material in their proper time slots. History says Ninus the first King of Nineveh, was Nimrod, the greatgrandson of Noah. The name "NINEVEH" means "THE HABITATION OF NINUS."[8] And the Scriptures say it was Nimrod who built Nineveh (Genesis 10:11). Ninus (Nimrod) the first King of Nineveh WAS THE FIRST MORTAL TO BE DEIFIED AT HIS DEATH, AND WAS THE ACTUAL FATHER OF THE GODS.* This pagan belief of kings being deified at their death was adopted from Mesopotamia to Egypt, to the North and South Americas. One such god who has been traced to Nimrod, the original deified god, was the pagan ill-omened black god of the Anglo-Saxons. His name was "ZERNEBOGUS." This man-headed bull god name is almost pure Chaldee, and his name means: "THE SEED OF THE PROPHET CUSH."[9] In the Bible, it says: "CUSH BEGOT NIMROD." Genesis 10:8. Hence, the beginning of the part-man and part-animal symbols of gods, that have guarded the places of kings and pharaohs all over the world. The Assyrian Hercules, who has been traced to Nimrod also, "BEGAN TO BE A MIGHTY ONE IN THE EARTH," Genesis 10:8, without club, spear, or weapons of any kind, attacked a bull. Having overcome it, he sets the bulls horns on his head as a trophy of victory and a symbol of power.[10] The Vikings, the Anglo-Saxons, the Africans, and even the American Indians wore horned headdresses to display their might and power. The bull or calf became a symbol of divinity as in Exodus 32:1-28.

Three thousand Israelites lost their lives because while they were professing to be the Lord's people they demanded Aaron to make them a

---

[7] See *The Quest for Sumer*, by Leonard Cottrell, pp. 47-56.
[8] See *The Two Babylons*, by Alexander Hislop, pp. 23, 25.
* *Ibid.*, p. 32.
[9] See *The Two Babylons*, by Alexander Hislop, p. 34.
[10] *Ibid.*, p. 34.

This is a Cuneiform Tablet that describes a portion of the Gilgamesh Epic, which contains a flood account with remarkable parallels to the account in Genesis. Courtesy of the British Museum.

Gilgamesh, the giant mythical hero who built the walls of Erech (Uruk). Gilgamesh's name appears at many sites throughout the "Land of Nimrod" (Mesopotamia). It is believed by many, that Gilgamesh was just another of the multitude of names for Nimrod. It was Nimrod according to Genesis 10:10, who built Erech. Courtesy of the Louvre.

This photo shows the entire victory stele of Naram-Sin. Notice how he is pictured as a giant. Courtesy of the Louvre.

Naram-Sin, the grandson of Sargon of Akkad (Accad). The City of Accad has not been discovered as of this date. It is the third city Nimrod built in Genesis 10:10. In the legend of Nimrod, Nimrod killed a bull without any weapons and placed the horns of the bull on his head as a symbol of his strength. Notice the horned headdress of Naram-Sin; a version of this traditional headdress was worn by the Vikings, Africans and ancient American Indians. Courtesy of the Louvre.

One of the many part-man, part-bull symbols of gods uncovered from Mesopotamia. This one was found by Layard at Nimroud (Calah), one of the cities Nimrod, the greatgrandson of Noah, built (Genesis 10:11). Courtesy of the British Museum.

The Winged Bull found at Khorsabad. Courtesy of the Oriental Institute.

The Winged Bulls discovered at the Gate of Xerxes in Persepolis (Iran). Courtesy of the Oriental Institute.

golden calf, which was the Egyptian symbol of the god-king Pharaoh Osiris.[11]

Throughout the Holy Scriptures, the Bible reveals there are two Spirits in the world in which we live. One is working for our good, and the other is working for our destruction. There is a Spirit of Christ (Philippians 1:19), and a Spirit of Antichrist (I John 4:1-4). There is a Mystery of Godliness (I Timothy 3:16) and a Mystery of Iniquity (II Thessalonians 2:7). The purpose of this book is to expose to the reader both systems; and to prove to the Jew first, that Jesus of Nazareth, was, is, and is to come The Mighty God, The Everlasting Father, The Prince of Peace. Isaiah 9:6.

Just as the Lord had ancient Patriarchs before the written word was given proclaiming the Gospel verbally to the first inhabitants of the world after the flood; so did Satan have his Patriarchs spreading his gospel of the Mystery of Iniquity. It started at Babel, on this side of the flood, and Nimrod the greatgrandson of Noah, was used by Satan to promote it. Revelation the twelfth chapter traces the history of the Mystery of Godliness from Christ's war with Satan in Heaven, to his Second Coming. The symbol used as His church is a pure woman. Jeremiah 6:2. "I have likened the daughter of Zion to a comely and delicate woman." This can be seen also in Isaiah 62:5, II Corinthians 11:2, and Revelation 19:7, 8.

Just as God used a pure woman to symbolize His chosen people and His movement in the world, so does the "HARLOT OF REVELATION" in the seventeenth chapter, represent Satan's huge system of false worship, and his movement in the world. She is the Mother of all pagan religions of the world. That is why in divine language she is called:

"MYSTERY, BABYLON THE GREAT, THE MOTHER OF HARLOTS AND ABOMINATIONS OF THE EARTH." Revelation 17:5.

History records the greatest influence to man outside the Bible, was Sun worship. In the Bible, Sun worship is called Baalim, and to the Israelites the Sun God was simply called Baal. I Kings 16:31. The term Baal is the highest name the pagan gave his god. It meant Lord or Master. The pagan Babylonians and other ancient nations usually traced the origin of their nation to their chief deity. Not always, but in most cases the sun was the main deity of the Old and New World. He was usually regarded as the ancestor god of the Royal family and his worship

[11] See *The Masks of God: Occidental Mythology,* by Joseph Campbell, p. 59.

was imposed on conquered nations. Their earthly kings pretended to be the true incarnate of their Baal, and to identify with Baal, the kings, to show their earthly authority bestowed upon themselves, claimed their god's name; as "Ethbaal," who was Jezebel's father, king of the Zidonians. I Kings 16:31.

Ethbaal means: "with Baal or Baal's man." Pagans also named their towns and cities after Baal as in Numbers 32:38. Baalmelon — which means: "Lord of the Habitation;" and Baalhamon — which means: "Lord of the Multitude." Song of Solomon 8:11.

The Canaanite kings often used the name "Adonis" before their names. Adonis was simply the divine word "ADON," which means: "LORD." A Canaanite king in Jerusalem in Joshua's day was called "Adoni-zedec," which means: "Lord of Justice." Joshua 10:1. As Baal or Belus was the name of the great male divinity of Babylon; so the female divinity was called Beltis or Baalath.[12] In Joshua 19:8 she is called "BAALATHBEER," which means: "Lady of the Well." Baalath's son was "Baalberith," which means: "LORD OF THE COVENANT," and the Israelites worshipped him in their apostasy. Judges 8:33. Baalzebub or Beelzebub, means: "Lord of the Fly." This is the chief Oriental name for Satan. It also means: "The Restless One." Just as a fly is never stable and has no resting place and travels to and fro in the earth, so has Satan. "And the Lord said unto Satan, Whence cometh thou? Then Satan answered the Lord, and said from going to and fro in the earth, and from walking up and down in it." Job 1:7.

In Isaiah 14:4-26, Satan's first seat after the flood was in Babylon. As Satan moves from place to place finding no rest: his system of pagan worship has moved from place to place. In Ezekiel 28:1-19, Satan moved to Tyrus; in Revelation 2:13, Satan's seat was in Pergamos. In these last days, if you hunger after truth and righteousness, you shall see where Satan's seat is today.

The King-Priest of Sun worship had a clergy. They were responsible for performing the duties of the temple services. Women, who were virgins, were employed, and were bound by oath to single life. Traces of this pagan priestess order are found in history and archaeological findings from all over the world. In Alexander Hislop's *The Two Babylons*, we read the following on page 223:

"In Scandinavia, the Priestesses of Freya, who were generally king's daughters, whose duty it was to watch the sacred fire, and who were bound to perpetual virginity, were just an order of Nuns. In Athens there were virgins maintained at the public expense, who were strictly bound

---

[12] See *The Two Babylons*, by Alexander Hislop, p. 264.

to single life. In pagan Rome, the Vestal virgins, who had the same duty to perform as the priestesses of Freya, occupied a similar position. Even in Peru, during the reign of the Incas, the same system prevailed, and showed so remarkable an analogy, as to indicate that the Vestal of Rome, the Nuns of the Papacy, and the holy virgins of Peru, must have sprung from a common origin." (by permission, Loizeaux Brothers, Neptune, N.J.)

The ancient temple virgins had to enroll in a school for women that taught the duties of the pagan religious rites, as well as their duties. In Hislop's *The Two Babylons,* he shows the reader what happens to a virgin if she breaks her vow:

"The moment they enter the establishment they were cut off from all communication with the world, even with their own family and friends. . . . Woe to the unhappy maiden who was detected in an intrigue! By the stern law of the Incas she was to be buried alive. This was precisely the fate of the Roman Vestal who was proved to have violated her "vow." *The Two Babylons,* by Alexander Hislop, pp. 223, 224. (by permission Loizeaux Brothers, Neptune, N.J.)

Men were set to watch over them that they might not lose their consecrated virginity to the Sun god and his king. They were called eunuchs. Eunuchs often held important positions in the king's court. In order to keep the eunuch from touching the virgins, they were castrated, and promised a better hereafter.

When drought and famine came, some pagans believed this was due to disobedience to the fertility god or goddess. In order to appease the wrath of the god or goddess, human sacrifices were offered to the gods. Some pagans believed their gods were nourished by the blood of human beings, and a daily hunt for victims was not uncommon.[13] Because of the many different languages throughout the world, the chief sky god had many names and many variations to his worship. Nimrod, to the Zidonians and to the Israelites, was Baal. In Moab their chief deity was Chemosh, in Ammon it was Moloch. I Kings 11:5-7. Even Solomon worshipped a form of this pagan deity. If you read the Old Testament, you find that this is why God destroyed the Israelites down through the centuries and left only a remnant of them.

In Sun worship, two very important festivals were observed by most pagans throughout the world. They were held two times in the year when the sun is at its greatest distance from the celestial equator. To the Astronomers, these two days are known as the Winter and Summer solstice. But to the pagan Sun worshiper, the shortest day of the year was

---

[13] See *The Earth Mother,* by Erich Neumann, pp. 71, 72.

the day the sun god was reborn, and the Nativity of the Sun fell on December 25th. According to legend, the Sun after its birth on December 25th, began to mature and his light and heat would grow until the sun god would reach full maturity at mid-summer. The ignorant pagans believed they played an important part in the growth of the Sun, and in the winter solstice, fires were kindled to help the sun's expiring light. The logs used in the fires to help the sun regenerate its light and heat were called Yule logs.

Fires were also lighted during the mid-summer solstice, when the sun's annual declension began. This festival was held on June 24th, and it was called the Mid-Summer Festival. Children were employed to go through the streets begging for contributions for lighting the fires for this joyous event. Huge piles of combustible substances were placed all over the countryside. And to honor the dead, seats were placed for them close to the piles. The pagans believed the spirits of the dead would come and listen to their native songs, and recall the days of their youth. At a given moment around sundown, all the fires were kindled at once. Like huge bonfires, these fires were seen all over by the inhabitants of the surrounding area. After the fires burned for several hours, then came the purification ritual. To be forgiven for the past sins committed against the chief deity, everyone present had to pass through the fire. Infants were thrown across the sparkling embers, while older children, men and women, either walked through or leaped over the still hot ashes.[1]

In the Babylonian and Assyrian legend, Nimrod died in his prime leaving a queen named Semiramis. At his death, Nimrod according to legend, became immortal, and his spirit flew up to the sun and took possession of it. Hence, he became Beel-saman, "Lord of Heaven."

After Nimrod had died and became the Sun God, Semiramis his queen became pregnant, she claimed to be a virgin, and after Nimrod's death, according to legend, begot a child by Nimrod's spirit coming down on her from the sun. She proclaimed to her subjects that her husband's spirit entered into her womb through a sunbeam and begot the legendary god-child Tammuz (Ezekiel 8:14), he was born December 25th.[2]

Tammuz has been traced to be the origin of other pagan heroes such as, Adonis, Osiris, Attis, Hercules, Krishna and the ancient incarnate Sun god Quetzalcoatl of Mexico. His Mayan name was Kukulcan.

Genesis 11:1-9, states the account given of the first Ziggurat (tower) built by Nimrod's supervision in defiance to God. Pyramidal towers to the sun have been uncovered from many parts of the Old World, and also in the Americas. The temple to the sun in Teotihuacan, Mexico, is one of

---

[1] See *The Golden Bough*, by Sir James G. Frazer, pp. 745-47.

[2] See *The Two Babylons*, by Alexander Hislop, p. 115, 305.

A seal showing Ishtar (right), the mother of gods, and Tammuz, the god of vegetation. Notice the bow and arrows. Tammuz, like his father, Nimrod, was a mighty hunter. Courtesy of the British Museum.

the largest structures in the world. We will investigate the religion, and the amazing history of the origin of the American Indians later.

Genesis 11:7, 8 also states that because the inhabitants of Nimrod's first city built this tower and became united against God, the Lord confused their language and scattered them ALL OVER the Earth. Archaeological findings have proved early man indeed came from the Babylonian and Northern Assyrian areas.

To the first inhabitants of the world after the flood, Nimrod (Ninus), the first King of Babel, his queen Semiramis, and their miraculously born god-child Tammuz, (the son of the sun) was the first pagan Trinity. A multitude of various names have covered their true identity, but the discoveries of the ancient ruins of Babylon, Assyria, Egypt, Mexico, etc., have enabled scholars to trace their worship from Babylon and Assyria, to the Hindus; and across the ocean to the early American Indians. Their pattern of worship is usually the same, only the names are different because of the various languages in the world.

Comparing Bible doctrine with pagan mythology, scholars, both Christian and non-Christian, will agree that some of the most cherished traditions and ordinances kept by both Catholic and Protestant churches, have their origin from Sun worship, and not from the Old and New Testaments.

SUNDAY SACREDNESS, CHRISTMAS, THE CHRISTMAS TREE, EASTER, THE EASTER EGG, AND BUNNY, HOT CROSS BUNS AND GOOD FRIDAY, are not Holy days and ordinances to be kept sacred from the Bible; but were sacred to the ancient Babylonian gods: NIMROD (BAAL) I Kings 16:30-33, SEMIRAMIS (ASHTAROTH) Judges 2:13 AND TAMMUZ (ADONIS) Ezekiel 8:14.

This mixture of Sun worship and the true worship of God brought judgments from God on the Israelites during their apostasy. We will also study this later. These festivals to the heathen Trinity were observed centuries before the birth of Jesus in Babylon, Persia, Egypt, Greece, Rome, Scandinavia, and other remote areas of the world.

When the Lord brought Israel out of the land of heathenism He said: "AND THE LORD SPAKE UNTO MOSES, SAYING, SPEAK UNTO THE CHILDREN OF ISRAEL, AND SAY UNTO THEM, I AM THE LORD YOUR GOD. AFTER THE DOINGS OF THE LAND OF EGYPT, WHEREIN YE DWELT, SHALL YE NOT DO: AND AFTER THE DOINGS OF THE LAND OF CANAAN, WHITHER I BRING YOU, SHALL YE NOT DO: NEITHER SHALL YE WALK IN THEIR ORDINANCES." Leviticus 18:1-3.

Now, heathen philosophy says when Semiramis died, her spirit, like her husband's Ninus' (Nimrod), became immortal and flew up to the moon and took possession of it. She became the Moon Goddess, The Mother of gods, The Queen of Heaven. When her god-child Tammuz died, the pagans claimed his spirit became immortal and took possession of the East Star (Venus), that appears together with the sun and moon in the spring. This was also known as the New Year Festival. The reason they called it the New Year Festival was because in ancient times pagans began their New Year in the spring, not in January. As Baal, the Lord of Heaven had his visible home, The Sun, so did Semiramis as the Queen of heaven have her visible home, The Moon.[3] Tammuz, like his parents, took possession of the brightest lights in the sky, (Venus), the East Star. This Vegetation God was known as the bright and morning star. One of the multitude of names given to the Vegetation God was Athtar. In *Near Eastern Mythology,* by John Gray, p. 22, we read the following:

"Ishtar the war goddess name is also identified with this east star, the most significant star in the near east, called by the Arabs in Palestine An-najim, "The Star." It was the home of the god of Vegetation of the Semitic people who was known as Athtar."

During the month of Abib was the Jewish Passover Festival. This was held in the spring also. The Jews were commanded by the Lord to eat the

[3] See *The Two Babylons,* by Alexander Hislop, p. 309.

passover lamb. Exodus 12:1-51, Leviticus 23:5. However, just as the Jews celebrated the passover so did the pagans around them have their New Year Festival. It was and is known today as Holy Week, the time of the resurrection of the dead Vegetation God, who died in the autumn and came back to life in the spring. Just as the Jews had their sacrifical lamb and were commanded to eat it, so did the Cahna-Bal have his sacrifice. Cahna-Bal was a priest of Baal. The priests of Baal sacrificed humans, most of whom were little children. They sat these little ones on altars of brick or wood, and set them on fire as a burnt offering to Baal. Then, as the Israelites were commanded to eat the passover lamb, so did Cahna-Bal, the priest of Baal eat his sacrifice. Cahna-Bal is where we get our word cannibal — one who eats human flesh.[4]

Satan invented these cruel gods and its cruel clergy, to guide those who worshipped them to destroy themselves. Everything from cannibalism, sacred prostitution, rape, incest, homosexuality, murder, lying, stealing, self-emasculation, and suicide, did these gods in their myths commit; therefore, those who worshipped them were led to follow in their footsteps. Here is who accepted the heathen sacrifices:

"THEY JOINED THEMSELVES ALSO UNTO BAALPEOR, AND ATE THE SACRIFICES OF THE DEAD. YEA, THEY SACRIFICED THEIR SONS AND DAUGHTERS UNTO DEVILS." Psalm 106:28, 37.

In the legend of the Tauric Goddess Diana, it is said that every stranger who landed on her shore, was sacrificed on her altar.[5] Have you ever wondered what the Christmas Tree has to do with the Birth of Christ? Or the ornaments you place on the tree, or the meaning of the word "YULETIDE"? Or where the tradition of mistletoe came from and how it became a symbol of Christmas? Reader, they have nothing whatsoever to do with the birth of Jesus, but are some of the traditions observed to honor the birth of pagan god-child TAMMUZ. There is not one single Scriptural evidence that supports the Birth of Christ as being December 25th; but history says December 25th was kept thousands of years before the birth of Jesus, in honor of the pagan Messiah. Another name for Tammuz, the pagan god-child was "Baal-bereth," which means: "Lord of the Fir-Tree."

The Sun God, the Mother goddess, and their son, according to Babylonian mythology were mystically changed into trees. This is the origin of burning the Yule log. Nimrod deified as the Sun god was symbolized by a big fir tree stripped of all its branches and cut almost to

---

[4] See *The Two Babylons,* by Alexander Hislop, p. 232.
[5] See *The Golden Bough,* by Sir James G. Frazer, p. 3.

Nimrod was killed in his prime of life and Nimrod's myth was that his death was to be avenged by the incarnation of his son Tammuz, who was born at the winter solstice (December 25th). Nimrod the great god of the Babylonians and Assyrians and his son Tammuz were symbolized in the form of trees. Nimrod, cut off in the midst of his power and glory, "was symbolised as a huge tree, stripped of all its branches, and cut down almost to the ground, but the great serpent, the symbol of the life restoring Aesculapius, twists itself around the dead stock (as shown above), and lo, at its side, up sprouts a young tree — a tree of an entirely different kind, that is destined never to be cut down by hostile power." This was a palm tree and it became the symbol of Tammuz, the pagan messiah, because it was a symbol of victory. This could explain the custom of the heathen of hanging their enemies' heads from their sacred trees. For it not only showed a sign of victory, but also to avenge both Nimrod and Tammuz, for Tammuz, in his myth, like his father, was killed in his prime of life. See *The Two Babylons,* by Alexander Hislop, p. 98. Courtesy of Loizeaux Brothers, Neptune, N.J.

the ground. But the great serpent which symbolized the life restorer, whose name is Aesculapius, twists itself around the dead stock and lo, at its side sprouts a young tree — a tree of an entirely different kind, which is destined never to be cut down by hostile power; even the palm tree, the well known symbol of victory.[6] People of Aryan stock who believed that the oak tree was a symbol of Zeus or Jupiter; believed that this Branch was of Mistletoe which grew on the oak tree, and to be kissed under the mistletoe would insure fertility. The Branch was a name given to the Christ in Isaiah 11:1 — "AND THERE SHALL COME FORTH A ROD OUT OF THE STEM OF JESSE, AND A BRANCH SHALL GROW OUT OF HIS ROOTS."

Now take the word "Yuletide." The word yule is as Babylonian as Tammuz. The word yule is the Chaldee word for infant or little child, and the 25th of December was called by the pagan Anglo-Saxons,

[6] See *The Two Babylons,* by Alexander Hislop, p. 98.

"Yule-day" or Child's Day. The pagan Egyptians, and the Persians both observed the 25th of December as the birthday of their god.[7]

In Germanic Mythology, they too, had a supreme god to whom they gave sacrifice. These war-like people promised their god, whose name was TIWAZ, that if he would give them victory over their enemy, they would give to their god all the spoils of the battle. Like the Babylonians, they believed their gods could transform themselves into trees. If their god answered their prayers, they took their dead victims along with their spoils of war, and dragged them to their sacred grove, and there hung them on their sacred trees. Such offerings have been recovered from bogs in Germany.[8] This begot the origin of hanging ornaments from the Christmas Tree.

Little sheep of the Lord's pasture, it is impossible to ignore the pagan Festival of Christmas. The World is commemorating the Birth of Christ, not Tammuz. There is an advantage during the Christmas season to preach the real Jesus of the Bible. However, we should keep ourselves from the vanities of the pagan Festival, not to mention the cost, and the deaths caused by lighted Christmas Trees.

There is, however, an opportunity during the Christmas Season, with its beautiful music, to make others aware that Christ is no longer a helpless babe in a manger, but is the Saviour of the world, the King of Kings, Lord of Lords. Many who think the Bible and its message is foolishness can be reached during the Christmas Season where it would be almost impossible to talk to them at another time. Even the Christmas Tree can be used to teach the children a great lesson. The children should be taught that it is a historical fact that placing bulbs, tinsel, and lights on a Christmas tree is pure pagan heathenism.

This pagan custom got its start from killing enemies and hanging their heads and their spoils from pagan sacred trees. It would not be a sin if an evergreen tree was set up in a church during the Christmas Season if it was done to be an object lesson. If the parents would take the money they spend each year on Christmas trees, bulbs, lights, and expensive presents, and give the money as an offering to advance the preaching of the gospel, would not the Lord be pleased with such a self-sacrifice?

Rex Warner, a noted authority about ancient mythology, wrote many interesting facts about the Mother Goddess, her son, and how their worship spread through the Old World. Here from, *Encyclopedia of World Mythology,* we read the following:

---

[7] See *The Two Babylons,* by Alexander Hislop, pp. 97, 98.
[8] See *Encyclopedia of World Mythology,* by Rex Warner, pp. 73, 98.

"However, the most authoritative evidence concerning the worship of the mother goddess comes from the Mediterranean area, from Iran in the east to Rome in the west, and covering Mesopotamia, Egypt and Greece. Indeed, in this area, the names and functions of the great goddesses were so interchangeable as to make comparative study a highly complex undertaking. The primary identification of the goddess with the fruitful earth is unquestionable, but starting from Mesopotamia there is an involved pattern, in which celestial elements combine with those of the underworld in such a way as to suggest that the Great Mother may be a composite figure, as complex as the human mind.

"The Semitic names for the greatest mother goddess were Inanna in Sumeria, Ishtar in Babylon, and Astarte or Anat among the Canaanites. Commonly identified with the planet Venus, her most typical title is 'Queen of Heaven,' though she is also known as Mistress of the gods and the lady of the world. In time, she gathered to herself the attributes of a host of other goddesses so that in Mesopotamia the word Ishtar came to mean simply goddess. She was believed to be the giver of vegetation; a hymn contains these words:

"In the heavens I take my place and send the rain, in the earth I take my place and cause green to spring forth." She was the creator of the animals, and the goddess of sexual love, marriage, and maternity. In another hymn it was said: "I turn the male to the female. I turn the female to the male; I am she who adorneth the female for the male."

"Her worship was frequently connected with the practice of sacred prostitution. Two other characteristics of the Semitic mother goddess are worth mentioning in this context. The first, concerned her connection with the male figure who could be described as son, brother or husband. The best known of these figures was Tammuz (Sumerian Dumu-zi), a god of vegetation and in particular of the growing corn. Every year a festival was held at which his death and resurrection was celebrated.

"The vegetation god was believed to die and rise again annually, and in the myths of the descent of the mother goddess into the land of the dead there is a dramatic image of the search of the mother for her lost son and lover, the search of the earth for the temporarily lost fertility which the new spring restores. A Sumerian version of this myth, Inanna Descent to the Nether World, is one of the earliest examples.

"Inanna descends, perhaps in order to free Dumu-zi; she approaches the subterranean temple of Ereshkigal, the god-of-the-dead, through seven gates, at each one of which she has to remove part of her clothing, until she finally stands before him naked. An interesting feature of this myth is that on her return, she brings with her all manner of evil and malevolent beings: They who preceded her, they who preceded Inanna,

Alabaster bas-relief — Ashurbanipal and his wife resting under the vine. This is the King of Nineveh whose royal palace was first excavated by Austen H. Layard, and his assistant and successor Hormudz Rassam. Notice to your far left, an enemy's head hanging from the tree. This is believed to be the origin of hanging bulbs and ornaments from the Christmas tree. Nineveh, 7th century B.C., Courtesy of the British Museum.

were beings who knew not food, who knew not water, who eat not sprinkled flour, who drink not libated wine, who take away the wife from the loins of man, who take away the child from the breast of the nursing mother. Similar myths were current all over the Semitic world, for instance in Canaan, where the mother attacks and conquers Mot (death) in order to free the fertility god Baal.

"The cult of the mother goddess moved westward, perhaps through Cyprus and Crete, into Anatolia and Greece. Significantly, the most popular image of Venus, the Greek Aphrodite, depicts her emerging from the sea on the coast of Cyprus, while from her consort, Adonis, is a Semitic figure, with a Semitic name. In her purely Greek form, as Aphrodite, the goddess' cult was fairly decorous, but on the borders of the Greek world, in Corinth, sacred prostitution was practiced." Reproduced by arrangement with Phoebus Publishing Company from *Encyclopedia of World Mythology,* Copyrighted 1970, 71, 75, pp. 33, 34 BPC Publishing, Limited. (by permission).

As clearly shown to the reader, this worship can be found in all parts of the ancient world. It will be shown later, this pagan abomination even made its way to the New World before the arrival of Columbus in 1492.

Nimrod the greatgrandson of Noah, was the son of Cush who was the son of Ham, Genesis 10:6. Nimrod's father Cush has also been traced to be the origin of a pagan god. When Austen Layard found over twenty-five thousand tablets at Nineveh, some of the tablets had colophons inscribed upon them and had belonged to the library of the Temple of Nebo (Nabu) the Divine Scribe, god of art, science, and writing.[1]

The Divine Scribe was Hermes to the Egyptians, he was Mercury to the Romans, Bel to the Babylonians and many other names throughout the world. Here again, some astonishing discoveries by the late Alexander Hislop:

"According to Genesis 10:8, Cush begot Nimrod. Cush was the son of Ham who settled in Africa. Cush as the son of Ham, was Hermes or Mercury: for Hermes is just an Egyptian synonym for the son of Ham. Now, Hermes was the great original prophet of idolatry: for he was recognized by the pagans as the author of their religious rites and the interpreter of the gods."

"Cush was the founder of the Cushites, or better known as the Ethiopians. Now, Nimrod, as the son of Cush, was black, in other words, was a Negro. 'Can the Ethiopian change his skin? is in the original, Can the Cushite do so?' " "Bigotry was just as active among the pagans as it is among the Christians today. Semiramis gained glory

---

[1] See *Road to Nineveh,* by Nora Benjamin Kubie, p. 263.

The mother goddess of Babylon with her divine son. Courtesy of Loizeaux Brothers, Neptune, N.J.

from her dead and deified husband: and in the course of time both of them, under the names of Rhea and Nin, or Goddess Mother and Son, were worshipped with an enthusiasm that was incredible and their images were everywhere set up and adored. Whenever the negro aspect of Nimrod was found an obstacle to his worship, this was very easily obviated. According to the Chaldean doctrine of the transmigration of souls all the attributes, and all that was needful was just to teach that Ninus has reappeared in the person of a posthumous son, of a fair complexion, supernaturally borne by his widowed wife after the father had gone to glory."

"This son, thus worshipped in his mother's arms, was looked upon as invested with all the attributes, and called by almost all the names of the promised Messiah. As Christ, in the Old Testament was Adonai, the

A goddess and child from India. Courtesy of Loizeaux Brothers, Neptune, N.J.

Lord, so Tammuz was called Adon or Adonis. Under the name of Mirthras, he was worshipped as the Mediator. As Mediator and head of the covenant of grace, he was styled Baal-Berith, THE LORD OF THE COVENANT." (All the above quotes are given by permission — Loizeaux Brothers, Neptune, N.J., publishers of *The Two Babylons,* by Alexander Hislop, pp. 25, 26, 34, 69, 70.)

Let the reader not misunderstand. Alexander Hislop in his historical records, is not promoting racialism, but historical facts. It is true the Negroes are descendants of Ham. The Bible says Egypt which is in Africa is the Land of Ham. "Israel also came into Egypt: and Jacob sojourned in the land of Ham. They shewed his signs among them, and wonders in the land of Ham." Psalms 105:23.

Let the reader remember, one of the first Christians was an Ethiopian eunuch who was a descendant of Cush, the father of the land, and the father of Nimrod. Acts 8:27; Genesis 10:8.

All Gentiles — Blacks, Whites, Latins, Chinese, Indian, etc., were: "Aliens from the commonwealth of Israel, and strangers from the covenants of promise, having no hope, and without God in the world: But now in Christ Jesus ye who sometimes were far off are made nigh by the blood of Christ." Ephesians 2:12, 13.

Nimrod was believed to be a giant, who was black. However, Nimrod was worshipped as a white and black god throughout the world. And not all descendants of Ham are Negroid. The second son of Ham was Mizraim. Genesis 10:6. His descendants are the Egyptians. Mizraim's son Casluhim, had descendants called Philistim. Genesis 10:14. They migrated north from Egypt and settled on the coast of Cannan. They were later called the Philistines. The city of Gath of the Philistines is where the Giant Goliath came from, whom David killed. I Samuel 17:4, 48-51. The word "India," commonly means "Ethiopia," or the land of Cush.[1] The Hindu god, Vishnu, was black, and the Black Indian god was to have ten incarnations. Nine have come, and one is believed to be still future according to the myth. Devaki, the Mother goddess, conceived two saviors of the Hindu belief. One was white and one was black. Like the Christ, they were born miraculously. One hair was plucked from a white multi-headed snake named Anata, and one hair was plucked from the black god Vishnu; and the white hair begot the white incarnate of Vishnu, Balarama and the blue-black hair begot Krishna.[2]

In Egypt, the Mother goddess and the white god-child were worshipped under the names of Isis and Horus. Horus the falcon-headed god according to the gospel of Egyptian Mythology, like Jesus, was born miraculously. As the Holy Spirit of God begot our Lord, the Incarnate of the God of Israel; pagan philosophy says this too happened in the legend of the Egyptian Trinity. However, it was not the Holy Spirit of God that conceived Horus, but the spirit of the dead black Pharaoh Osiris, his father, who was mystically represented as a young bull or calf.[3] This is where the Israelites got the idea of making the golden calf as a sign that divinity was among them. Exodus 32:1-35.

"THUS SAITH THE LORD, LEARN NOT THE WAY OF THE HEATHEN, AND BE NOT DISMAYED AT THE SIGNS OF HEAVEN; FOR THE HEATHEN ARE DISMAYED AT THEM. FOR THE CUSTOMS

---

[1] See *The Two Babylons*, by Alexander Hislop, p. 56.
[2] See *Indian Mythology*, by Veronica Ions, p. 62.
[3] See *The Two Babylons*, by Alexander Hislop, p. 45.

Here pictured, are the two saviors of the world in the Hindu myth in their adolescence. Balarama (left), and the more popular black savior Krishna (right). Courtesy of the Victoria and Albert Museum.

OF THE PEOPLE ARE VAIN. FOR ONE CUTTETH A TREE OUT OF THE FOREST, THE WORK OF THE HANDS OF THE WORKMAN, WITH THE AXE, THEY DECK IT WITH SILVER AND WITH GOLD: THEY FASTEN IT WITH NAILS AND WITH HAMMERS, THAT IT MOVE NOT. THEY ARE UPRIGHT AS THE PALM TREE, BUT THEY SPEAK NOT. THEY MUST NEEDS BE BORN, BECAUSE THEY CANNOT GO. BE NOT

Vishnu the black god is pictured in the middle of the photo surrounded by his incarnations. Nine have come, and one more is still to come. Courtesy of the Victoria and Albert Museum.

An incarnation of Vishnu, the black god of the Hindus. Courtesy of the Victoria and Albert Museum.

AFRAID OF THEM; FOR THEY CANNOT DO EVIL NEITHER ALSO IS IT IN THEM TO DO GOOD. YE ARE MY WITNESSES, SAITH THE LORD, AND MY SERVANT WHOM I HAVE CHOSEN: THAT YE MAY KNOW AND BELIEVE ME, AND UNDERSTAND THAT I AM HE: BEFORE ME THERE WAS NO GOD FORMED, NEITHER SHALL THERE BE AFTER ME. I, EVEN I, AM THE LORD; AND BESIDE ME THERE IS NO SAVIOUR.'' Jeremiah 10:2-5; Isaiah 43:10, 11.

The black Egyptian god Osiris, dressed in his spotted royal dress. The upper part was of leopard skin. The under part was also spotted to match the upper part. Nimrod, the black god and first king of the first city (Babel) was worshipped as his name signifies. Nimrod's name means - "The Subduer of the Leopard." It appears that the Egyptian black god Osiris was nothing less but the original black god Ninus (Nimrod), under another name. Courtesy Loizeaux Brothers, Neptune, N.J.

Here are just a few names that identify with the original pagan trio of **NIMROD, SEMIRAMIS, AND TAMMUZ.**

	NIMROD THE LORD OF HEAVEN	**TAMMUZ THE PAGAN MESSIAH**	**SEMIRAMIS THE QUEEN OF HEAVEN**
APOSTATE ISRAEL	Baal	Tammuz	Ashtoreth
PHOENICIA	IL	Bacchus	Astarte
BABYLON	Belus	Tammuz	Rhea, Ishtar
ASSYRIA	Ninus	Hercules	Beltis
GREECE	Zeus	Dionysus	Aphrodite
ROME	Jupiter	Attis	Cybele, Diana
EGYPT	Ra	Osiris, Horus	Isis, Hathor
INDIA	Vishnu	Krishna	Isi, Devaki
CHINA	Pan-Ku	Yi	Heng-O, Ma Tsoopo
MEXICO	Teotl	Quetzalcoatl	Coatlicue
SCANDINAVIA	Odin	Balder	Frigg, Freyia

Space does not allow to place all the names that identify with this pagan trio. Although the worship may vary, the same pattern usually can be found in their worship. Semiramis' first deified name is believed to be Rhea, however under her mortal name she was believed to have built Babylon,[4] a continuation of her husband's Babel.

If the reader would explore the books on North American Indian Mythology, he would find much of the same pattern of worship as above. Among the Eskimo, Cherokee, Apache, the Crow, Navaho, etc., many of the Indian tribes regarded themselves as descendants of the Sun. Sometimes the sun was thought as a female. The Eskimo tale of the Sun sister and Moon Brother relates how a brother has incestuous relations with his sister; she discovers her lover's identity and flees to the sky to become the Sun, while the brother pursues her and becomes the Moon.[5]

Turn in your Bibles to Ezekiel the 8th chapter. There are many abominations of Sun worship, shown in these following verses:

"THEN HE BROUGHT ME TO THE DOOR OF THE GATE OF THE LORD'S HOUSE WHICH WAS TOWARD THE NORTH; AND, BEHOLD, THERE SAT WOMEN WEEPING FOR TAMMUZ. THEN SAID HE UNTO ME, HAST THOU SEEN THIS, O SON OF MAN? TURN THEE YET AGAIN, AND THOU SHALT SEE GREATER ABOMINATIONS THAN THESE. AND HE BROUGHT ME INTO THE INNER COURT OF THE LORD'S HOUSE, AND, BEHOLD, AT THE DOOR OF THE TEMPLE OF THE LORD, BETWEEN THE PORCH AND THE ALTAR, WERE ABOUT FIVE AND TWENTY MEN, WITH THEIR BACKS TOWARD THE TEMPLE OF THE LORD, AND THEIR FACES TOWARD THE EAST; AND THEY WORSHIPPED THE SUN TOWARD THE EAST." Ezekiel 8:14-16.

The Vernal Equinox or the New Year Festival was the most celebrated festival of the pagan year, for it was the time of the resurrection of the dead god Tammuz, who was "THE LORD OF DEATH AND REBIRTH." Centuries before the birth of Jesus, pagans in Babylon, Egypt, Persia, and Greece, all had their version of the RESURRECTION before our Lord's death and resurrection.[6]

This New Year Festival also known as HOLY WEEK, was started by 40 days of weeping and fasting. This 40 days of fasting and weeping was to bring back Tammuz from the grave. It was very necessary because the great Vegetation God, Tammuz, had control over the seasons, and it was he that brought the spring (the regeneration of life). Because

---

[4] See *The American College Dictionary*, C. L. Barnhart, editor in chief, p. 1101.
[5] See *Standard Dictionary of Fokelore Mythology and Legend*, p. 1087.
[6] See *Adonis Attis Osiris*, by Sir James George Frazer, p. 6.

Tammuz was killed and suffered much pain, the men would identify with their god by self-flagellation. This was usually done with knives. While the men would cut themselves to show their sincerity, the women would weep for their god's return. They believed because Tammuz died in the fall, vegetation died also, and if he was resurrected, this too would cause the regeneration of plant life in the spring.

Tammuz was known as the SON OF THE SUN, and the ignorant pagan saw life beyond the grave. If they proved faithful, at death they would shed their mortal bodies and become like the spirits of gods, and live in Paradise.

One of the strict observances a follower had to keep in the worship of Baal, often with the pain of death if broken, was a (Day) to give honor, and to recognize the Sun God as the Creator and Lord of Heaven. This day was to be kept Holy, and the people were commanded by Law not to do any servile work on this Holy Day. This day was to be a Holy Convocation; a day to be set aside from earning a livelihood. It was a day to give Thanks to the Sun God for the Bounties from Heaven. On this day, the pagans would face the east at sunrise as the sun appeared, and they worshipped the Sun toward the east, on what was called "Sun-day," which is the first day of the week. However, during the New Year Festival, Sunday had a double observance at this time of the year. It was the day Tammuz was resurrected from the dead. This was the time of Tammuz's appearance with the Sun, and the Moon, who were believed to be the homes of Baal, and the Queen of Heaven. Tammuz's star was the East Star (Venus).

This Sunday was the Holiest of Holy to the pagan. This pagan observance was called "Easter," and on this special day the followers of the gods would hold what modern Christian Churches call today "Sun-rise Services." The same New Year Festival that was held in Mesopotamia, was also held in Western Asia and Greece under the name of "Adonis." He too was mourned, with bitter wailing, and the East Star was his symbol.[7]

Has the reader ever wondered what the Easter Bunny has to do with the Resurrection of Christ? Or the Easter Egg? Like the Festival of Christmas and The Christmas Tree, they have nothing whatsoever to do with the Gospel of Christ. The Queen of Heaven was also a goddess of Fertility, and because the rabbit and the hen were noted for their many off-springs, they were her symbols.[8] Even the word "EASTER" is of

---

[7] See *Adonis Attis Osiris*, by Sir James George Frazer, pp. 223, 258, 259.

[8] See *The Two Babylons*, by Alexander Hislop, pp. 103-112.

pagan origin. It is Chaldean and means "ASTARTE;" this is one of the titles of BELTIS, the QUEEN OF HEAVEN at Nineveh.[9]

There were many symbols that identified with Pagan worship, and one of them was the letter "T".[10] This was the symbol of life beyond the grave, and it was also the symbol of Tammuz, the Lord of Death and Rebirth. In Egypt, this symbol was called the ANKH. As we established earlier, Baal worship, sacrificed human beings, and because Tammuz's name began with a "T" they would make wooden piles in the shape of a "T" and then placed their sacrifices on them. In due time, miniature amulets were made as symbols of Sun worship, they looked like this:

When Solomon began to worship a form of this system of Satan's, it was primarily because of the pagan wives he married. "And he had seven hundred wives, princesses, and three hundred concubines: And his wives turned his heart. For it came to pass, when Solomon was old, that his wives turned away his heart after other gods: and his heart was not perfect with the Lord his God, as was the heart of David his father. For Solomon went after Ashtoreth the goddess of the Zidonians, and after Milcom the abomination of the children of Ammonites. And Solomon did evil in the sight of the Lord, and went not fully after the Lord, as did David his father. Then did Solomon build an high place for Chemosh, the abomination of Moab, in the hill that is before Jerusalem, and for Molech, the abomination of the children of Ammon." I Kings 11:3-7.

Solomon, noted for his wisdom and understanding, who had been called "Jedidiah," which means "Beloved of the Lord" (II Samuel 12:25), who wrote in his youth, "There is a way which seemeth right unto a man, but the end thereof are the ways of death," (Proverbs 14:12), because of his lust for Women and Wealth, eventually separated himself from the Lord and practiced the most abominable rites of paganism. It was Solomon who was the first of many kings of Israel, to allow the sacrifice of little children.

This hill he built was in the valley of the son of Hinnom. This area lies at the entry of the east gate of Jerusalem (Jeremiah 19:2). In verses 5, and 6, of the same chapter we read:

---

[9] *Ibid.*, p. 103.

[10] See *The Mask of God*, by Joseph Campbell, pp. 469, 479, 480.

"They have built also the high places of Baal, to burn their sons with fire for burnt offerings unto Baal which I commanded not, nor spake it, neither came it into my mind: Therefore, behold, the days come, saith the Lord, that this place shall no more be called Tophet, nor The valley of the son of Hinnom, but The valley of slaughter."

The heathen sacrifices always featured incense. Ezekiel wrote of its use in his vision found in Ezekiel 8:11.

"And there stood before them seventy men of the ancients of the house of Israel, and in the midst of them stood Jaazaniah the son of Shaphan, with every man his censer in his hand; and a thick cloud of incense went up."

Just as the Hebrew priests were commanded to use incense as prayers rising up to heaven (Exodus 30:1-9); so did the pagan burn his incense to the Sun God. When the Israelites burnt their children with fire, they too, burnt strange incense upon the altars of Baal. "As they called them, so they went from them: they sacrificed unto Baalim, and burnt incense to graven images." "And they burnt incense in all the high places, as did the heathen whom the Lord carried away before them: and wrought wicked things to provoke the Lord's anger." Hosea 11:2, II Kings 17:11.

One of the Basest idolatries existed during the reign of Judah's King Manasseh. You can read about his evil deeds and his repentance in II Kings 21 and II Chronicles 33:1-20.

"For he built again the high places which Hezekiah his father had broken down, and he reared up altars for Baalim, and made groves, and worshipped all the host of heaven, and served them. And he caused his children to pass through the fire in the valley of the son of Hinnom: also he observed times, and used enchantments, and used witchcraft, and dealt with a familiar spirit, and with wizards: he wrought much evil in the sight of the Lord, to provoke him to anger. And he set a carved image, the idol which he had made, in the house of God, of which God had said to David and to Solomon his son, In this house, and in Jerusalem, which I have chosen before all the tribes of Israel, will I put my name for ever." II Chronicles 33:3, 6, 7.

In the Ten Commandments the Lord has commanded us to never make graven images of anything that is in Heaven; on Earth, or under. "Thou shalt not make unto thee any graven image, or any likeness of any thing that is in heaven above, or that is in the earth beneath, or that is in the water under the earth." Exodus 20:4.

"They that make a graven image are all of them vanity: and their delectable things shall not profit; and they are their own witnesses; they see not, nor know: that they may be ashamed. Who hath formed a god, or molten a graven image that is profitable for nothing?'' Isaiah 44:9,10.

"I am the Lord: that is my name: and my glory will I not give to another, neither my praise to graven images.'' Isaiah 42:8.

But, nevertheless, this was Israel's history from Mt. Sinai all the way down through the centuries until they left their captivity in Babylon. "YE SHALL MAKE YOU NO IDOLS NOR GRAVEN IMAGE, NEITHER REAR YOU UP A STANDING IMAGE, NEITHER SHALL YE SET UP ANY IMAGE OF STONE IN YOUR LAND, TO BOW DOWN UNTO IT: FOR I AM THE LORD YOUR GOD,'' Leviticus 26:1.

But like the pagans around them, the Israelites made idols of gods. They made bulls, which we saw earlier were symbols of divine strength, as in Exodus 32:1-35, and I Kings 12:28,29; made molten images in the likeness of men, Isaiah 44:13-15.

Psalm 115:4-8 says: "Their idols are silver and gold, the work of men's hands. They have mouths, but they speak not: eyes have they, but they see not: They have ears but they hear not: noses have they, but they smell not: they have hands, but they handle not: feet have they, but they walk not: neither speak they through their throat: they that make them are like unto them: so is every one that trusteth in them.''

But Israel made gods out of stone with human forms with heads of various animals or birds, sometimes of snakes and fish. They went to the extent of leaving food and drink to graven images. In Ezekiel 16:17-19 we read:

"Thou hast also taken thy fair jewels of my gold and my silver which I had given thee, and madest to thyself images of men, and didst commit whoredom with them, and tookest thy broidered garments, and coveredst them: and thou hast set mine oil and mine incense before them. My meat also which I gave thee, fine flour, and oil, and honey, wherewith I fed thee, thou hast even set it before them for a sweet savour, and thus it was, saith the Lord God.''

Jeremiah 44:16,17 reveals another important part of the system of Baalim. Described is the Israelites exaltation of the "QUEEN OF HEAVEN,'' who was SEMIRAMIS, the pagan goddess, identified with ASHTORETH to the Israelites. "As for the word that thou hast spoken unto us in the name of the Lord, we will not hearken unto thee. But we will certainly do whatsoever thing goeth forth out of our own mouths, to burn incense to the queen of heaven, and pour out drink offerings unto her, as we have done, we, and our fathers, our kings, and our princes, in the cities of Judah, and in the streets of Jerusalem: for then had we plenty of victuals, and were well, and saw no evil.''

As we have seen, the Queen of Heaven was also known as the Mother of gods, the goddess of love and war, the goddess of fertility, etc. Sacred prostitution was a very active part in this pagan abomination. In the *New Laroussee Encyclopedia of Mythology* we read the following:

"One story has it when she descended to earth she was accompanied by courtesans, harlots and strumpets. Her holy city was Erech (Gen. 10:10) and was called also the town of the sacred courtesans. She was known as Ishtar and moreover she was the courtesan of the gods, and she was the first to experience the desires which she inspired. She was also known to the Assyrians as the daughter of Sin and the sister of Shamash, the Lady of Battles valiant among goddesses." *New Laroussee Encyclopedia of Mythology,* introduced by Robert Graves, p. 58, Laroussee & Co., Inc., New York.

The famous gate of Ishtar of Babylon is named after this Queen of Heaven. Ishtar or Semiramis was also identified with "Diana of Ephesus," whose Temple was one of the ancient seven wonders of the world. The apostle Paul ran head on with this pagan cult in Acts 19:24-35. One of the customs the pagan women observed each year was and is making cakes or buns with a symbol of a cross to represent the Queen of Heaven and give honor to her son Tammuz. This custom was condemned by God in Jeremiah 7:18:

"The children gather wood, and the fathers kindled the fire, and the women knead their dough, to make cakes to the queen of heaven, and to pour out drink offerings unto other gods, that they may provoke me to anger." This very custom of making cakes with a cross is observed in modern Christianity. The cakes with a cross are called HOT CROSS BUNS. Some of the drink offerings the pagans offered to their gods were of Blood.

"Their sorrows will be multiplied that hasten after another god: their drink offerings of blood will I not offer, nor take up their names into my lips." Psalm 16:4.

The Israelites were forbidden by death to eat any manner of blood. The Israelites were allowed to eat the flesh of clean animals only when the blood was drained out. For this was a practice of their pagan neighbors, that led to cannibalism during famines. Before the Israelites were heard of, God commanded Noah that he and his family were not to eat the blood of the animals. Genesis 9:4.

"But flesh with the life thereof, which is the blood thereof, shall ye not eat." Moses was commanded later to tell the Israelites which animals were clean, and not clean to eat. Leviticus 11:1-47. But never were they to eat blood of any sort, or the fat. "It shall be a perpetual statute for your generations throughout all your dwelling, that ye eat neither fat nor blood." Leviticus 3:17.

"And whatsoever man there be of the house of Israel, or of the strangers that sojourn among you, that eateth any manner of blood; I will even set my face against that soul that eateth blood, and will cut him off from among the people." Leviticus 17:10.

The Israelites soaked the meat in brine, which is water and salt, until the blood was drained completely, then they would restore the flavor by using spices. The blood is sacred to God, it is the Life.

"For the life of the flesh is in the blood: and I have given it to you upon the altar to make an atonement for your souls: . . . Therefore I said unto the children of Israel, No soul of you shall eat blood, neither shall any stranger that sojourneth among you eat blood." Leviticus 17:11,12.

The apostle Paul knew the importance of avoiding blood, as found in Acts 15:20, also Acts 21:25. "But that we write unto them, that they abstain from pollutions of idols, and from fornication, and from things strangled, and from blood." Acts 15:29. "That ye abstain from meats offered to idols, and from blood, and from things strangled, and from fornication: from which if you keep yourselves, ye shall do well. Fare ye well."

Many professed Doctors of Divinity will tell us the Christian who is a Gentile is not subject to this; but the same God in the Old Testament is the same God in the New Testament. Paul again, speaking to both Jew and Gentile, said, "AS TOUCHING THE GENTILES WHICH BELIEVE WE HAVE WRITTEN AND CONCLUDED THAT THEY OBSERVE NO SUCH THING, SAVE ONLY THAT THEY KEEP THEMSELVES FROM THINGS OFFERED TO IDOLS, AND FROM BLOOD, AND FROM STRANGLED, AND FROM FORNICATION." Acts 21:25.

But the Israelites like the pagans often did just the opposite of what God commanded, because the spirit that controlled them in their apostasy is the opposite from God.

"And the people flew upon the spoil, and took sheep, and oxen, and calves and slew them on the ground: and the people did eat them with the blood. Then they told Saul, saying, Behold, the people sin against the Lord, in that they eat with the blood, and he said, Ye have transgressed, roll a great stone unto me this day. And Saul said, Disperse yourselves among the people, and say unto them, Bring me hither every man his ox, and every man his sheep, and slay them here, and eat: sin not against the Lord in eating with blood. And all the people brought every man his ox with him that night, and slew them there." I Samuel 14:32-34.

Drink and blood offerings were the toast the pagans would give to Baal and other gods for victory in war, or on other occasions. Some pagans believed that in eating the flesh of humans they would gain the wisdom of their victim. Even Israel ate their sons and their daughters during a famine. This was foretold by Moses in Deuteronomy 28:56, 57:

"The tender and delicate woman among you, which would not adventure to set the sole of her foot upon the ground for delicateness and tenderness, her eye shall be evil toward the husband of her bosom, and toward her son and toward her daughter, and toward her young one that cometh out from between her feet, and toward her children which she shall bear; for she shall eat them for want of all things secretly in the siege and straitness, wherewith thine enemy shall distress thee in thy gates."

Brothers and sisters, we have come to the last remaining years of this age of Satanic dominion. These things that came upon the Israelites of old shall be repeated in our time. "Now all these things happened unto them for ensamples: and they are written for our admonition, upon whom the ends of the world are come." I Corinthians 10:11.

"Speak unto the children of Israel saying, Ye shall eat no manner of fat of ox, or of sheep, or of goat. And the fat of the beast that dieth of itself, and the fat of that which is torn with beasts, may be used in any other use: but ye shall in no wise eat of it. For whosoever eateth the fat of the beast, of which men offer an offering made by fire unto the Lord, even the soul that eateth it shall be cut off from his people. Moreover ye shall eat no manner of blood, whether it be of fowl or of beast, in any of your dwelling. Whatsoever soul it be that eateth any manner of blood, even that soul shall be cut off from his people." Leviticus 7:23-27.

"And if ye will not for all this hearken unto me, but walk contary unto me: Then I will walk contrary unto you also in fury: and I, even I, will chastise you seven times for your sins, And ye shall eat the flesh of your sons, and the flesh of your daughters shall ye eat." Leviticus 26:27-29.

Israel did not hearken and in II Kings 6:28, 29, we read:

"And the king said unto her, What aileth thee? And she answered, This women said unto me, Give thy son, that we may eat him today, and we will eat my son tomorrow, So we boiled my son, and did eat him: and I said unto her on the next day, Give thy son, that we may eat him: and she hath hid her son." "The hands of the pitiful women have sodden their own children: they were their meat in the destruction of the daughter of my people." Lamentations 4:10.

During the destruction of Jerusalem in 70 A.D. by the Roman General Titus the Jews again fulfilled the Scriptures for want of flesh. There too, Israel ate their sons and daughters. And this warning is for us until the second coming of Christ. How about the meat shortage a few years ago when horse meat was sold in the super markets in Detroit, Michigan. All who bought it were aware that it was horse meat, but bought over 10,000 lbs. as a beef supplement. What would happen under a famine?

"For nation shall rise against nation, and kingdom against kingdom:

and there shall be famines, and pestilences, and earthquakes, in divers places." Matthew 24:7.

"Thus saith the Lord, thy Redeemer, the Holy One of Israel; I am the Lord thy God which teacheth thee to profit, which leadeth thee by the way that thou shouldest go. O that thou hadst hearkened to my commandments! then had thy peace been as a river, and thy righteousness as the waves of the sea." Isaiah 48:17, 18

"Wherefore come out from among them, and be ye separate, saith the Lord, and touch not the unclean thing; and I will receive you. And will be a Father unto you, and ye shall be my sons and daughters, saith the Lord Almighty." 2 Corinthians 6:17, 18

"For all that is in the world, the lust of the flesh, and the lust of the eyes, and the pride of life, is not of the Father, but is of the world. And the world passeth away, and the lust thereof: but he that doeth the will of God abideth forever." I John 2:16, 17

"Forasmuch as ye know that ye were not redeemed with corruptible things, as silver and gold, from your vain conversation received by tradition from your fathers; But with the precious blood of Christ, as of a lamb without blemish, and without spot." I Peter 1:18, 19

In the sacrificial Law, Moses instructed the Israelite priests to take the blood of the sacrificed animals and sprinkle the altar and the people as a covenant that by the blood was atonement for sin. Leviticus 4:2-8; Exodus 30:10

This foreshadowed Christ pouring out his blood for us. "For it is not possible that the blood of bulls and of goats should take away sins. Wherefore when he cometh into the world, he saith, Sacrifice and offering thou wouldest not, but a body hast thou prepared me: In burnt offerings and sacrifices for sin thou hast had no pleasure. Then said I, Lo, I come (in the volume of the book it is written of me,) to do thy will, O God. He that despised Moses' law died without mercy under two or three witnesses: Of how much sorer punishment, suppose ye, shall he be thought worthy, who hath trodden under foot the Son of God, and hath counted the blood of the covenant, wherewith he was sanctified, an unholy thing, and hath done despite unto the Spirit of grace?" Hebrews 10:4-7, 28, 29

The sacrifices of animals by Moses' Law, until Christ had come, was a temporary system of forgiveness of sin. "For when Moses had spoken every precept to all the people according to the law, he took the blood of calves and of goats, with water, and scarlet wool, and hyssop, and sprinkled both the book, and all the people, Saying, This is the blood of the testament which God hath enjoined unto you. Moreover he sprinkled with blood both the tabernacle, and all the vessels of this ministry. And almost all things are by law purged with blood; and without shedding of blood is no remission. So Christ was once offered to bear the sins of many: and unto them that look for him shall he appear the second time without sin unto salvation. Hebrews 9:19-28.

As the Blood of Jesus saves us from all sin, so did the pagan believe there is no remission of sin unless by the shedding of blood. In a study of the customs and people who worshipped Attis, who was nothing less but the god, Tammuz, under another name, Sir James George Frazer a noted scholar, has a chapter in his book *The Golden Bough,* the life styles of the worshippers of Attis, who was the god of Vegetation to the Romans. With the publisher's permission, here is the legend of Attis:

"Like Adonis, he appears to have been a god of vegetation, and his death and resurrection were annually mourned and rejoiced over at a festival in spring. The legends and rites of the two gods were so much alike that the ancients themselves sometimes identified them. Attis was said to have been a fair young shepherd or herdsman beloved by Cybele, the Mother of Gods, a great Asiatic goddess of fertility who had her chief home in Phrygia.

"Some held that Attis was her son. His birth, like that of many other heroes, is said to have been miraculous. His mother, Nana, was a virgin, who conceived by putting a ripe almond or a pomegranate in her bosom. Indeed in the Phrygian cosmogony an almond figured as the father of all things, perhaps because its delicate lilac blossom is one of the first heralds of spring, appearing on the bare boughs before the leaves have opened. Such tales of virgin mothers are relics of an age of childish ignorance when men had not yet recognized the intercourse as the true cause of the offspring. That ignorance, still by the lowest of existing savages, the aboriginal tribes of central Australia, was doubtless at one time universal among mankind. Even in later times, when people are better acquainted with the laws of nature, they sometime imagine that these laws may be subject to exceptions and that miraculous beings may be born in miraculous ways by women who have never known man. In Palestine to this day it is believed that women may conceive by a Jinnee or by the spirit of her dead husband. There is, or was lately, a man at Nebk who is currently supposed to be the offspring of such a union, and the simple folk have never suspected his mother's virtue. Two different accounts of the death of Attis were current. According to the one he was killed by a boar, like Adonis. According to the other, he unmanned himself under a pinetree, and bled to death on the spot. The latter is said to have been the local story told by the people of Pessinus, a great seat of the worship of Cybele, and the whole legend of which the story forms a part is stamped with a character of rudeness and savagery that speaks strongly for its antiquity. Both tales might claim the support of the custom, or rather both were probably invented to explain certain customs observed by the worshippers. The story of the self-mutilation of Attis is clearly an attempt to account for the self-mutilation of his priests, who regularly castrated themselves on entering the service of the goddess. The story of his death by the boar may have been told to explain why his worshippers, especially the people of Pessinus, abstained from eating swine. In like manner the worshippers of Adonis abstained from pork, because a boar had killed their god. After his death Attis is said to have been changed into a pinetree.

"The worship of the Phrygian Mother of the Gods was adopted by the Romans in 204 B.C., towards the close of their long struggle with Hannibal. For their drooping spirits had been opportunely cheered by a prophecy, alleged to be drawn from that convenient farrago of nonsense, the Sibylline Books, that the foreign invader would be driven from Italy if the great Oriental goddess were brought to Rome. Accordingly ambassadors were despatched to her sacred city Pessinus in Phrygia. The small black stone which embodied the mighty divinity was entrusted to them and conveyed to Rome, where it was received with great respect and installed in the temple of Victory on the Palatine Hill. It was the middle of April when the goddess arrived, and she went to work at once. For the harvest that year was such as had not been seen for many a long day, and in the very next year Hannibal and his veterans embarked for Africa.

"As he looked his last on the coast of Italy, fading behind him in the distance, he could not foresee that Europe, which had repelled the arms, would yet yield to the gods of the Orient. The vanguard of the conquerors had already encamped in the heart of Italy before the rearguard of the beaten army fell suddenly back from its shores. We may conjecture, though we are not told, that the Mother of the Gods brought with her the worship of her youthful lover or son to her new home in the West. Certainly the Romans were familiar with the Galli, the emasculated priests of Attis, before the close of the Republic. These unsexed beings, in their Oriental costume, with little images suspended on their breasts, appear to have been a familiar sight in the streets of Rome which they traversed in procession, carrying the image of the goddess and chanting their hymns to the music of cymbals and tambourines, flutes and horns, which the people, impressed by the fantastic show and moved by the wild strains, flung alms to them in abundance, and buried the image and its bearers under showers of roses. A further step was taken by the Emperor Claudius when he incorporated the Phrygian worship of the sacred tree, and with it probably the orgiastic rites of Attis, in Rome. This great spring festival of Cybele and Attis is best known to us in the form in which it was celebrated at Rome; but as we are informed that the Roman ceremonies were also Phrygian, we may assume that they differed hardly, if at all, from their Asiatic original. The order of the festival seems to have been as follows.

"On the twenty-second day of March, a pine tree was cut in the woods and brought into the sanctuary of Cybele, where it was treated as a great divinity. The duty of carrying the sacred tree was entrusted to a guild of Tree-bearers. The trunk was swathed like a corpse with woollen bands and decked with wreaths of violets, for violets were said to have sprung from the blood of Attis, as roses and anemones from the blood of Adonis; and the effigy of a young man, doubtless Attis himself, was tied to the middle of the stem. On the second day of the festival, the twenty-third of March, was known as the Day of Blood: the Archigallus or the high-priest drew blood from his arms and presented it as an offering. Nor was he alone in making this bloody sacrifice. Stirred by the wild barbaric music of clashing cymbols, rumbling drums, droning horns, and screaming flutes, the inferior clergy whirled about in the dance with waggling heads and streaked hair, until, rapt into a frenzy of excitement and insensible to pain, they gashed their bodies with potsherds or slashed them with knives in order to bespatter the altar and the sacred tree with their flowing blood. The ghastly rite probably formed part of the mourning for Attis and may have been intended to strengthen him for the resurrection. The Australian aborigines cut themselves in like manner over the graves of their friends for the purpose, perhaps, of enabling them to be born again. Further, we may conjecture, though we are not expressly told, that it was on the same Day of Blood and for the same purpose that the novices sacrificed their virility. Wrought up to the highest pitch of religous excitement they dashed the severed portions of themselves against the image of the cruel goddess. These broken instruments of fertility were afterwards reverently wrapped and buried in the earth or in subterranean chambers sacred to Cybele, where, like the offering of blood, they may have been deemed instrumental in recalling Attis to Life and hastening the general resurrection of nature, which was then bursting into leaf and blossom in the vernal sunshine. Some confirmation of this conjecture is furnished by the savage story that the mother of Attis conceived by putting in her bosom a pomegranate sprung from the severed genitals of a man-monster named Agdestis, a sort of double of Attis.

"If there is any truth in this conjecture explanation of the custom, we can readily understand why other Asiatic goddesses of fertility were served in like manner by the eunuch priests. These feminine deities required to receive from their male ministers, who personated the divine lovers the means of discharging their beneficent functions: they had themselves to be impregnated by the life-giving energy before they could transmit it to the world. Goddesses thus ministered to by eunuch priests were the great Artemis of Ephesus and the great Syrian Astarte of Hierapolis, whose sanctuary, frequented by swarms of pilgrims and enriched by the offerings of Assyria and Babylonia, or Arabia and Phoenicia, was perhaps in the days of its glory the most popular in the East. Now the unsexed priests of this Syrian goddess resembled those of Cybele so closely that some people took them to be the same. And the mode in which they dedicated themselves to the religous life was similar. The greatest festival of the year at Hierapolis fell at the beginning of spring, when multitudes thronged to the sanctuary from Syria and the regions round about. While flutes played, the drums beat, and the eunuch priests slashed themselves with knives, the religious excitement gradually spread like a wave among the crowd of onlookers, and many a one did that which he little thought to do when he came as a holiday spectator to the festival. For man after man, his vains throbbing with the music, his eyes fascinated by the sight of the streaming blood, flung his garments from him, leaped forth with a shout, and seizing one of the swords which stood ready for the purpose, castrated himself on the spot. Then he ran through the city, holding the bloody pieces in his hand, till he threw them into one of the houses which he passed in his mad career. The household thus honoured had to furnish him with a suit of female attire and female ornaments, which he wore for the rest of his life. When the tumult of emotion had subsided, and the man had come to himself again, the irrevocable sacrifice must often have been followed by passionate sorrow and lifelong regret. This revulsion of natural human feeling after the frenzies of a fanatical religion is powerfully depicted by Catullus in a celebrated poem.

"The parallel of these Syrian devotees confirms the view that in the similar worship of CYBELE the sacrifice of virility took place on the DAY of BLOOD at the vernal rites of the goddess, when the violets, supposed to spring from the red drops of her wounded lover, were in bloom among the pines. Indeed the story that ATTIS unmanned himself under a PINE-TREE was clearly devised to explain why his priests did the same beside the sacred violet wreath tree at his festival. At all events, we can hardly doubt that the Day of Blood witnessed the mourning for Attis over an effigy of him which was afterwards buried. The image thus laid in the sepulchre was probably the same which had hung upon the tree. Throughout the period of mourning the worshippers fasted from bread, nominally because Cybele had done so in her grief for the death of Attis, but really perhaps for the same reason which induced the women of

Harran to abstain from eating anything ground in a mill while they wept for Tammuz. To partake of bread or flour at such a season might have been deemed a wanton profanation of the bruised and broken body of the God. Or the fast may possibly have been a preparation for a sacramental meal.

"But when night had fallen, the sorrow of the worshippers was turned to joy. For suddenly a light shown in the darkness: the tomb was opened: the god had risen from the dead: and as the priest touched the lips of the weeping mourners with balm, he softly whispered in their ears the glad tidings of salvation. The resurrection of the god was hailed by his disciples as a promise that they too would issue triumphant from the corruption of the grave. On the morrow, the twenty-fifth day of March, which was reckoned the vernal equinox, the divine resurrection was celebrated with a wild outburst of glee. At Rome, and probably elsewhere, the celebration took the form of a carnival. It was the Festival of Joy (Hilaria). A universal license prevailed. Every man might say and do what he pleased. People went about the streets in disguise. No dignity was too high or too sacred for the humblest citizen to assume with impunity. In the reign of Commodus a band of conspirators thought to take advantage of the masquerade by dressing in the uniform of the Imperial Guard, and so, mingling with the crowd of merrymakers, to get within stabbing distance of the emperor. But the plot miscarried. Even the stern Alexander Severus used to relax so far on the joyous day as to admit a peasant to his frugal board. The next day, the twenty-sixth of March, was given to repose, which must have been much needed after the varied excitements and fatigues of the preceding days. Finally, the Roman festival closed on the twenty-seventh of March with a procession to the brook Almo. The silver image of the goddess, with its face of jagged black stone, sat in a wagon drawn by oxen. Preceded by the nobles walking barefoot, it moved slowly, to the loud music of pipes and tambourines, out by the Porta Capena, and so down to the banks of the Almo, which flows into the Tiber just below the walls of Rome. There the high priest, robed in purple, washed the wagon, the image, and the other sacred objects in the water of the stream. On returning from their bath, the wain and the oxen were strewn with fresh spring flowers. All was mirth and gaiety. No one thought of the blood that had flowed so lately. Even the eunuch priests forgot their wounds.

"Such, then, appears to have been the annual solemnization of the death and resurrection of Attis in the spring, but besides these public rites, his worship is known to have comprised certain secret or mystic ceremonies, which probably aimed at bringing the worshipper, and especially the novice, into closer communication with his god. Our information as to the nature of these mysteries and the date of their celebration is unfortunately very scanty, but they seem to have included a sacramental meal and a baptism of blood. In the sacrament the novice became a partaker of the mysteries by eating out of a drum and drinking out of a cymbal, two instruments of music figuring prominently in the thrilling orchestra of Attis. The fast which accompanied the mourning for the dead god may perhaps have been designed to prepare the body of the communicant for the reception of the blessed sacrament by purging it of all that could defile by contact the sacred elements. In the baptism the devotee, crowned with gold and wreathed with fillets, descended into a pit, the mouth of which was covered with a wooden grating. A bull, adorned with garlands of flowers, its forehead glittering with gold leaf, was then driven on to the grating and there stabbed to death with a consecrated spear. Its hot reeking blood poured in torrents through the apertures, and was received with devout eagerness by the worshipper on every part of his person and garments, till he emerged from the pit, drenched, dripping, and scarlet from head to foot to receive the homage, nay the adoration, of his fellows as one who had been born again to eternal life and had washed away his sins in the blood of the bull. For some time afterwards the fiction of a new birth was kept up by dieting him on milk like a new-born babe. The regeneration of the worshipper took place at the same time as the regeneration of his god, namely the vernal equinox. At Rome the new birth and the remission of sins by the shedding of bulls blood appear to have been carried out above all at the sanctuary of the Phrygian goddess on the Vatican Hill, at or near the spot where the great basilica of St. Peter now stands; for many inscriptions relating to the rites were found when the church was being enlarged in 1608 or 1609. From the Vatican as a centre this barbarous system of superstition seems to have spread to other parts of the Roman empire. Inscriptions found in Gaul and Germany prove that provincial sanctuaries modelled their ritual on that of the Vatican. From the same source we learn that the Testicles as well as the blood of the bull played an important part in the ceremonies. Probably they were regarded as a powerful charm to promote fertility and hasten new birth." *The Golden Bough,* by Sir James G. Frazer, pp. 403-409, Macmillan Company, New York, 1958 (by permission).

CHAPTER II

The Mystery Of Iniquity – Continued

Hell the burning place of torment, not a doctrine from the Old or New Testament. Borrowed from Sun Worship – The false doctrine of a thousand year reign of peace with Christ on earth – The false doctrine of the Secret Rapture – Divination: Astrology, Hypnotism, Spiritualism, Inventions of Satan Himself – The False Sabbath, Sunday, Borrowed from Sun Worship, and not from the Old and New Testaments – The ancient Sun worship of the Aztecs and Mayans traced to Nimrod – Pagan Baptism and Pagan Communion Observed Among Multitudes of Christian Churches – Jesus Christ the Real Bright and Morning Star

Like the worshippers of Tammuz, in the resurrection of Osiris; the Egyptians saw the pledge of a life everlasting for themselves beyond the grave. At the death of kings, pagans would leave provisions for the dead monarch, and in many instances slaves were murdered at the site of the monarch's tomb, to serve him in the spirit world. There are many from the ancient past and MODERN DAY SOCIETIES that claim to receive messages from the spirits of dead friends, relatives, and of the Saints. Many are there among the intellectual and the ignorant people who believe they have a SOUL that flies out of them at their death. And the burning place of torment "HELL," has been the teaching of both pagan and Christian since the tower of Babel and apostolic times. The Great God of the Underworld, has burned so many people in HELL down through the centuries according to priests and pastors, that it's almost impossible to imagine where the Devil put them all. This teaching of HELL FIRE has also been the leading cause of ATHEISM. Do we fly up to Heaven, at death, as Nimrod did in his myth? Or, are we cast down to a living Hell? Are there multitudes of people who died since Adam, being burned in Hell, having to suffer longer than those who die today? Is God a tyrant? This doctrine makes Him out to be one. Let's forget the traditions of the pagans and the Christians handed down to us through the centuries and find out what the Bible says about the dead. Now let us question this doctrine of Hell Fire in the Under World. If the dead are in Hell Fire and are receiving the torture and pain as screamed by most priests and pastors, wouldn't those who are receiving this torment feel pain and be conscious of what is happening to them?

"Whatsoever thy hand findeth to do, do it with thy might: for there is no work, nor device, nor knowledge, nor wisdom, in the grave, whither thou goest." Ecclesiastes 9:10

Let's ask the Lord another question. When a man dies, does he go to Heaven immediately at death?

"The dead praise not the Lord, neither any that go down into silence." Psalm 115:17

"For the living know that they shall die: but the dead know not any thing, neither have they any more a reward; for the memory of them is forgotten. Also their love, and their hatred, and their envy, is now perished; neither have they any more a portion forever in anything that is done under the sun." Ecclesiastes 9:5, 6

Lord, there are those who go to the grave sites of their departed loved ones and talk to them; can they hear them?

"His sons come to honour, and he knoweth it not; and they are brought low, but he perceiveth it not of them." Job 14:21

Lord, some religions say a man will come back from the dead as a human or be reincarnated as an animal; is this true?

"So man lieth down, and riseth not: till the heavens be no more, they shall not awake, nor be raised out of their sleep." Job 14:12

Lord, there are those who claim to receive thoughts from the spirits of dead people called spirit guides (familiar spirits); is this true?

"REGARD NOT THEM THAT HAVE FAMILIAR SPIRITS, NEITHER SEEK AFTER WIZARDS, TO BE DEFILED BY THEM: I AM THE LORD YOUR GOD. FOR ALL THAT DO THESE THINGS ARE AN ABOMINATION UNTO THE LORD: AND BECAUSE OF THESE ABOMINATIONS THE LORD THY GOD DOTH DRIVE THEM OUT FROM BEFORE THEE. FOR IN DEATH THERE IS NO REMEMBRANCE OF THEE: IN THE GRAVE WHO SHALL GIVE THEE THANKS? HIS BREATH GOETH FORTH, HE RETURNETH TO HIS EARTH; IN THAT VERY DAY HIS THOUGHTS PERISH." Leviticus 19:31; Deuteronomy 18:12; Psalm 6:5, Psalm 146:4

Lord, you have clearly established the dead cannot hear us, nor can they project their thoughts to us. However, mediums have received messages which they claim to be from the supernatural. If the dead are not sending these messages, who is?

"NOW THE SPIRIT SPEAKETH EXPRESSLY, THAT IN THE LATTER TIMES SOME SHALL DEPART FROM THE FAITH, GIVING HEED TO SEDUCING SPIRITS, AND DOCTRINES OF DEVILS. AND NO MARVEL; FOR SATAN HIMSELF IS TRANSFORMED INTO AN ANGEL OF LIGHT." I Timothy 4:1, II Corinthians 11:14

Lord, there are those who will argue that these preceding Scriptures refer to the body only, it's the Soul that lives on after death. Is this true?

"BEHOLD, ALL SOULS ARE MINE; AS THE SOUL OF THE FATHER, SO ALSO THE SOUL OF THE SON IS MINE: THE SOUL THAT SINNETH, IT SHALL DIE." Ezekiel 18:4

The word "Soul" has been twisted to mean a spirit, or ghost. However, in the Bible it simply means a Living person. "And the Lord God formed man of the dust of the ground, and breathed into his NOSTRILS THE BREATH OF LIFE; AND MAN BECAME A LIVING SOUL." Genesis 2:7.

The spirit and the breath of life are the same, and it is the breath of life (spirit), that returns to God. It has no conscience. "The spirit of God hath made me, and the breath of the Almighty hath given me life." Job 33:4. "Cease ye from man, whose breath is in his nostrils: for wherein is he to be accounted of?" Isaiah 2:22. "All the while my breath is in me, and the SPIRIT of God IS IN MY NOSTRILS;" Job 27:3. "Then shall the dust return to the earth as it was: and the spirit shall return unto God who gave it." Ecclesiastes 12:7.

WHEN WILL WE GO TO HEAVEN?

"For the Lord himself shall descend from heaven with a shout, with the voice of the archangel, and with the trump of God: and the dead in Christ shall rise first: Then we which are alive and remain shall be caught up together with them in the clouds to meet the Lord in the air: and so shall we ever be with the Lord." I Thessalonians 4:16,17.

Those who died believing in the promises of Christ from Adam's time, to the final days of earth's history, will be resurrected to life at Christ's second coming. Here is another truth. If the righteous dead are in Heaven, why is Jesus coming to resurrect them out of their graves?

"MARVEL NOT AT THIS: FOR THE HOUR IS COMING, IN WHICH ALL THAT ARE IN THE GRAVES SHALL HEAR HIS VOICE, AND SHALL COME FORTH; THEY THAT HAVE DONE GOOD, UNTO THE RESURRECTION OF LIFE AND THEY THAT HAVE DONE EVIL, UNTO TO RESURRECTION OF DAMNATION." John 5:28,29.

Jesus clearly shows that the dead shall hear his voice from the grave, and will receive the promise of immortality at Christ's second coming, not immediately at death.

Even King David is still in his grave waiting to be raised at Christ's second coming.

"Men and brethren, let me freely speak unto you of the patriarch David, that he is both dead and buried, and his sepulchre is with us this day. For David is not ascended into the heavens: but he saith himself, the Lord said unto my Lord, Sit thou on my right hand.'' Acts 2:29,34.

The apostle Paul was very aware when the dead shall be raised from the grave. Paul said at the ''LAST TRUMP.''

''Behold I shew you a mystery; We shall not all sleep, but we shall all be changed, in a moment, in the twinkling of an eye, at the last trump: for the trumpet shall sound, and the dead shall be raised incorruptible, and we shall be changed. For this corruptible must put on incorruption, and this mortal must put on immortality. So when this corruptible shall have put on incorruption, and this mortal shall have put on immortality, then shall be brought to pass the saying that is written, Death is swallowed up in victory. O death, where is thy sting? O grave, where is thy victory?'' I Corinthians 15:51-56.

At the ''Last Trump'' we will receive immortality, not at death. You may ask then, what is the meaning of Hell in the Bible that even Jesus talked about in Matthew 11:23; 16:18?

If you go to a Greek Lexicon and look up the word Hell, the word originally meant ''GRAVE,'' not a burning torment, or a place of punishment. The word in Hebrew for grave is ''SHEOL.'' Like the word Soul, both words have been twisted to mean something entirely different.

You still might ask, what is the Hell Fire that Jesus also spoke of in Matthew 18:8,9?

Jesus said to the Pharisees that what happened to Sodom and Gomorrah, is what will happen at His second coming.

''Likewise also as it was in the days of Lot: they did eat, they drank, they bought, they sold, they planted, they builded; But the same day that Lot went out of Sodom it rained fire and brimstone from heaven, and destroyed them all. Even thus shall it be in the day when the Son of man is revealed.'' Luke 17:28-30.

God destroyed Sodom and Gomorrah with fire and brimstone as Jesus said. This can be found in Genesis 19:4. ''Then the Lord rained upon Sodom and Gomorrah brimstone and fire from the Lord out of heaven.'' Jesus referred to this as a shadow of what is to come upon the whole world. This was also foretold by the Prophets.

''For, behold, the day cometh, that shall burn as an oven: and all the proud, yea, and all that do wickedly, shall be stubble: and the day that cometh shall burn them up, saith the Lord of hosts, that it shall leave them neither root nor Branch.'' Malachi 4:1.

The wicked are destroyed at Christ's second coming by fire. The apostle Paul foretold this in II Thessalonians 1:7-9.

''And to you who are troubled rest with us, when the Lord Jesus shall be revealed from heaven with his mighty angels, in flaming fire taking vengeance on them that know not God, and that obey not the gospel of our Lord Jesus Christ, who shall be punished with everlasting destruction from the presence of the Lord, and from the glory of his power."

The fire and brimstone comes from Heaven, not under the earth as a burning place of torment, as it has been screamed to you. At Christ's second coming it will be a destruction from the Almighty, not a 1,000 year's reign of peace here on the earth as erring Evangelists and Preachers have taught. For the face of the earth shall totally be made a waste at the appearance of Christ in the Heavens.

"OUR GOD SHALL COME, AND SHALL NOT KEEP SILENCE: A FIRE SHALL DEVOUR BEFORE HIM, AND IT SHALL BE TEMPESTOUS ROUND ABOUT HIM. HE SHALL CALL TO THE HEAVENS FROM ABOVE, AND TO EARTH, THAT HE MAY JUDGE HIS PEOPLE. GATHER MY SAINTS TOGETHER UNTO ME: THOSE THAT HAVE MADE A COVENANT WITH ME BY SACRIFICE." Psalm 50:3-5.

This also destroys the false doctrine about a SECRET RAPTURE, that the followers of Christ will not go through the GREAT TRIBULATION period just before Christ's return (Matthew 24:21). God's people shall go through this time, and there is nothing secret about Jesus' Second Coming: "AND EXCEPT THOSE DAYS SHOULD BE SHORTENED, THERE SHOULD NO FLESH BE SAVED: BUT FOR THE ELECT'S SAKE THOSE DAYS SHALL BE SHORTENED. AND THEN SHALL APPEAR THE SIGN OF THE SON OF MAN IN HEAVEN: AND THEN SHALL ALL THE TRIBES OF THE EARTH MOURN, AND THEY SHALL SEE THE SON OF MAN COMING IN THE CLOUDS OF HEAVEN WITH POWER AND GREAT GLORY. AND HE SHALL SEND HIS ANGELS WITH A GREAT SOUND OF A TRUMPET, AND THEY SHALL GATHER TOGETHER HIS ELECT FROM THE FOUR WINDS, FROM ONE END OF HEAVEN TO THE OTHER." Matthew 24:22,30,31.

All the people of the earth will know about Christ's appearance at the end of the world. There is nothing secret at all about Christ's Second Coming: "FOR AS THE LIGHTNING COMETH OUT OF THE EAST, AND SHINETH EVEN UNTO THE WEST; SO SHALL ALSO THE COMING OF THE SON OF MAN BE. AND THE KINGS OF THE EARTH, AND THE GREAT MEN, AND THE RICH MEN, AND THE CHIEF CAPTAINS, AND THE MIGHTY MEN, AND EVERY BONDMAN, AND EVERY FREE MAN, HID THEMSELVES IN THE DENS AND IN THE ROCKS OF THE MOUNTAIN; AND SAID TO THE MOUNTAINS AND ROCKS, FALL ON US, AND HIDE US FROM THE FACE OF HIM THAT SITTETH ON THE THRONE, AND FROM THE WRATH OF THE LAMB: FOR THE GREAT

DAY OF HIS WRATH IS COME; AND WHO SHALL BE ABLE TO STAND?" Matthew 24:27; Revelation 6:15-17

King David and all the prophets of the Old Testament foretold Christ's Second Coming would be a destruction from the Almighty, not a reign of peace:

"THE GREAT DAY OF THE LORD IS NEAR, IT IS NEAR, AND HASTETH GREATLY, EVEN THE VOICE OF THE DAY OF THE LORD: THE MIGHTY MAN SHALL CRY THERE BITTERLY. THAT DAY IS A DAY OF WRATH, A DAY OF TROUBLE AND DISTRESS, A DAY OF WASTENESS AND DESOLATION, A DAY OF DARKNESS AND GLOOMINESS, A DAY OF CLOUDS AND THICK DARKNESS, A DAY OF THE TRUMPET AND ALARM AGAINST THE FENCED CITIES, AND AGAINST THE HIGH TOWERS." Zephaniah 1:14-16

"HOWL YE: FOR THE DAY OF THE LORD IS AT HAND; IT SHALL COME AS A DESTRUCTION FROM THE ALMIGHTY." Isaiah 13:6

"BEHOLD, THE DAY OF THE LORD COMETH, CRUEL BOTH WITH WRATH AND FIERCE ANGER, TO LAY THE LAND DESOLATE: AND HE SHALL DESTROY THE SINNERS THEREOF OUT OF IT." Isaiah 13:9

"BEHOLD, THE LORD MAKETH THE EARTH EMPTY, AND MAKETH IT WASTE, AND TURNETH IT UPSIDE DOWN, AND SCATTERETH ABROAD THE INHABITANTS THEREOF. THE LAND SHALL BE UTTERLY EMPTIED, AND UTTERLY SPOILED: FOR THE LORD HATH SPOKEN THIS WORD. THE EARTH IS UTTERLY BROKEN DOWN, THE EARTH IS CLEAN DISSOLVED, THE EARTH IS MOVED EXCEEDINGLY. THE EARTH SHALL REEL TO AND FRO LIKE A DRUNKARD, AND SHALL BE REMOVED LIKE A COTTAGE; AND THE TRANSGRESSION THEREOF SHALL BE HEAVY UPON IT; AND IT SHALL FALL, AND NOT RISE AGAIN." Isaiah 24:1, 3, 19, 20

"THOU SHALT BE VISITED OF THE LORD OF HOSTS WITH THUNDER, AND WITH EARTHQUAKE, AND GREAT NOISE, WITH STORM AND TEMPEST, AND THE FLAME OF DEVOURING FIRE." Isaiah 29:6

"FOR BEHOLD, THE LORD WILL COME WITH FIRE, AND WITH HIS CHARIOTS LIKE A WHIRLWIND, TO RENDER HIS ANGER WITH FURY, AND HIS REBUKE WITH FLAMES OF FIRE. FOR BY FIRE AND BY HIS SWORD WILL THE LORD PLEAD WITH ALL FLESH: AND THE SLAIN OF THE LORD SHALL BE MANY. THEY THAT SANCTIFY THEMSELVES, AND PURIFY THEMSELVES IN THE GARDENS BEHIND ONE TREE IN THE MIDST, EATING SWINE'S FLESH, AND THE

ABOMINATION, AND THE MOUSE, SHALL BE CONSUMED TOGETHER, SAITH THE LORD." Isaiah 66:15-17.

"THE LORD IS NOT SLACK CONCERNING HIS PROMISE, AS SOME MEN COUNT SLACKNESS; BUT IS LONGSUFFERING TO USWARD NOT WILLING THAT ANY SHOULD PERISH, BUT THAT ALL SHOULD COME TO REPENTANCE. BUT THE DAY OF THE LORD WILL COME AS A THIEF IN THE NIGHT: IN THE WHICH THE HEAVENS SHALL PASS AWAY WITH A GREAT NOISE, AND THE ELEMENTS SHALL MELT WITH FERVENT HEAT, THE EARTH ALSO AND THE WORKS THAT ARE THEREIN SHALL BE BURNED UP." II Peter 3:9,10.

Both the prophets in the Old Testament and the apostles in the New Testament say the world will be destroyed at Christ's second coming and He will save His people out of it. So the fire that Jesus said would come is from HEAVEN, not from under the earth. There are TWO periods of this devouring fire. The first is at Jesus' second coming, as the Scriptures clearly describe. The second time will be after the thousand year millennium described in Revelation 20:1-6,9,10. This is when the wicked will be raised from the dead, and come to destroy the NEW JERUSALEM.

"AND THEY WENT UP ON THE BREATH OF THE EARTH, AND COMPASSED THE CAMP OF THE SAINTS ABOUT, AND THE BELOVED CITY, AND FIRE CAME DOWN FROM GOD OUT OF HEAVEN, AND DEVOURED THEM. AND THE DEVIL THAT DECEIVED THEM WAS CAST INTO THE LAKE OF FIRE AND BRIMSTONE, WHERE THE BEAST AND THE FALSE PROPHET ARE, AND SHALL BE TORMENTED DAY AND NIGHT FOR EVER AND EVER." Revelation 20:9, 10.

This whole earth is going to be covered with fire just as the waters in Noah's day destroyed the world. Christ will not set up His Kingdom in this present polluted world. This is one of the reasons the Jews rejected the Son of God. They believed Christ was to set up His Kingdom in this world, but Jesus said in John 18:36:

"JESUS ANSWERED, MY KINGDOM IS NOT OF THIS WORLD: IF MY KINGDOM WERE OF THIS WORLD, THEN WOULD MY SERVANTS FIGHT, THAT I SHOULD NOT BE DELIVERED TO THE JEWS: BUT NOW IS MY KINGDOM NOT FROM HENCE." "I HAVE GIVEN THEM THY WORD: AND THE WORLD HATH HATED THEM, BECAUSE THEY ARE NOT OF THE WORLD, EVEN AS I AM NOT OF THE WORLD." John 8:22,23. "THEN SAID THE JEWS, WILL HE KILL HIMSELF? BECAUSE HE SAITH, WHITHER I GO YE CANNOT COME,

AND HE SAID UNTO THEM, YE ARE FROM BENEATH: I AM FROM ABOVE: YE ARE OF THIS WORLD: I AM NOT OF THIS WORLD." Speaking of His disciples Jesus said: "IF YE WERE OF THE WORLD, THE WORLD WOULD LOVE HIS OWN: BUT BECAUSE YE ARE NOT OF THE WORLD, BUT I HAVE CHOSEN YOU OUT OF THE WORLD, THEREFORE THE WORLD HATETH YOU." John 15:19. I John 2:15-17, "LOVE NOT THE WORLD, NEITHER THE THINGS THAT ARE IN THE WORLD. IF ANY MAN LOVE THE WORLD, THE LOVE OF THE FATHER IS NOT IN HIM, FOR ALL THAT IS IN THE WORLD, THE LUST OF THE FLESH, AND THE LUST OF THE EYES, AND THE PRIDE OF LIFE, IS NOT OF THE FATHER, BUT IS OF THE WORLD. AND THE WORLD PASSETH AWAY, AND THE LUST THEREOF: BUT HE THAT DOETH THE WILL OF GOD ABIDETH FOREVER." James 4:4, "YE ADULTERERS AND ADULTERESSES, KNOW YE NOT THAT FRIENDSHIP OF THE WORLD IS ENMITY WITH GOD? WHOSOEVER THEREFORE WILL BE A FRIEND OF THE WORLD IS THE ENEMY OF GOD." "HE THAT LOVETH HIS LIFE SHALL LOSE IT: AND HE THAT HATETH HIS LIFE IN THIS WORLD SHALL KEEP IT UNTO LIFE ETERNAL," John 12:25. "LET NOT YOUR HEART BE TROUBLED: YE BELIEVE IN GOD, BELIEVE ALSO IN ME, IN MY FATHER'S HOUSE ARE MANY MANSIONS: IF IT WERE NOT SO, I WOULD HAVE TOLD YOU. I GO TO PREPARE A PLACE FOR YOU. AND IF I GO AND PREPARE A PLACE FOR YOU, I WILL COME AGAIN, AND RECEIVE YOU UNTO MYSELF; THAT WHERE I AM, THERE YE MAY BE ALSO." John 14:1-3.

Jesus promises to come again and take us to where He is, at His Second Coming. I Thessalonians 4:16,17 says we will meet Him in the air. Where do you think we could go from there? TO HEAVEN, where Jesus said He has many mansions: not back down immediately to here on earth, but to Heaven. We will reign with Christ a thousand years in Heaven, not here on the earth. The face of the earth will be utterly destroyed at Christ's Second Coming as the Scriptures clearly foretell. The Lord will make a NEW HEAVEN and a NEW EARTH, this one will pass away, and God will dwell here on earth after this present evil world is purified of its pollutions by fire. "FOR BEHOLD, I CREATE NEW HEAVENS AND A NEW EARTH: AND THE FORMER SHALL NOT BE REMEMBERED, NOR COME INTO MIND." Isaiah 65:17. "FOR AS THE NEW HEAVENS AND THE NEW EARTH WHICH I WILL MAKE, SHALL REMAIN BEFORE ME, SAITH THE LORD, SO SHALL YOUR SEED AND YOUR NAME REMAIN, AND IT SHALL COME TO PASS, THAT FROM ONE NEW MOON TO ANOTHER, AND FROM ONE SABBATH TO

ANOTHER, SHALL ALL FLESH COME TO WORSHIP BEFORE ME, SAITH THE LORD." Isaiah 66:22,23.

"AND I SAW A NEW HEAVEN AND A NEW EARTH: FOR THE FIRST HEAVEN AND THE FIRST EARTH WERE PASSED AWAY: AND THERE WAS NO MORE SEA, AND I JOHN SAW THE HOLY CITY, NEW JERUSALEM, COMING DOWN FROM GOD OUT OF HEAVEN, PREPARED AS A BRIDE ADORNED FOR HER HUSBAND, AND I HEARD A GREAT VOICE OUT OF HEAVEN SAYING, BEHOLD THE TABERNACLE OF GOD IS WITH MEN, AND HE WILL DWELL WITH THEM, AND THEY SHALL BE HIS PEOPLE, AND GOD HIMSELF SHALL BE WITH THEM, AND BE THEIR GOD. AND GOD SHALL WIPE AWAY ALL TEARS FROM THEIR EYES: AND THERE SHALL BE NO MORE DEATH, NEITHER SORROW, NOR CRYING, NEITHER SHALL THERE BE ANY MORE PAIN: FOR THE FORMER THINGS ARE PASSED AWAY." Revelation 21:1-4.

The Lord with His purifying agent will purify the earth of its pollution. Just as in Noah's day when He destroyed the world by water and it covered the whole world, so will God this last age we live in cover the world with fire. This was foretold by Peter in II Peter 3:5,6:

"FOR THIS THEY WILLINGLY ARE IGNORANT OF, THAT BY THE WORD OF GOD THE HEAVENS WERE OF OLD, AND THE EARTH STANDING OUT OF THE WATER AND IN THE WATER; WHEREBY THE WORLD THAT THEN WAS, BEING OVERFLOWED WITH WATER, PERISHED. BUT THE HEAVENS AND THE EARTH, WHICH ARE NOW, BY THE SAME WORD ARE KEPT IN STORE, RESERVED UNTO FIRE AGAINST THE DAY OF JUDGMENT AND PERDITION OF UNGODLY MEN."

It will be SATAN, THE ANTICHRIST, who will try to establish his kingdom on this earth, NOT CHRIST! This has been foretold and it will come to pass. These two doctrines of IMMORTALITY OF THE SOUL, and the 1,000 YEAR REIGN OF CHRIST ON EARTH, ARE NOT FROM THE TEACHING OF JESUS CHRIST OF NAZARETH, but from another "Jesus" who will make his appearance shortly.

There will not be peace in the world until Satan is destroyed with all the wicked after the 1,000 year reign in Heaven, and NEW JERUSALEM is established here on earth, Revelation 20:9,10. As we pointed out earlier, there are two periods of the fire and brimstone of the Bible. The first is at Jesus' Second Coming; (II Peter 3:9,10; II Thessalonians 1:7-9; Luke 17:28-30).

The second period of fire and brimstone is after all the wicked are raised from the dead and destroyed forever. This is called the second death. "AND I SAW THRONES, AND THEY SAT UPON THEM, AND JUDGMENT WAS GIVEN UNTO THEM: AND I SAW THE SOULS OF THEM THAT WERE BEHEADED FOR THE WITNESS OF JESUS, AND FOR THE WORD OF GOD, AND WHICH HAD NOT WORSHIPPED THE BEAST, NEITHER HAD RECEIVED HIS MARK UPON THEIR FOREHEADS, OR IN THEIR HANDS: AND THEY LIVED AND REIGNED WITH CHRIST A THOUSAND YEARS. BUT THE REST OF THE DEAD LIVED NOT AGAIN UNTIL THE THOUSAND YEARS WERE FINISHED. THIS IS THE FIRST RESURRECTION. BLESSED AND HOLY IS HE THAT HATH PART IN THE FIRST RESURRECTION: ON SUCH THE SECOND DEATH HATH NO POWER, BUT THEY SHALL BE PRIESTS OF GOD AND OF CHRIST, AND SHALL REIGN WITH HIM A THOUSAND YEARS. AND WHEN THE THOUSAND YEARS ARE EXPIRED, SATAN SHALL BE LOOSED OUT OF HIS PRISON." Revelation 20:4-7.

Satan's prison will be the earth when it has been made desolate by Jesus' Second Coming. Satan for 1,000 years will study the death and destruction he caused down through the centuries. He shall be bound here on earth with no one to tempt, for the wicked will be destroyed at Christ's Second Coming. However, before all these things shall come to pass, there will be men in this present evil world predicting peace will come on the earth as in Jeremiah 8:11: "FOR THEY HAVE HEALED THE HURT OF THE DAUGHTER OF MY PEOPLE SLIGHTLY, SAYING, PEACE, PEACE; WHEN THERE IS NO PEACE."

Paul also warned us about this in I Thessalonians 5:3:

"FOR WHEN THEY SHALL SAY, PEACE AND SAFETY: THEN SUDDEN DESTRUCTION COMETH UPON THEM, AS TRAVAIL UPON A WOMEN WITH CHILD: AND THEY SHALL NOT ESCAPE. THUS SAITH THE LORD GOD: WOE UNTO THE FOOLISH PROPHETS, THAT FOLLOW THEIR OWN SPIRIT, AND HAVE SEEN NOTHING! BECAUSE, EVEN BECAUSE THEY HAVE SEDUCED MY PEOPLE, SAYING, PEACE; AND THERE WAS NO PEACE: AND BUILT UP A WALL, AND LO, OTHERS DAUBED IT WITH UNTEMPERED MORTAR. BECAUSE WITH LIES YE HAVE MADE THE HEART OF THE RIGHTEOUS SAD, WHOM I HAVE NOT MADE SAD: AND STRENGTHENED THE HANDS OF THE WICKED, THAT HE SHOULD NOT RETURN FROM THE WICKED WAY, BY PROMISING HIM LIFE." Ezekiel 13:3,10,22.

Another part of Baal worship that holds millions today in a snare of the devil, is DIVINATION. Very few even know what the word means, much less know that it is an abomination to the Lord to practice it.

Deuteronomy 18:10-12 shows that divination is not from God, it is an abomination to Him. This is one of the multitude of reasons the Lord told Joshua to destroy the Canaanites both women and children, in Deuteronomy 7:1-26. What is divination? Divination is foretelling the future by crystal visions in a crystal ball, palm reading, by arranging cards, by reading one's handwriting, by studying flight patterns of birds, and predicting certain events, by reading and studying the lines on calf livers, etc. The most popular system of divination was and is believed by many sent from God. To the pagan, the person that could perform this system of divination was not only considered wise and holy, but had the spirits of the living gods in him. Many would not even venture to travel out the door of their house unless they consulted with the diviner. By using mathematics and by the way the stars moved across the sky these diviners would predict certain events which would happen to people. Kings and rulers used their services to gain courage in the time of war, and also in peace. To the ancient man it was called Chaldaic Wisdom, or "Astrology."

In all pagan philosophies, the doctrine of immortality of the soul was the foundation and center of their whole pagan belief and worship. Pagans believed that when they died they too, like Nimrod, became immortal and their spirit that lived inside them was a divine spark that took possession of one of the stars.* The ancient Babylonians taught that the fate of everything was dependent on the sky. Babylonians, as most ancient people, believed that each mortal was like the gods and had his own star in the sky.[1] This will help us to understand the cosmic religion of Astrology, and how Astrology ties in with Sun Worship. And why John, in the book of Revelation, was given the sacred number 666, of Astrology, to identify the beast of Revelation 13:1-17, 18.

In the Babylonian astrological system, all the gods of heaven (the stars), were considered offspring or emanations of the Sun God. Now astrology claims to interpret the will of the star gods that control the fate of mankind by the position of the chief star gods in the zodiac. The chief gods of the zodiac were 7 planets who serpentine their way through the narrow band of the zodiac. You see, according to astrology, the zodiacal band was divided into 12 houses, one for each month of the year and each house was divided into three rooms making 36 rooms in all, one for each 10 degrees of the zodiacal circle.[2] The entire remainder of the sky outside of the zodiacal band was also divided into 36 constellations, 15

---

* *Mythology of All Races*, Vol. 3, Louis H. Gray, Ed., Cooper Square Publishers, 1964, p. 273.

[1] *Ibid.*, Vol. III, p. 273; VII, pp. 17, 94; Vol. XII, pp. 54, 55.

[2] *Encyclopedia of Religion and Ethics*, James Hastings, Ed., Vol. 12, Charles Scribner's Sons, N.Y., No Date, p. 49.

on the south side, and 21 on the north side, and a god of each constellation was appointed to rule over each of the 36 rooms of the zodiac.[3] Thus we see that every star in the sky, each considered as a god and the abode of departed spirits, was included in a constellation over whom was appointed a god who ruled over a zodiacal room. Each zodiacal house-god thus had 3 room-gods under him. The 12 house-gods (signs of the zodiac), each ruled over a month of the year, and the 7 planetary gods who serpentine their way through the zodiacal band who were the Sun, Moon, Mercury, Venus, Mars, Jupiter, and Saturn, regulated, according to astrology, the affairs of mankind by their relative positions in the various rooms of the zodiac.[4] Over them all ruled the Sun God, who was considered the central fire from which each had sprung, because all the gods of the sky were but emanations of the one god, the Sun.

Now, the origin of this number 666 also derived from astrology. As we have seen, astrology used the number 36 to divide the stars. If you add the numbers 1 to 36, they will add to 666. No ancient or modern day witch can cast a spell, no sorcerer can perform an enchantment, no fortuneteller can predict the future without the aid of astrology. Astrology is the basic foundation of all sciences of the occult, and the origin of all pagan religious systems.

God warned Israel about the worship of the stars, the host of heaven. We should worship the Lord who created those stars, not the stars! This is another way Satan has directed the thoughts of people from God to created things. "Thus saith the Lord, Learn not the way of the heathen, and be not dismayed at the signs of heaven: for the heathen are dismayed at them." Jeremiah 10:2.

Just as God foretold certain events through His prophets, so did the astrologers foretell certain events by their system. When God sent prophets to warn the Israelites of coming judgments from God, there were always false prophets telling the same people the opposite thing would come. Astrology, sorcery, magic, witchcraft, and soothsaying always were the main features in most systems of paganism. To counterfeit the miracles by God through His prophets, the false prophets would use astrology, magic, etc. "For thus saith the Lord of hosts, the God of Israel; Let not your prophets and your diviners, that be in the midst of you, deceive you, neither hearken to your dreams which ye cause to be dreamed. For they prophesy falsely unto you in my name: I have not sent them, saith the Lord." Jeremiah 29:8, 9.

---

[3] *Ibid.*, pp. 50-67.

[4] *Encyclopedia of Religion and Ethics,* Vol. 12, Ed., James Hastings, No Date, p. 86.

The Lord Himself has clearly foretold 750 years before Christ, what is to happen to all astrologers, sorcerers, etc., and all of those who seek and trust their counsels:

"THOU ARE WEARIED IN THE MULTITUDE OF THY COUNSELS. LET NOW THE ASTROLOGERS, THE STARGAZERS, THE MONTHLY PROGNOSTICATORS, STAND UP, AND SAVE THEE FROM THESE

6	32	3	34	35	1
7	11	27	28	8	30
19	14	16	15	23	24
18	20	22	21	17	13
25	29	10	9	26	12
36	5	33	4	2	31

1	32	34	3	35	6
30	8	27	28	11	7
20	24	15	16	13	23
19	17	21	22	18	14
10	26	12	9	29	25
31	4	2	33	5	36

Diagram of mystic numbers.

These are two astrological charts pagan high priests used to predict certain future events.

Any direction the columns are added, they will add to 111. There are 6 spaces, and 6×111=666. Any direction the numbers (1 to 36) are added together, the numbers of both charts will add to 666.

THINGS THAT SHALL COME UPON THEE. BEHOLD, THEY SHALL BE AS STUBBLE: THE FIRE SHALL BURN THEM; THEY SHALL NOT DELIVER THEMSELVES FROM THE POWER OF THE FLAME: THERE SHALL NOT BE A COAL TO WARM AT, NOR FIRE TO SIT BEFORE IT." Isaiah 47:13,14.

The same wonders that Satan used in the past he can use today, but he will always come short of the power of the Lord, and so will they who represent Satan's agents.

Here are astrological charts the pagan high priests used in their claim to foretell the future. These can be seen on display at the Berlin Museum. Any way you multiply the six columns times the number that it will add to, which is 111, it will come to 666. (6×111=666). Any way you add all the numbers in the columns together, it will add to 666. This is Satan's number (Revelation 13:18), and we will investigate more of this later. Another King of Israel who caused the Israelites to fall into a national apostasy was Ahab.

"And Ahab the son of Omri did evil in the sight of the Lord above all that were before him. And it came to pass, as if it had been a light thing for him to walk in the sins of Jeroboam the son of Nebat, that he took to wife Jezebel the daughter of Ethbaal king of the Zidonians, and went and served Baal, and worshipped him. And he reared up an altar for Baal in the house of Baal, which he had built in Samaria. And Ahab made a grove: and Ahab did more to provoke the Lord God of Israel to anger than all the kings of Israel that were before him." I Kings 16:30-33.

Chapters 16, 17, 18, and 19 of I Kings, tell the Great deception Baal worship had on the Israelites. The Israelites were so degraded and blinded by this counterfeit religion of Satan that they did not know the difference between Jehovah as the Lord; or Baal as the Lord; or whether the prophets of Baal were genuine, or the mighty Elijah was a genuine Prophet.

Because the worship of Baal satisfied the desires of the flesh, the Israelites did not heed the message the prophet Elijah first gave to Ahab. The Israelites committed the same atrocities the pagan worshippers of Tammuz and Attis, practiced in their worship as we showed earlier. Even those who saw through this false system of Satan dared not to expose it for what it was. "Who changed the truth of God into a lie, and worshipped and served the creature more than the Creator, who is blessed for ever. Amen." "God is a spirit: and they that worship him must worship him in spirit and in truth." Romans 1:25; John 4:24.

In the worship of Baal, followers carried amulets or charms, or the crosses of Tammuz, little idols carved out of wood, or some kind of symbol of their gods around their necks; and on their chariots, camels and donkeys. Sometimes they were made in images of dogs, chickens, snakes, crocodiles, crescents, etc. These were used as a magical or religious power to scare away evil spirits or protection from harm. As you probably know, this is done today in the Christian religion. Instead of depending on the Holy Spirit of God, people's minds are drawn to their religous helps and pictures. It is the purpose of Satan to keep our thoughts out of Heaven, and have them focussed on the material things of this world. Satan's aim is to train the human mind through various mediums, to keep our desires and thoughts on the things of this world, and not on the spiritual things of God. Jesus warned us not to get involved with the cares of this world where God is secondary and the material things first, for this was the condition of the people before the flood, and they were lost because they heeded not the warning of Noah, to turn from their sins. "BUT AS THE DAYS OF NOAH WERE, SO SHALL ALSO THE COMING OF THE SON OF MAN BE. FOR AS IN THE DAYS THAT WERE BEFORE THE FLOOD THEY WERE EATING AND DRINKING, MARRYING AND GIVING IN MARRIAGE, UNTIL THE DAY NOE ENTERED INTO THE ARK, AND KNEW NOT UNTIL THE FLOOD CAME, AND TOOK THEM AWAY; SO SHALL ALSO THE COMING OF THE SON OF MAN BE." Matthew 24:37-39.

The condition of the people before the flood and the conditon of the people just before the END OF THE WORLD can be vividly seen in the apostasy of Israel in the day of Elijah. Just as the Israelites were conditioned by Satan, through erring teachers, to worship false gods, so has Satan used erring teachers, priests, pastors, and evangelists to preach a false conception of the Christ and cause many to trust in a false system of Christianity.

Elijah was struck deep in his heart with astonishment and great sorrow when he saw how ignorant God's people were in his days. God in His mercy sent Elijah to expose the deceptions of Baal worship, and to turn the Israelites back to the true worship of the real Creator. However, Elijah was rejected and turned away. But Elijah went before the Lord and pleaded with God to save His people anyway. Even though they rejected his message, God was able to turn His people; even if it had to be through judgments from the Almighty. Here was to be the first test between the prophets of Baal and the prophets of the Queen of Heaven (Ashtoreth), and the prophet Elijah. The rain and dew which comes from Heaven, that the Israelites were deceived into believing came from these gods of nature, would stop. "And Elijah the Tishbite, who was of the inhabitants of Gilead, said unto Ahab, As the Lord God of Israel liveth before whom I stand, there shall not be dew nor rain these years, but according to my word.'' I Kings 17:1.

While Israel was apostatizing, Elijah remained a loyal and true prophet of God. He knew the only way to bring Israel back to God was by much suffering. And this is the case today. We have many avenues that lead away from God. When we do not hear and obey His call, He will cut them off leaving nowhere to turn but to Him. He does this for our own good. It sometimes makes our whole world fall in on us, but if He didn't do this to us we wouldn't be writing this book to you, or worshipping our Lord. Sometimes it takes something terrible to happen in our lives before we turn to God. When things are going well, that seems to be the time we call on God less. Such was the case of Israel. You that have ears to hear, listen and take heed to these words of wisdom:

''My son, despise not the chastening of the Lord; neither be weary of his correction: For whom the Lord loveth he correcteth; even as a father the son in whom he delighteth. Happy is the man that findeth wisdom, and the man that getteth understanding. For the merchandise of it is better than the merchandise of silver, and the gain thereof than fine gold.'' Proverbs 3:11-14.

The instrument of the Lord's chastisement stood suddenly before the evil King Ahab. The king was stunned over the sudden appearance of Elijah and by what the prophet said: ''There shall not be dew nor rain these years, but according to my word.'' I Kings 17:1. The king, not over the shock and the power of the words spoken by the prophet, was left standing in amazement, and Elijah left King Ahab as sudden as he came.

Then the Lord told Elijah: ''Get thee hence, and turn thee eastward, and hide thyself by the brook: that is before Jordan.'' I Kings 17:3.

Elijah was told to hide himself in the wilderness. The Lord knew there would follow persecution because of the straight testimony and his denunciations against Israel. In the meantime rain and dew did stop according to Elijah's word. Trees and plants began to wither and streams began to dry up. The earth started to crack and their cattle began to die.

Jezebel's prophets, who were prophets of the Queen of Heaven, along with the prophets of Baal, offered sacrifices to their gods, and called upon them both day and night to bring rain. The gods they used to deceive the people did not answer. The priests did everything they could think of so their gods would hear, but still no rain fell from heaven. The Cahna-Bal could be heard in the streets of Samaria crying; ''O Baal hear us, but there was no voice, nor any that answered.'' I Kings 18:26.

However, Israel still could not see the false security in trusting in the gods of the Zidonians, and did not turn to the God of Elijah. Meantime Jezebel, who made an all out effort to evangelize and to preach Baalim throughout the Nation of Israel, is filled with vengeance and madness. The god she supported did not answer, and she did not recognize the God of Elijah. Baal's prophets, Ahab, Jezebel, and just about all of Israel blamed Elijah for their troubles. King Ahab sent messengers all over the land and other kingdoms to search for Elijah the prophet, and even required an oath from the kingdoms, that they knew nothing of Elijah's whereabouts. When they couldn't find Elijah, Jezebel's anger turned against the other prophets of God. Anyone professing to be a prophet of Jehovah was to be killed. After two years of famine, with all of its sickness and death, Israel still did not repent from its sins and apostasy.

"And it came to pass after many days, that the word of the Lord came to Elijah in the third year, saying, Go, shew thyself unto Ahab; and I will send rain upon the earth." I Kings 18:1.

During this time Ahab sent Obadiah who was the governor of his house, and also was the one who hid the prophets of God from Jezebel and Ahab, to go throughout the kingdom and find water. On his way he met Elijah.

"And as Obadiah was in the way, behold, Elijah met him: and he knew him, and fell on his face, and said, Art thou that my Lord Elijah? And he answered him, I am; go, tell thy Lord, Behold, Elijah is here." I Kings 18:7,8.

Obadiah recognized Elijah, but as Elijah sends him with a message to the king, Obadiah is terrified. Because for the past three years, Elijah has been on the most wanted list of the government of Israel and Elijah was hunted down as a criminal. Elijah promises Obadiah things will be all right when he sees Ahab. When Ahab met eye to eye with Elijah, who he hated and hunted for, he was shocked and almost speechless at Elijah's sudden appearance again. He says: "Art thou he that troubleth Israel? And he answered, I have not troubled Israel; but thou, and thy father's house, in that ye have forsaken the commandments of the Lord, and thou hast followed Baalim." I Kings 17:18,19.

To show the blindness of Israel, Elijah challenged the prophets of Baal and the prophets of the groves that he was the only real prophet among them. So Ahab sent unto all the children of Israel, and gathered the prophets together unto Mount Carmel.

"And Elijah came unto the people, and said, How long halt ye between two opinions? If the Lord be God, follow him: but if Baal, then follow him. And the people answered him not a word. Then said Elijah unto the people, I, even I only, remain a prophet of the Lord; but Baal's prophets are four hundred and fifty men." I Kings 18:21,22.

Elijah picked Mount Carmel which was the very meeting place the prophets of Baal had had their pagan rites for Baal in times past. Elijah told the prophets to place on their altar a sacrifice, a bullock and cut it in pieces, and lay it on wood without a fire, and he would do the same. This was early in the morning.

Elijah then told the pagan prophets, that if Baal was God, tell him to send fire down from heaven to burn the sacrifice. They agreed. Elijah told them the God who brought fire down from heaven was the true God. They said it was well spoken.

Elijah let the Cahna-Bal go first while the full light of the Sun god was seen. The prophets of Baal called for Baal from early morning to noon, but still there was no fire from heaven. Elijah then started to mock them because their god wouldn't answer them.

"And it came to pass at noon, that Elijah mocked them, and said, Cry aloud: for he is a god; either he is talking, or he is pursuing, or he is in a journey, or peradventure he sleepeth, and must be awaked." I Kings 18:27. This stirred these false prophets to go into their wild dance and frenzy we saw earlier. The madness of this, is also recorded in Scripture.

"And they cried aloud, and cut themselves after their manner with knives and lancets, till the blood gushed out upon them." I Kings 18:28.

God told the priests of Israel never to practice this madness in the worship of Him. "They shall not make baldness upon their head, neither shall they shave off the corner of their beard, nor make any cuttings in their flesh." Leviticus 21:5.

False worship always will have with it an insane display of religious fervor, for the spirit in the midst of it is such. Those today who roll on floors from one side of the church to the other, and say, "I have the spirit," ought to remember there are two Spirits in the World.

"And it came to pass, when midday was past, and they prophesied until the time of the offering of the evening sacrifice, that there was neither voice, nor any to answer, nor any that regarded." I Kings 18:29.

The prophets of Baal called on their Sun God from early morning to evening and still no answer. Elijah sat patiently the whole day and watched the sun rise from the east and set in the west. Elijah allowed the pagan priests to call on the sun as it traveled across the sky all day. Not until it set in the west did Elijah say it was his turn. The Israelites witnessed the terrible demonstrations of the frantic priests all day.

"And Elijah said unto the people, Come unto me. And all the people came near unto him. And he repaired the altar of the Lord that was broken down. And Elijah took twelve stones, according to the number of the tribes of the sons of Jacob, unto whom the word of the Lord came saying, Israel shall be thy name." I Kings 18:30,31.

Elijah's turn had now come. After Elijah rebuilt the Lord's altar that was there before, he made a trench around the altar, he laid wood on the altar, placing his sacrifice on the wood, as did the Baal prophets, but he told the Israelites to pour four barrels of water on the altar, the wood, and sacrifice. They did this three times. And the water ran about the altar, and filled the trench also with water. Then Elijah called upon Jehovah to bring down fire out of Heaven.

"Then the fire of the Lord fell, and consumed the burnt sacrifice, and the wood, and the stones, and the dust, and licked up the water that was in the trench." I Kings 18:38.

Elijah did not have to make loud shrieks, cut himself with knives, dance himself into a frenzy, or threaten his God that he would leave His service if not answered. But with a humble short prayer, as soon as Elijah's prayer was finished, the fire of the Lord fell, and consumed the burned sacrifice, and the wood, and the dust, and licked up the water that was in the trench. "And when all the people saw it, they fell on their faces; and said, The Lord, He is the God: the Lord, He is the God." I Kings 18:38,39.

The Israelites had been conditioned by the false prophets of Baal that to receive answers to their prayers they must demonstrate sincerity by the acts of these false teachers. Baal's priests had screamed, and foamed, and danced and prayed to their Sun god. What a contrast it was to the Israelites who drifted from the pure worship of God, to hear and see Elijah seek God in a meek and lowly spirit. So is it with some Christians today. Many have been conditioned to sit and hear sermons screamed, danced, and dramatized as in Elijah's day, but this is not the spirit of the Lord. To act in such manner of the prophets of Baal, is just the opposite of what the Bible teaches. The Spirit of the Lord says:

"Ask, and it shall be given you; seek, and ye shall find; knock, and it shall be opened unto you." Matthew 7:7.

This is what prayer is all about. Prayer is asking God for help in the time of need and for His power to live according to His will. Never once will you read that Christ jumped, danced, screamed, or did any violent act to be heard by His heavenly Father. Elijah just spoke his petition to our God and it was answered. But to the pagan, prayer was chanting prayers in repetition, beating their chests, cutting their flesh and many other sad gestures of showing sincerity.

"Therefore I say unto you, What things soever ye desire, when ye pray, believe that ye receive them, and ye shall have them." Mark 11:24.

We need not demonstrate our sincerity by an outward show.

"BUT THOU, WHEN THOU PRAYEST, ENTER INTO THY CLOSET,

AND WHEN THOU HAST SHUT THY DOOR, PRAY TO THY FATHER WHICH IS IN SECRET; AND THY FATHER WHICH SEETH IN SECRET SHALL REWARD THEE OPENLY. BUT WHEN YE PRAY, USE NOT VAIN REPETITIONS, AS THE HEATHEN DO: FOR THEY THINK THAT THEY SHALL BE HEARD FOR THEIR MUCH SPEAKING. BE NOT YE THEREFORE LIKE UNTO THEM: FOR YOUR FATHER KNOWETH WHAT THINGS YE HAVE NEED OF, BEFORE YE ASK HIM." Matthew 6:6-8.

"But without faith it is impossible to please him; for he that cometh to God must believe that he is, and that he is a rewarder of them that diligently seek Him." Hebrews 11:6. "God is not a man, that he would lie; neither the son of man, that he should repent: hath he said, and shall he not do it? or hath he spoken, and shall he not make it good?" Numbers 23:19.

When the Israelites saw the fire they knew that God of Elijah was God. The darkness of Baalim had been exposed. The craftiness and the falsehood of the Cahna-Bal had been unmasked. Israel was shown their blindness, and their apostasy. Now they began to think of all the things they were led to do against the Most High, while under the influence of prophets of Baal. Now the anger they had towards Elijah, was turned on the prophets of Baal. "And Elijah said unto them, Take the prophets of Baal; let not one of them escape. And they took them: and Elijah brought them down to the brook Kishon, and slew them there." I Kings 18:40.

Elijah slew everyone of the false prophets by his own hand. God rewarded these false prophets according to their own works. Many of these high priests of Baal led the Israelites to sacrifice their sons and their daughters to this Sun god.

"But there were false prophets also among the people, even as there shall be false teachers among you, who privily shall bring in damnable heresies, even denying the Lord that bought them, and bring upon themselves swift destruction. And many shall follow their pernicious ways; by reason of whom the way of the truth shall be evil spoken of. And through covetousness shall they with feigned words make merchandise of you: whose judgment now of a long time lingereth not, and their damnation slumbereth not!" II Peter 2:1-3.

"For there shall arise false Christs, and false prophets, and shall shew great signs and wonders; insomuch that, if it were possible, they shall deceive the very elect." Matthew 24:24.

Millions believe anything that is from God has the name Christian or Jesus stamped on it, but this is what Christ Himself warned us about. "For many shall come in my name, saying, I am Christ; and shall deceive many." Matthew 24:5. We should never take for granted anything spoken by any religious leader or books written about salvation and doctrines of Christ. "Prove all things: hold fast that which is good." "Beloved, believe not every spirit, but try the spirits whether they are of God: because many false prophets are gone out into the world." I Thessalonians 5:21; I John 4:1.

But how do we check the credentials of religious leaders if they be of God or are being used by Satan? The only standard of measuring truth is the Holy Bible. Our only safeguard from falsehood is to study the Holy Scripture "OURSELVES," and not to rely on Pastors and Bible teachers. Those who do not see the seriousness in studying God's word in these last days, will accept this False Christ who will come upon the earth. "Even him, whose coming is after the working of Satan with all power and signs and lying wonders, and with all deceivableness of unrighteousness in them that perish BECAUSE THEY RECEIVED NOT THE LOVE OF THE TRUTH, THAT THEY MIGHT BE SAVED." II Thessalonians 2:9,10.

There are well over 300 Christian denominations in the world. But the Scriptures reveal only two, the small remnant of followers symbolized as a Virgin Woman (who is free of doctrines of BAALIM); and the people of The Mother of Harlots (who is full of doctrines of BAALIM). Most people today are like a string of seaweed which is swept away with the current of the tide. It is human nature to follow the crowd or majority in the paths of life. But this is just the opposite of the teaching of our Saviour.

"ENTER YE IN AT THE STRAIT GATE: FOR WIDE IS THE GATE, AND BROAD IS THE WAY, THAT LEADETH TO DESTRUCTION, AND MANY THERE BE WHICH GO IN THEREAT: BECAUSE STRAIT IS THE GATE, AND NARROW IS THE WAY, WHICH LEADETH UNTO LIFE, AND FEW THERE BE THAT FIND IT." Matthew 7:13,14.

We should never take the attitude in religious matters of Christ, that because everybody's doing it, "it's right;" or think, "he's a pastor, he should know what he's talking about."

The Rev. Jim Jones, leader of the People's Temple was a pastor. His movement began as a fundamentalist Christian group, seeking racial harmony and social justice. He exhorted his followers to hark back to the days of Christianity, when Jesus' followers lived by their commitment to universal equality and social justice. He set up a soup kitchen for the hungry, clothed the poor, found jobs for the unemployed, and eventually was named director of a city's human rights commission.

However, when his modest flock began to increase, his sermons focused less and less on the Christian gospel of love and developed into hours-long sermons about how he had been chosen by God, and his lust for power and recognition grew in the poor man, until he completely deceived himself, and in 1962 began to tell his followers that he himself was Jesus Christ. His followers were taught to call him "FATHER" and "PROPHET," and commanded that they go out and preach that Jim Jones was Christ, and he would back it up with miracles.

Fake cancers were plucked from startled old women. He had his accomplices rise from wheelchairs and walk on what he tried to make people believe were crippled legs. Jones stuffed a plastic bag filled with blood under his shirt, and when an accomplice shot him with blanks, Jones burst the bag and fell to the floor as if dead before his stunned congregation. A short time later he reappeared, waving the bullet plucked from his wound, and said he had raised himself from the dead

San Francisco was his headquarters and was a supply depot for his tropical paradise in Guyana. Here, one of the most gruesome events in history took place. Some followers of Rev. Jones finally began to see through this devil possessed man and began to leave Jonestown. Fearing for their relatives still in Jonestown, the Temple defectors sought help from the U.S. State Department and from Congressman Lee Ryan. Ryan and some People's Temple defectors set out with some press representatives to investigate Jones and his Jonestown, which had become a virtual concentration camp.

After Ryan arrived in Jonestown, and during his brief visit, some of Jones followers also wanted to leave with Ryan, and Jones sent his "AVENGING ANGELS" to the airport at Port Kaituma. In a hail of gunfire, Ryan and four members of his party were murdered. Later, Jones led his followers to commit suicide by drinking Flavour-Aide laced with cyanide. Nearly 1,000 members of the People's Temple died in November, 1978, including Jones and some of his immediate family. See the American Annual 1979, pp. 34-37, by Gerald Lubenow; San Francisco Bureau Chief, *Newsweek Magazine*.

"BEWARE OF FALSE PROPHETS, WHICH COME TO YOU IN SHEEP'S CLOTHING, BUT INWARDLY THEY ARE RAVENING WOLVES." Matthew 7:15.

False Christs and false prophets have arisen from Babel and will continue to arise until Jesus comes. Let the reader always remember, Christ will not walk this earth at his Second Coming. The Jesus of the Bible will meet his followers in the air. I Thessalonians 4:16, 17. And it shall come as a destruction upon the world, not a reign of Peace. II Peter 3:9, 10. Jesus will destroy the wicked at His Second Coming (II Thessalonians 1:7-9). But at the same time, the righteous who have died in the Lord, and the righteous who are living at Christ's Second Coming, will meet Him in the air and be taken to Heaven (I Corinthians 15:51-56). The earth will be completely emptied of the human race at the presence of the Lord (Isaiah 24:1-3; II Peter 3:10). Jeremiah the prophet, makes this very clear to us also in his vision of the Lord's Second Coming:

"I BEHELD THE EARTH, AND LO, IT WAS WITHOUT FORM, AND VOID; AND THE HEAVENS, AND THEY HAD NO LIGHT. I BEHELD THE MOUNTAINS, AND LO, THEY TREMBLED, AND ALL THE HILLS MOVED LIGHTLY. I BEHELD, AND LO, THERE WAS NO MAN, AND ALL THE BIRDS OF THE HEAVENS WERE FLED. I BEHELD, AND LO, THE FRUITFUL PLACE WAS A WILDERNESS, AND ALL THE CITIES THEREOF WERE BROKEN DOWN AT THE PRESENCE OF THE LORD, AND BY HIS FIERCE ANGER. FOR THUS HATH THE LORD SAID, THE WHOLE LAND SHALL BE DESOLATE; YET WILL I NOT MAKE A FULL END. FOR THIS SHALL THE EARTH MOURN, AND THE HEAVENS ABOVE BE BLACK: BECAUSE I HAVE SPOKEN IT, I HAVE PURPOSED IT, AND WILL NOT REPENT, NEITHER WILL I TURN BACK FROM IT." Jeremiah 4:23-28.

It was the lack of study of the Scriptures that led Israel to worship false gods, and reject Jesus as the Messiah. It is the lack of studying the Scriptures which causes multitudes of Christians to follow in the footsteps of the Antichrist, who has conditioned the world through a false system of Christianity. The same message that Elijah gave to the deceived Israelites is the same message to be given to deceived Christians today. "HOW LONG HALT YE BETWEEN TWO OPINIONS? IF THE LORD BE GOD, FOLLOW HIM: BUT IF BAAL, THEN FOLLOW HIM." I Kings 18:21. Just as Elijah was called by God in the Old Testament to turn Israel from idolatry, so is Jesus calling a people to preach the real Gospel unmixed with paganism. The same Spirit that led Elijah in days of old, is the same Spirit that will lead the small remnant of the True Faith in these last days. "AND IT SHALL COME TO PASS AFTERWARD, THAT I WILL POUR OUT MY SPIRIT UPON ALL FLESH; AND YOUR SONS AND DAUGHTERS SHALL PROPHESY, YOUR OLD MEN SHALL DREAM DREAMS, YOUR YOUNG MEN SHALL SEE VISIONS: AND ALSO UPON THE SERVANTS AND UPON THE HANDMAIDS IN THOSE DAYS WILL I POUR OUT MY SPIRIT." Joel 2:28, 29.

And, as Elijah was translated to Heaven (Mark 9:1-13), and was taken up to Heaven and saw no death (II Kings 2:11, 12), so will those in these last days be translated to Heaven at Jesus' Second Coming, when He comes in a chariot of fire. Isaiah 66:15-17; I Thessalonians 4:16-18.

The fire Elijah brought down from Heaven will be counterfeited by the SECOND BEAST of Revelation 13:13, whom we will study in the last chapter. The miracles of Christ will be counterfeited, while at the same time genuine manifestations will be performed. Only by the knowledge of the Scriptures will a believer see who is led by the Holy Spirit and who is being used by the Spirit of Satan. Miracles will not be the sign of the true Church, but those who are preaching the FAITH OF JESUS without human theory and paganism. Unless we know the Scriptures and the Will of God for ourselves, these great counterfeits of the power of darkness shall deceive the very elect of God, if possible (Matthew 24:24).

"FOR THEN SHALL BE GREAT TRIBULATION, SUCH AS WAS NOT SINCE THE BEGINNING OF THE WORLD TO THIS TIME, NO, NOR EVER SHALL BE. AND EXCEPT THOSE DAYS SHOULD BE SHORTENED, THERE SHOULD NO FLESH BE SAVED: BUT FOR THE ELECT'S SAKE THOSE DAYS SHALL BE SHORTENED." Matthew 24:21,22.

This passage of Scripture has a TWO-FOLD meaning; there are two periods of the Great Tribulation. The first was during the Dark Ages and the second is when Michael, who is Christ, shall stand up. Daniel 12:1,2. There are two periods of the Antichrist which, the first, history does record; and second, the unfulfilled prophecies which are still future. But for us to understand the prophecies of the Antichrist, we must understand fully the great apostasy of Israel, which is also history.

When light from the Bible is rejected, darkness of Satan sets in. The Lord has foretold that the world will be covered by spiritual darkness, but those who seek Him with all their hearts will find light and shine like lights to the world.

"FOR, BEHOLD, THE DARKNESS SHALL COVER THE EARTH, AND GROSS DARKNESS THE PEOPLE: BUT THE LORD SHALL ARISE UPON THEE, AND HIS GLORY SHALL BE SEEN UPON THEE." Isaiah 60:2.

Then spake Jesus again unto them, saying, "I AM THE LIGHT OF THE WORLD: HE THAT FOLLOWETH ME SHALL NOT WALK IN DARKNESS, BUT SHALL HAVE THE LIGHT OF LIFE." John 8:12.

The Bible, the Word of God, reveals that by beholding we become changed. By beholding the evils of the world, people can be transformed into the very likeness of what he has been observing. A good example of this is the changing fashions of dress and appearance. We are not saying dress and appearance is evil, but the love of display and self-glorification is. Satan is the chief designer who has invented the ever changing fashions that are a snare to most, to both Christian and the unbeliever. The love of display or self-glorification develops and cultivates the attributes of the author of self-glorification, which are pride, envy, jealousy, hatred, conceit, etc. There is no such thing as Christian jewelry. The wearing of gold and silver ornaments by men and women, was most strikingly condemned after the Israelites made the golden calf.

"YE ARE A STIFFNECKED PEOPLE: I WILL COME UP INTO THE MIDST OF THEE IN A MOMENT, AND CONSUME THEE: THEREFORE NOW PUT OFF THY ORNAMENTS FROM THEE: THAT I MAY KNOW WHAT TO DO UNTO THEE. AND THE CHILDREN OF ISRAEL STRIPPED THEMSELVES OF THEIR ORNAMENTS BY THE MOUNT OF HOREB." Exodus 33:5,6.

Paul writing to Timothy in the New Testament states:

"IN LIKE MANNER ALSO, THAT WOMEN ADORN THEMSELVES IN MODEST APPAREL, WITH SHAMEFACEDNESS AND SOBRIETY; NOT WITH BROIDED HAIR, OR GOLD, OR PEARLS, OR COSTLY ARRAY. BUT (WHICH BECOMETH WOMEN PROFESSING GODLINESS) WITH GOOD WORKS." I Timothy 2:9,10.

In ancient times, the prince of the air led the human race to commit cannabalism, to sacrifice children, to commit suicide, to inflict self-mutilation, because the gods the people worshipped committed these things. By beholding these immoral gods, the people were led to commit the same atrocious acts. In our modern times, millions waste away their lives in front of television sets and in front of movie screens beholding every evil, sickness, horror, and monstrous act the pagan worshippers of Baal committed in the times past. From cannibalism to mass murders, the youth receive a steady diet of this daily, as well as do the adults. If you don't believe T.V. programs have an influence on people, try turning it off for a week. Many would rather go without many things than be without television. However, God has given us another image to behold. This image is a revelation of His own nature. It is found in His Son Jesus Christ. "Who is the image of the invisible God, the firstborn of every creature." Colossians 1:15. We should spend as much time as our day allows in study and in meditation about the things of Christ's. By beholding Jesus we are changed into His Image, instead of the other image that is very dominant in the human race. "BUT WE ALL, WITH OPEN FACE BEHOLDING AS IN A GLASS THE GLORY OF THE LORD, ARE CHANGED INTO THE SAME IMAGE FROM GLORY TO GLORY, EVEN BY AS THE SPIRIT OF THE LORD." II Corinthians 3:18.

Paul knew the struggle a person goes through once he sees his own miserable life. He knew he wanted to do good, but did that which he didn't want to do.

"For I know that in me (that is, in my flesh) dwelleth no good thing: for to will is present with me; but how to perform that which is good I find not." Romans 7:18.

This is what the good news of the Gospel of Jesus Christ is all about. Jesus will save us from that which we cannot save ourselves. Jesus will give us power to overcome our evil habits that have been the ruin of many lives. This is why the angels called Mary blessed, for she would bring forth the one that would save us from our sins. (Matthew 1:21).

Every good gift and every perfect gift is from God; but all suffering, sickness, and death is from Satan. Our Adversary does not want us to know the promises of God, found in the Scriptures, made known to anyone who will search and claim them. Satan knows the Scriptures better than we do. Remember the temptation of Christ in the fourth chapter of Matthew, how Satan used Scriptures to tempt the Lord? But Christ again used Scripture to rebuke Satan. The Bible reveals a blueprint of the salvation of man through Jesus Christ. It shows what we must do to be forgiven of past sin.

"AND THAT THEY MAY RECOVER THEMSELVES OUT OF THE SNARE OF THE DEVIL, WHO ARE TAKEN CAPTIVE BY HIM AT HIS WILL." II Timothy 2:26.

But Satan has made sin popular by using T.V., movies, magazines, books, and newspapers. Satan is taking away the natural affection of many people today. The filthy four letter words that even hardened criminals might be ashamed to speak around certain people, have become every day language in many families, both poor and rich. With the lust of amusement and pleasure in the world, Satan has tucked away the name of Jesus Christ unless used in a "cuss" word. But the Bible has revealed that at the name of Jesus every knee shall bow. Philippians 2:10.

"Wherefore I give you to understand, that no man speaking by the Spirit of God calleth Jesus accursed: and that no man can say that Jesus is the Lord, But by the Holy Ghost." I Corinthians 12:3.

Either we are led by the Spirit of God or led by the spirit of Satan. "Therefore if any man be in Christ, he is a new creature: old things are passed away; behold all things are become new." II Corinthians 5:17. "In this the children of God are manifest, and the children of the devil;

whosoever doeth not righteousness is not of God, neither he that loveth not his brother." I John 3:10.

Until we come to God through Jesus Christ, we are all children of the devil according to Scripture. We also have the attributes of the god of this world and reflect Satan's image by our deeds.

"Little children, let no man deceive you: he that doeth righteousness is righteous, even as he is righteous. He that committeth sin is of the devil; for the devil sinneth from the beginning. For this purpose the Son of God was manifested, that he might destroy the works of the devil." I John 3:7, 8.

We have not the power to do good, or to stop doing the evil we have committed in the past, or the sins we are committing this present day, outside the help of Christ. The word of God reveals that because of our evil hearts we cannot do righteousness.

"The heart is deceitful above all things, and desperately wicked: who can know it? I the Lord search the heart, I try the reins, even to give every man according to his ways, and according to the fruit of his doings." Jeremiah 17:9,10.

But as the Scriptures proclaim, punishment to the evil doer which is death; so do they reveal forgiveness and life if claimed by faith.

"For the wages of sin is death; but the gift of God is eternal life through Jesus Christ our Lord." Romans 6:23.

To you who have already accepted Christ, and who are fighting a hand to hand combat with your own evil heart, listen to the words of our Saviour through Ezekiel 36:25,26; Jeremiah 32:38-40.

"THEN WILL I SPRINKLE CLEAN WATER UPON YOU, AND YE SHALL BE CLEAN: FROM ALL YOUR FILTHINESS, AND FROM ALL YOUR IDOLS, WILL I CLEANSE YOU. A NEW HEART ALSO WILL I GIVE YOU, AND A NEW SPIRIT WILL I PUT WITHIN YOU: AND I WILL TAKE AWAY THE STONY HEART OUT OF YOUR FLESH, AND I WILL GIVE YOU A HEART OF FLESH. AND THEY SHALL BE MY PEOPLE, AND I WILL BE THEIR GOD: AND I WILL GIVE THEM ONE HEART, AND ONE WAY, THAT THEY MAY FEAR ME FOR EVER, FOR THE GOOD OF THEM, AND OF THEIR CHILDREN AFTER THEM: AND I WILL MAKE AN EVERLASTING COVENANT WITH THEM, THAT I WILL NOT TURN AWAY FROM THEM, TO DO THEM GOOD; BUT I WILL PUT MY FEAR IN THEIR HEARTS, THAT THEY SHALL NOT DEPART FROM ME."

The promise is that we will receive a new heart from God so that we can do his will. When King David took a good look at his life and how he sinned greatly against the Lord, he prayed:

"Have mercy upon me, O God, according to thy loving kindness: according unto the multitude of thy tender mercies blot out my transgressions . . . . For I acknowledge my transgressions: and my sin is ever before me. Against thee, thee only, have I sinned, and done this evil in thy sight: that thou mightest be justified when thou speakest, and be clear when thou judgest . . . . Hide thy face from my sins, and blot out all mine iniquities. Create in me a clean heart, O God: and renew a right spirit within me. Cast me not away from thy presence; and take not thy holy spirit from me. Restore unto me the joy of thy salvation; and uphold me with thy free spirit. Then will I teach transgressors thy ways; and sinners shall be converted unto thee." Psalm 51:1, 3, 4, 9-13

When we see our state of sin and its shame, we too might come to feel as David about our hearts and agree with Scripture: "The heart is deceitful above all things, and desperately wicked: who can know it?" Jeremiah 17:9

"For from within, out of the heart of men, proceed evil thoughts, adulteries, fornications, murders, Thefts, covetousness, wickedness, deceit, lasciviousness, an evil eye, blasphemy, pride, foolishness." Mark 7:21, 22

Like Israel in the days of Elijah, Christ is seeking to draw men's minds away from the vanities of the world to Him. Elijah was the instrument the Lord used to call His people to repentance and turn them to Him. As many wander to and fro to seek help for their troubled minds and problems, they seek love and comfort from friends, but find rejection and hate because, in most cases, their friends are as bad off as they. Nevertheless, many will not find the path that leads to life, including some who have been pastors and priests for years, because they are filled with pride and cannot humble themselves at the feet of the Saviour. They have enjoyed for many years pointing out the errors of other denominations, but when their error has been exposed, they will refuse to listen. Like Jezebel, they will not believe the message of Elijah.

"The fool hath said in his heart, There is no God. Corrupt are they, and have done abominable iniquity: there is none that doeth good. God looked down from heaven upon the children of men, to see if there were any that did understand, that did seek God." Psalm 53:1, 2

Such was the case of Israel in the days of Ahab, king of Israel. From shortly after Joshua's time to Elijah the prophet, we can read where the Israelites turned to worship other gods and committed many abominations. From Elijah's time to Daniel's time, the Israelites both in the North and in the South worshipped Baal. Each time a reformation was secured, shortly afterwards, they fell back into idolatry. This went on until God removed both the Northern Kingdom of Israel, and the Kingdom of Judah in the south. They were scattered throughout the land of Nimrod. The Northern Ten Tribes were taken to Assyria by King Shalmaneser of Assyria (II Kings 17:1-24), and Judah later was taken captive, and the Jews were brought to Babylon by King Nebuchadnezzar. (II Kings 25:1-12).

Step by step, Satan's religion drifted into the whole land of the Israelites. Images of Baal and Ashtoreth were everywhere to be seen. Pagan temples and sacred trees (Groves) of this man-made religion, directed by Satan, were multiplied. Human sacrifices, sacred prostitution, sorcery, astrology, and most of all, the evils of the seven nations God told Moses to command the children of Israel to destroy in Canaan, did the Israelites commit.

Instead of casting Baalim out of their sight as the Lord commanded, they eventually became worse than their pagan neighbors.

As pointed out to you earlier, Jezebel was the daughter of a pagan priest King named Ethbaal, King of the Zidonians, whom Ahab married. I Kings 16:31. The Zidonians were named after the founder of their city, Zidon, who was the son of Canaan. Genesis 10:15, I Chronicles 1:13.

It was the Zidonians who influenced Solomon into the worship of the pagan goddess Ashtoreth. I Kings 11:5. Ezekiel foretold Zidon's destruction and that it was a pricking brier to Israel, Ezekiel 28:22-24.

Because the worship of Baal gave reverence to the things of nature as the source of all bounties, the Israelites worshipped the created things instead of the Creator. By reasoning away truths, little by little the great deceiver had God's chosen people praying to rocks, posts, trees, and carved images that were symbols of Baalim and Ashtoreth. When a pagan bowed before his image and an unbeliever would ask why you worship stone, he would usually answer, "I am not worshipping stone, it's just a symbol of my god." The pagan claimed the image was just a reminder, or a help to remind them of the deity. But God clearly warned Israel not to make any image of Him.

"Take ye therefore good heed unto yourselves; for ye saw no manner of similitude on the day that the Lord spake unto you in Horeb out of the midst of the fire: lest ye corrupt yourselves, and make you a graven image, the similitude of any figure, the likeness of male or female, the likeness of any beast that is on the earth, the likeness of any winged fowl that flieth in the air, the likeness of anything that creepeth on the ground, the likeness of any fish that is in the waters beneath the earth: and lest thou lift up thine eyes unto heaven, and when thou seest the sun, and the moon, and the stars, even all the host of heaven, shouldest be driven to worship them, and serve them, which the Lord thy God hath divided unto all nations under the whole heaven." Deuteronomy 4:15-19.

The dependence on images and amulets leads to trusting more unto the symbol than the Lord. Instead of worshipping God in spirit and in truth, it leads to trusting in a symbol or amulet for some kind of magical power to keep from evil, or be delivered from, as pointed out earlier. But God did give the ancient world and the Israelites a special reminder or memorial that he is the Lord God, The Creator.

"REMEMBER THE SABBATH DAY, TO KEEP IT HOLY." Exodus 20:8.

What is the Sabbath Day? To the average person they never heard of it. Unless you are a Jew or a Christian or have studied the Old Testament, you probably never came across the word Sabbath. The word Sabbath means rest in Hebrew. What are we to do on the Sabbath Day?

"SIX DAYS SHALT THOU LABOUR, AND DO ALL THY WORK: BUT THE SEVENTH DAY IS THE SABBATH OF THE LORD THY GOD: IN IT THOU SHALT NOT DO ANY WORK, THOU, NOR THY SON, NOR THY DAUGHTER, THY MANSERVANT, NOR THY MAIDSERVANT, NOR THY CATTLE, NOR THY STRANGER THAT IS WITHIN THY GATES:" Exodus 20:9,10.

Which day is the Sabbath Day? Look up in your dictionary the word Sunday; it will tell you that Sunday is the first day of the week, your calendar will also. The day Sunday was the Sabbath or rest day that the pagan Sun Worshippers knew all over the known world. The word "SUNDAY" means the Day of the SUN God. As a matter of fact, each day of the week is named after a pagan god. Here they are in Latin, Saxon, and English.

Latin	Saxon	English
1. Dies Solis	1. Sun's Day	1. Sunday
2. Dies Lunae	2. Moon's Day	2. Monday
3. Dies Martis	3. Tiw's Day	3. Tuesday
4. Dies Mercurii	4. Woden Day	4. Wednesday
5. Dies Jovis	5. Thor's Day	5. Thursday
6. Dies Veneris	6. Friga's Day	6. Friday
7. Dies Saturni	7. Saturn's Day	7. Saturday

The pagan had a day for each of the gods they worshipped. But the Lord at creation blessed one day to be set aside as His Holy Day; a Day on which we are to leave all worldly business transactions for money making and come to worship Him. Some who err in the Scriptures will tell you the Sabbath Day, the Seventh day, was only given in the Ten Commandments to the Jewish people by Moses. But the Holy Scriptures say just the opposite. God gave the Sabbath Day to the world over 2,000 years before the Jews ever existed.

"THUS THE HEAVEN AND THE EARTH WERE FINISHED, AND ALL THE HOST OF THEM. AND ON THE SEVENTH DAY GOD ENDED HIS WORK WHICH HE HAD MADE; AND HE RESTED ON THE SEVENTH DAY FROM ALL HIS WORK WHICH HE HAD MADE. AND GOD BLESSED THE SEVENTH DAY, AND SANCTIFIED IT: BECAUSE THAT IN IT HE HAD RESTED FROM ALL HIS WORK WHICH GOD CREATED AND MADE." Genesis 2:1-3.

Just as God had a day that recognized Him as Creator of Heaven and Earth, which He made in six days (Genesis 1:1-31), so did Satan create a worship day that recognized the Sun God Baal as the creator. The venerable day of the Sun, the first day of the week, was most sacred to the pagans as the Sabbath Day was and is to God's people. Known religious leaders all over the world will tell you the Sabbath Day, the seventh Day, was changed by Christ or His apostles to Sunday to commemorate the resurrection of Christ who arose from the dead on Sunday. But where in the Word Of God can we find such a transfer?

Let us forget what all the Catholics say, and most Protestants teach, and find out what the Scriptures say before the Catholic or Protestant Churches came into history. Not only does the Bible foretell the future, but it is also a history book as well. If you will study the Old Testament closely, which the New Testament magnifies, you will come to the conclusion there were two main reasons for God punishing Israel. They were idolatrous and they had broken away from the sacred observance of the Sabbath of the Lord. As most times in the past, it was the religous leaders that caused the ordinary people to err.

"The priests said not, Where is the Lord? and they that handle the law knew me not: the pastors also transgressed against me, and the prophets prophesied by Baal, walked after things that do not profit. The prophets prophesy falsely, and the priests bear rule by their means; and my people love to have it so: and what will ye do in the end thereof?" Jeremiah 2:8; 5:31.

The Lord commanded God's chosen people to always put a difference between the common and the Holy, the profane and the sacred, the clean and the unclean. Israel was warned not to mingle the common everyday occurences with the sacred things of Jehovah.

"For thou art an holy people unto the Lord thy God, and the Lord hath chosen thee to be a peculiar people unto himself, above all the nations that are upon the earth. Thou shall not eat any abominable thing. Moreover also I gave them my sabbaths, to be a sign between me and them, that they might know that I am the Lord that sanctify them." Deuteronomy 14:2,3; Ezekiel 20:12.

The word "SANCTIFY" means to set apart, to make Holy. God gave the Israelites a command to keep the Sabbath Day as a memorial to the Lord for creating the Heavens and the Earth. The seventh day was blessed at creation and sanctified by God Himself to be set aside from all other days of the week, as the Holy Day of the Lord our God. The Seventh Day Sabbath is a mark or a Sign that the Lord makes us Holy to Himself, and it was and is distinct from Baal Worship.

"And hallow my sabbaths; and they shall be a sign between me and you, that ye may know that I am the Lord your God. Notwithstanding the children rebelled against me: they walked not in my statues, neither kept my judgments to do them, which if a man do, he shall even live in them; they polluted my sabbaths: then I said, I would pour out my fury upon them, to accomplish my anger against them in the wilderness. Her priests have violated my law, and have profaned mine holy things: they have put no difference between the holy and profane, neither have they shewed difference between the unclean and the clean, and have hid their eyes from my sabbaths, and I am profaned among them." Ezekiel 20:20,21; 22:26.

Nehemiah prayed to the Lord to remember him, how he restored the Sabbath Day among the Jews after their 70 year captivity in Babylon. He mentioned how the Jews bought and sold on the Sabbath before, like their father before, like their fathers before them, and that this was one of the reasons why God destroyed the city of Jerusalem. Nehemiah commanded that the gates of the city of Jerusalem be shut on the Sabbath so the heathen who did not observe the rest day of the Lord wouldn't tempt the Jews to buy and sell during the Sabbath hours. Nehemiah 13:14-22.

All through the Old Testament we find Scripture where Israel despised the Holy things of God.

"Thou hast despised mine holy things, and hast profaned my sabbaths." Ezekiel 22:8.

God, who commanded that no buying or selling is to be done on the Sabbath, is the same God today. "For I am the Lord, I change not;" Malachi 3:6. "I know that whatsoever God doeth, it shall be forever: nothing can be put to it, nor any thing taken from it: and God doeth it, that men should fear before him." Ecclesiastes 3:14.

If God's word never changes, then you might say, how is it that most Christians keep Sunday as the Lord's Day? Well, it was changed, and in modern times this is one of the biggest stumbling blocks for the modern Jew to accept Jesus as the True Messiah. For the Jew knows that God's Word is not to be added to, or any thing taken from it.

"ADD THOU NOT UNTO HIS WORDS, LEST HE REPROVE THEE, AND THOU BE FOUND A LIAR. FOR THOU BLESSEST, O LORD, AND IT SHALL BE BLESSED FOREVER." Proverbs 30:6; I Chronicles 17:27.

"FOR IN SIX DAYS THE LORD MADE HEAVEN AND EARTH, THE SEA, AND ALL THAT IN THEM IS, AND RESTED THE SEVENTH DAY: WHEREFORE THE LORD BLESSED THE SABBATH DAY, AND HALLOWED IT." Exodus 20:11.

We will investigate more about the ancient Sabbath, and who was responsible for its change from the seventh day to the first day later. We have explored much of the worship of the Sun and its origin, now let's investigate Satan's invention in the Western Hemisphere.

The Aztecs as the Babylonians, Persians, Greeks, Romans, Egyptians, Hindus, etc. . . . believed in a chief God with a Mother goddess. There were lesser gods below the god and mother goddess, whose duty it was to govern the things of nature.

HUITZILOPOCHTLI was the Sun God and War God of the Aztec people. Just as Abraham was called by God to lead his family to the promised land, so did the prophets and chieftans of the Aztecs say HUITZILOPOCHTLI had called them to the central valley of Mexico. The Aztecs believed their place of origin was Chicomoztec, an Island in the middle of a lake, "The Place of Herons," located in their mythical homeland of Azlan.[1]

HUITZILOPOCHTLI, according to legend, told his followers to travel south until they reached another island in another lake that had the same magical properties of their original homeland. Renaming his Aztecas the Mexicas, he put a sign on their foreheads, gave them bows and arrows and promised that they would become Lords of the earth. The Aztecs also were to look for a sign from their god, that would show their final destination and promised land. They were to look for an eagle with a serpent in its beak, perched on a cactus, on a small island.[2]

The Aztecs penetrated the Central Valley of Mexico in 1248 A.D. For three or four generations the Aztecs served other tribes of Indians who were in the valley before they arrived. One such tribe was the Colhuacan. They were a principal ruling tribe of that time in Mexico. The Aztecs thinking they were paying the Colhuacan homage took a Toltec

---

[1] See *Mexico Mystique*, by Frank Waters, pp. 175,177.
[2] See *Mexico Mystique*, by Frank Waters, p. 177.

princess as a wife for their chief, and in 1323 A.D., sacrificed her, in the belief that she would then become a War Goddess. The Colhuacans were horrified when they heard of the sacrifice; and the Aztecs had to flee for their lives in 1325 A.D., into the salt water island of Lake Texcoco. Here they saw their sign, an eagle with a serpent in its beak, perched on a cactus, on a small island; they named the island after their chief Tenocha, who was their leader then. This scrubby little island became the Aztec's capital city called TENOCHTITLAN. Now, it's called Mexico City.[3]

When this became crowded, the Aztecs constructed artificial islands to help provide houses and vegetable gardens for their people. Each of the man-made islands connected with Tenochtitlan by causeways. Today they are called "The Floating Gardens." Also an Eagle with a Serpent in its beak, perched on a cactus on a small island is the National Emblem of Mexico. In the center of Mexico City (Tenochtitlan), is where the Aztecs erected a temple for HUITZILOPOCHTLI. In 1486 A.D. or 1487 A.D., the great temple of the Sun God was dedicated. For years humans were reserved from all over the city to be sacrificed at the dedication of the shrine to the Sun God. Captives who were to be sacrificed formed a procession two miles long. The ceremony sacrificed eighty thousand and four hundred humans during four days.[4]

The Aztecs sacrificed humans to their god HUITZILOPOCHTLI because the Sun and the Stars killed each other at night, and HUITZILOPOCHTLI was reborn every morning. Hence, the bloody sacrifices of the Aztecs were believed by them to be necessary to continue the world for HUTIZILOPOCHTLI the Sun God, being nourished by human blood.

In the process of time the Aztecs adopted other gods from Indian tribes of the Mexican Central Valley, who were there centuries before their arrival. QUETZALCOATL was one of them, who we will study later. By the time of the Spanish conquest, the Aztecs had thirteen principal deities, and more than two hundred lesser gods, to each of whom some special day, or appropriate festival, was consecrated.[5]

In the legends of the Aztecs it was believed the world went through four cycles or stages, and each consisted of several thousand years. At the end of each cycle the human family would be swept from the earth. During the first era, all the peoples of the world were destroyed by a flood, except a man named Cox Cox and his wife. Some of the neighbor-

---

[3] See *Man's Rise to Civilization,* by Peter Farb, pp. 164,165.
[4] See *The Aztecs,* by Fray Diego Duran, p. 199.
[5] See *The World of the Aztecs,* by William H. Prescott, p. 44.

ing people of the Aztecs far to the south were the MICHOACAN, who had a more complete story. Their Noah was TEZPI, WHO ESCAPED THE FLOOD IN A BOAT THAT WAS FILLED WITH VARIOUS KINDS OF ANIMALS AND BIRDS. AFTER SOME TIME A VULTURE WAS SENT OUT FROM IT, BUT REMAINED FEEDING ON THE BODIES OF GIANTS, WHICH HAD BEEN LEFT ON THE EARTH. As the waters subsided, the humming-bird, HUITZITZILIN WAS SENT FORTH, AND RETURNED WITH A TWIG IN ITS BEAK. As the descendants of Noah built a tower to the heavens after the flood, so did a family of giants near the city of Puebla build a pyramid rising almost to the height of one hundred and eighty feet. But the gods were offended with their presumptions; they sent fire from heaven on the pyramid.[6]

Before the arrival of the Aztecs, a race of giants was believed to have built the pyramids of the sun and the moon at TEOTIHUACAN. One race of giants was called CHICHIMECS. Other giants were said to be in TLAXCALA and CHOLULA and HUEXOTZINCO. The Cholultecs fought with the giants until they killed them or drove them from the country. In certain places of that region enormous skeletons of giants have been found.[7]

The amazing parallels to the Book of Genesis, startled the Conquistadores in the 16th century. Missionaries were sent to convert the Aztecs to Catholicism. Joseph de Acosta, a Jesuit, began to write in 1580 about the origin of the Indians in America. Since all men are descendants of Adam, they had to originally come from the Old World. And because all men were destroyed by the flood, save Noah's family, the American Indians were descendants from one of Noah's sons Shem, Ham, and Japheth. Genesis 9:18. Because the Mexican Indians had many parallels to the Bible, Acosta believed the American Indians were from the Ten Lost Tribes of Israel, who were from the Northern kingdom of Israel that were scattered in the land of Nimrod (Assyria), by Shalmaneser. II Kings 17:6, 26. However, if the Indians were Jewish, they had forgotten the lineage, their law, their ceremonies, and their entire religion, for the Indians never practiced any of these things save circumcision. Other theories said the Indians were from Carthage, Phoenicia, Ethiopia, China, Ophir, and other places in the Old World. The mystery of where the first settlers of America actually came from is still covered in the earth to this date, but the Bible says they got their start from Mesopotamia. The modern theory is that they came from Siberia, across a land bridge. But let us look again to the Bible to see if we can find any

---

[6] See *The Conquest of Mexico and The Conquest of Peru*, by William H. Prescott, pp. 693,694.
[7] See *The Aztecs* by Fray Diego Duran, pp. 11,12.

more evidence. The Lord says in Genesis 6:4, "THERE WERE GIANTS IN THE EARTH BEFORE THE FLOOD." Huge bones of both animals and men have been uncovered from different parts of the world, including Mexico. Man before the flood must have been of a huge stature, and degenerated through the years both in height and length of life. Noah was 600 years old when the flood came and he lived 350 years after the flood, making him 950 years old when he died. Genesis 9:29. Noah's children were the remnants of the people before the flood. Most of the giants of the Bible after the flood can be traced to Ham, the son of Noah.

Before entering Canaan, Moses sent twelve spies from the twelve tribes, one from each tribe, to spy out the land. They saw the children of ANAK, WHO WERE GIANTS. Numbers 13:33. Anak's descendants were called Anakims. Deuteronomy 9:2.

"A PEOPLE GREAT AND TALL, THE CHILDREN OF THE ANAKIMS, WHOM THOU KNOWEST, AND WHOM THOU HAST HEARD SAY, WHO CAN STAND BEFORE THE CHILDREN OF ANAK!" The giant Anak had three sons who were Animan, Sheshai, and Talmai. Joshua 15:14. The giant Anak's three sons had descendants who were the giants, the twelve spies Israel saw in Numbers 13:22-33.

Because they were afraid to go in the land, all the Israelites twenty years or older, who wandered in the wilderness forty years, died. Numbers 14:12-34. Only Joshua and Caleb went into Canaan from that generation. Numbers 32:8-13. In Joshua's day, the whole land was possessed by a race of giants. Joshua, after crossing over the Jordan, destroyed them from the mountains, and from Hebron, Debir, and Anab, so that a few were left in GAZA, GATH and ASHDOD, cities of the PHILISTINES. Joshua 11:21,22.

Anak, whose name means: (GIANT, LONG NECK) was the son of ARBA. Joshua 15:13. ARBA'S name means: (STRENGTH OF BAAL). Kir-jath-arba was named after ARBA, and later it was called HEBRON. Joshua 14:15. Arba founded the city and his descendants lived there and were called the Sons of Heth. Genesis 23:2,3,20. Heth was the second son of Canaan. Genesis 10:15. Canaan was the fourth son of HAM. Genesis 10:6. Canaan was the brother of CUSH, who begot NIMROD. In the Greek Septuagint, translated in Egypt, the term "MIGHTY" as applied in Genesis 10:8, to Nimrod, is rendered an ordinary name for GIANT. It was NIMROD WHO WAS "FIRST TO BE A MIGHTY ONE ON EARTH," who was the leader of the GIANTS that rebelled against Heaven.[8]

Let the reader remember, Genesis 11:8, says that the Lord scattered

---

[8] See *The Two Babylons,* by Alexander Hislop, pp. 31-37,55.

ABROAD THE FACE OF ALL THE EARTH the inhabitants of BABEL. Here is more evidence of the American Indian origin which began at Mesopotamia. Another god who was celebrated among the MEXICANS was WODEN, to whom they trace their race. In the legends found in the CHIAPANESE of the valley of Mexico, WODEN was the GREAT-GRANDSON of the old man, who at the time of the GREAT DELUGE, in which the greater part of the human race perished, was saved on a raft, together with his family. Woden contributed to the construction of a GREAT EDIFICE. The structure was begun as an effort to reach the skies. The execution of this rash project was interrupted. Each family received from that time a different language; and the great spirit TEOTL ordered Woden to go with his people to ANAHUAC (The Indian name for the valley of Mexico).

As the Saxons celebrated Woden's day, WHICH IS THE WEDNESDAY OF OUR CALENDAR TODAY, SO DID THE MEXICANS HAVE A DAY WHICH THEY CALLED WODEN'S DAY. To the Mexican Woden, and Odin to the Viking, and Adon to the Babylonians was Nimrod, who was the greatgrandson of Noah.[9]

The most astonishing facts about the Mexican past are found in their traditions about QUETZALCOATL, the Toltec, Colhuacan and the Mayan Messiah, who the Aztecs adopted in their religion. His Mayan name is Kukulcan. He was born of a virgin and the MORNING STAR VENUS WAS HIS SYMBOL. As Nimrod's incarnate son Tammuz was white, so was QUETZALCOATL. The Aztec Trinity was the Sun GOD HUITZILOPOCHTLI, QUETZALCOATL, AND THE MOON GODDESS COATLICUE.

QUETZALCOATL WAS A PRIEST-KING, AND COATLICUE was his mother and the Indian version of the Mother of gods. Coatlicue was one of the five moon goddesses of Mexico. In their myths Coatlicue could not make life possible without the help of certain mysterious magicians and the sun. Until the magicians solved the mystery of her existence, she remained hidden in a cloud, alone and sterile. But when the Sun appeared to take COATLICUE for a bride, all the instinctive forces of life came into being in QUETZALCOATL. [10]

As in all the pagan Messiahs — TAMMUZ, ADONIS, OSIRIS, ATTIS, HERCULES, GILGAMESH, KRISHNA, etc., QUETZALCOATL had many variations to his myth. Some say he was born in TEOTIHUACAN "THE CITY OF GODS." Quetzalcoatl was worshipped by the ancient Indian tribes of the valley of Mexico, "AS THE INCARNATE SON OF

---

[9] See *The Two Babylons,* Alexander Hislop, pp. 134,245.

[10] See *Mexican and Central American Mythology,* by Irene Nicholson, p. 85.

Quetzalcoatl the Mexican Messiah in his demonical form. In his human form, he was believed to have been white with a black beard and black hair. Courtesy of the Brooklyn Museum.

THE SUN, long before the arrival of the Aztecs. The pyramid to the Sun in Teotihuacan, is one of the largest pyramids in the world, in archeological discoveries to date. The pyramid to the sun stands 217 feet high on a base of 750 feet square. Symbols that represent Quetzalcoatl are sculptured at its base. The name Quetzalcoatl means BIRD-SERPENT, whose symbol is a plumed serpent. There is also a temple to the moon at Teotihuacan that is 149 feet high, with a courtyard surrounded by thirteen temples.

The Incarnate Sun God Quetzalcoatl, came to the Americas, according to legend, as mysterious as he left. As Jesus left the earth after his resurrection and promised to come back to destroy Satan, and overthrow the Kingdoms of the world, so did QUETZALCOATL have a similar belief among his followers in Mexico. Because Quetzalcoatl offended one of the principal gods of the land, he was compelled to abandon the country. On his way, he stopped at the city of Cholula, where a temple was dedicated to his worship. When he reached the shores of the Mexican Gulf, he told his small band of followers he would return and then, entering a skiff, made of serpent skins, embarked on the ocean for Tlapallan. Quetzalcoatl is said to have been tall with white skin, long, dark hair, and a flowing beard.[11] The son of the Sun during his residence on earth, instructed the natives in the use of metals, in agriculture, and in the arts of government. In his time maize grew so tall that every cob was as strong and firm as a human being. Pumpkins reached to a man's height and cotton grew in all colours.[12] A similar story is told in the Bible. When the twelve spies were sent into the land of Canaan, not only did they see giants in the land, but two of the spies cut one cluster of grapes from a vine, and it was so big, they had to carry it upon a staff. Numbers 14:23.

There are two main versions of the Quetzalcoatl legend. The first tells how the god-man fell from grace and allowed himself to be coaxed into a drunken orgy, during which he had sexual intercourse with his sister. When he recovered he repented, built his own funeral pyre, and rose to heaven as the planet Venus. Semiramis, the mother of Tammuz, is said to have burnt herself on a pyre out of grief at the death of a favorite horse. Oriental monarchs often died voluntarily by fire.[13]

As the Priest-King Ethbaal, Jezebel's father took on the supreme name of his god, so did the pagan priests of Quetzalcoatl. They were called by the same name. Just as the prophets and priests of Baal were considered by the people to be Baal's vicar here on earth, so were the

---

[11] See *The Conquest of Mexico and the Conquest of Peru,* by William H. Prescott, p. 39.
[12] See *Mexican and Central American Mythology,* by Irene Nicholson, p. 83.
[13] See *Adonis Attis Osiris* by Sir James George Fraser, p. 176.

priests of Quetzalcoatl and Huitzilopochtli. These blood thirsty priests who were supposed to be full of wisdom, to be perfect in all customs, who took a vow of celibacy were said to be loving, merciful, compassionate, friendly, devoted and god fearing. It is said by eye witnesses, that the Aztec priests sacrificed at least 20,000 human beings a year.[14]

Like Christianity, the Aztecs had the sign of the cross as a promise of eternal life, and had a form of Holy Communion, Baptism, and confession of sin. In their rite of Holy Communion, they also partook of bread to be kept in rememberance of their god.

In Bible truth,the bread represents a symbol of Christ's body being broken for us, and the juice from the grape as a symbol of Jesus' Blood that was shed for us. Luke 22:17-20; I Corinthians 11:24-26.

However, in the Aztec and the Egyptian communion, we see another meaning. The Aztecs would make an image of their god out of flour of maize, mixed with blood, and after consecration by the priests, it was distributed among the people, who as they ate it, showed signs of humiliation and sorrow, declaring it was the flesh of the deity. Although different in appearance, and substance, the bread used in the Egyptian Osiris communion had the same meaning. The Egyptians would eat the flesh of Osiris, the sun-divinity, in a form of a round disk wafer. The wafer was shaped as a round disk to be a symbol of the sun. The Aztec priest, as well as the Egyptians and Babylonian Cahna-Bal, taught the ignorant people that they had power to miraculously change the bread into their real deity. By eating the flesh and blood of their god they would receive food to feed the spirit inside them, better known today as the soul. Engraved on the Egyptian waver was I.H.S. It was the symbol for the Egyptian Trinity, "ISIS, HORUS, SEB" that is; THE MOTHER, THE CHILD and the FATHER OF GODS. Today in some Christian churches it means: "IESUS HOMINUM SALVATOR," Latin for — "JESUS THE SAVIOUR OF MEN."[15]

In the true faith of the Bible, Jesus said:

"VERILY, VERILY, I SAY UNTO YOU, EXCEPT YE EAT THE FLESH OF THE SON OF MAN, AND DRINK HIS BLOOD, YE HAVE NO LIFE IN YOU. I AM THE LIVING BREAD WHICH CAME DOWN FROM HEAVEN: IF ANY MAN EAT OF THIS BREAD, HE SHALL LIVE FOR EVER: AND THE BREAD THAT I WILL GIVE IS MY FLESH, WHICH I WILL GIVE FOR THE LIFE OF THE WORLD." John 6:53,51.

Just as the body needs physical food, so does the inward man need

---

[14] See *The World of Aztecs*, by William H. Prescott, p. 56.

[15] See *The Two Babylons*, by Alexander Hislop, pp. 133,162,164.

spiritual food. "It is the spirit that quickeneth; the flesh profiteth nothing; the words that I speak unto you, they are spirit and they are life." John 6:63. The backbone of pagan philosophy is that man consists of two beings; the physical and the "soul" which lives on after the death of the body. In Bible truth the soul dies: Ezekiel 18:4, "Behold, all souls are mine; as the soul of the father, so also the soul of the son is mine; THE SOUL THAT SINNETH, IT SHALL DIE."

The life Jesus teaches is eternal life in the flesh as He Himself arose from the dead in the flesh, NOT AS A GHOST OR SPIRIT. When Jesus appeared to the disciples they thought He might have been a GHOST (SPIRIT).

"AND HE SAID UNTO THEM, WHY ARE YE TROUBLED? AND WHY DO THOUGHTS ARISE IN YOUR HEARTS? BEHOLD MY HANDS AND MY FEET, THAT IT IS I MYSELF: HANDLE ME, AND SEE; FOR A SPIRIT HATH NOT FLESH AND BONES, AS YE SEE ME HAVE. AND WHEN HE HAD THUS SPOKEN, HE SHEWED THEM HIS HANDS AND HIS FEET. AND WHILE THEY YET BELIEVED NOT FOR JOY, AND WONDERED, HE SAID UNTO THEM, HAVE YE HERE ANY MEAT? AND THEY GAVE HIM A PIECE OF BROILED FISH, AND OF AN HONEYCOMB. AND HE TOOK IT, AND DID EAT BEFORE THEM." "BUT THOMAS, ONE OF THE TWELVE CALLED DIDYMUS, WAS NOT WITH THEM WHEN JESUS CAME. THE OTHER DISCIPLES, THEREFORE, SAID UNTO HIM, WE HAVE SEEN THE LORD. BUT HE SAID UNTO THEM, EXCEPT I SHALL SEE IN HIS HANDS THE PRINT OF THE NAILS, AND PUT MY FINGER INTO THE PRINT OF THE NAILS, AND THRUST MY HAND INTO HIS SIDE, I WILL NOT BELIEVE. AND AFTER EIGHT DAYS AGAIN HIS DISCIPLES WERE WITHIN, AND THOMAS WITH THEM: THEN CAME JESUS, THE DOORS BEING SHUT, AND STOOD IN THE MIDST, AND SAID, PEACE BE UNTO YOU. THEN SAID HE TO THOMAS, REACH HITHER THY FINGER AND BEHOLD MY HANDS; AND REACH HITHER THY HAND, AND THRUST IT INTO MY SIDE; AND BE NOT FAITHLESS, BUT BELIEVING. AND THOMAS ANSWERED AND SAID UNTO HIM, MY LORD AND MY GOD. JESUS SAITH UNTO HIM, THOMAS BECAUSE THOU HAST SEEN ME, THOU HAST BELIEVED: BLESSED ARE THEY THAT HAVE NOT SEEN, AND YET HAVE BELIEVED." Luke 24:38-43; John 20:24-29.

The great hope of Christianity is the "RESURRECTION OF THE DEAD," from Adam's time until Jesus' second coming. The great hope of paganism is to shed this mortal body and become as spirits or be reincarnated as humans, insects, animals, etc. . . . This is how priests of the sun gods led multitudes to be sacrificed, willing, in many cases. The pagans were great in the flesh, but dead inwardly (spiritually). They saw the elements of nature bring the bud, the plant, and the fruit. They were awed to see their Chief Deity, the Sun, send its beams to nourish the flowers and the plants. The Natural man saw that everything that had breath seemed to turn in the direction of the sun. The flowers turned their petals towards the sun to be painted by its beams into glorious patterns of beauty, and the birds and animals seemed to herald in the day star with their songs before sunrise. They had a god or goddess for rain, night, day, love, death, war, fertility, the seas, fire, the underworld, justice, liberty, scribes, and fortifications, etc. . . .

They paid homage to created things instead of the creator, "And worshipped and served the creature more than the Creator, who is blessed for ever. Amen." Romans 1:25.

To eat the Flesh and drink the Blood of the Son of God is to feast upon the Word of God found in the Bible. We are to eat the Word of God, digest it inwardly. Just as the natural body needs to be nourished, so must the spiritual or inward part of man be fed. People can make themselves look like angels of light on the outside, but inwardly could be mad men. "Beware of false prophets which come to you in sheep's clothing, but inwardly they are ravening wolves." Matthew 7:15.

It is the inward man that controls outward acts of the body. "Behold, thou desirest truth in the inward parts: and in the hidden part thou shall make me to know wisdom." Psalm 51:6. But the natural man, no matter how he whitewashes the flesh cannot be consistent in doing good. "For there is no faithfulness in their mouth; their inward part is very wickedness; their throat is an open sepulchre; they flatter with their tongue. Psalm 5:6. These six things doth the Lord hate! Yea, seven are an abomination unto him. a proud look, a lying tongue, and hands that shed innocent blood, an heart that deviseth wicked imaginations, feet that be swift in running to mischief, a false witness that speaketh lies, and he that soweth discord among brethren." Proverbs 6:16-19.

But the wicked person may make peace with His Maker by learning God's plan for man found in the scriptures. "All scripture is given by inspiration of God, and is profitable for doctrine, for reproof, for correction, for instruction in righteousness: that the man of God may be perfect, throughly furnished unto all good works." II Timothy 3:16,17.

"But the natural man receiveth not the things of the Spirit of God: for they are foolishness unto him: neither can he know them, because they are spiritually discerned. For the preaching of the cross is to them that perish foolishness: but unto us which are saved it is the power of god. For it is written, I will destroy the wisdom of the wise, and will bring to nothing the understanding of the prudent. Where is the wise? Where is the disputer of the world? Hath not God made foolish the wisdom of the world? for after that in the wisdom of God the world by wisdom knew not God, it pleased God by the foolishness of preaching to save them that believe." I Corinthians 2:14; 1:18-21.

Jesus said: "NO MAN CAN COME TO ME, EXCEPT THE FATHER WHICH HATH SENT ME DRAW HIM: AND I WILL RAISE HIM UP AT THE LAST DAY." John 6:44.

"JESUS ANSWERED, VERILY, VERILY, I SAY UNTO THEE, EXCEPT A MAN BE BORN OF THE WATER AND OF THE SPIRIT, HE CANNOT ENTER INTO THE KINGDOM OF GOD. THAT WHICH IS BORN OF THE FLESH IS FLESH, AND THAT WHICH IS BORN OF THE SPIRIT IS SPIRIT. FOR THEY THAT ARE AFTER THE FLESH, DO MIND THE THINGS OF THE FLESH: BUT THEY THAT ARE AFTER THE SPIRIT, THE THINGS OF THE SPIRIT." John 3:5, 6; Romans 8:5.

Until a person is born again spiritually, he cannot understand the Scriptures, or the plan of God for him or her in this world. It's foolishness to the unbeliever. The followers of Christ, in the days Jesus walked this earth, did not completely understand spiritual things. "Then he opened their understanding that they might understand the Scriptures." Luke 24:45.

The same Jesus who opened the understanding of the fisherman, about 1900 years ago, is the same Jesus who will open the understanding of anyone who seeks God's will for him found in the Scriptures.

"TURN YOU AT MY REPROOF: BEHOLD, I WILL POUR OUT MY SPIRIT UNTO YOU, I WILL MAKE KNOWN MY WORDS UNTO YOU. TRUST IN THE LORD WITH ALL THINE HEART; AND LEAN NOT UNTO THINE OWN UNDERSTANDING. IN ALL THY WAYS ACKNOWLEDGE HIM, AND HE SHALL DIRECT THY PATHS." Proverbs 1:23; 3:5,6.

It is the purpose of the Evil One to blind the spiritual perception of man by outward forms of religion, and the amusements of this world. Every human being in the past, present and future is influenced by the Spirit of God, or the spirit of the world. The Spirit of God leads the believer to Heavenly things, the god of this world seeks to lead us to worship worldly things.

There is one very important doctrine we will study before we go on to the next chapter. It is Baptism. We have seen throughout this chapter, many Messiahs and many religious doctrines which claim to lead to the Creator of the Universe. However, in Bible truth:

"Jesus saith unto him, I am the way, the truth, and the life: no man cometh unto the Father, but by me." John 14:6. Not through Buddah, Adonis, Osiris, Attis, Hercules, Krishna, Mohammed, Vishnu, Quetzalcoatl, or any other name does man come unto the Father.

"Neither is there salvation in any other: for there is none other name under heaven given among men, whereby we must be saved." Acts 4:12. There are also found in all religions, many forms of Baptism before a person can enter into the covenants of his god. Some, to become a partaker of his god's promises were baptized from head to toe in bull's blood. However, the main baptisms, both Christian and pagan, are by water. Some are splashed in the face or head with holy water, or baptized completely from head to toe in water by immersion. Others receive baptism by a cross drawn on their foreheads. Some are taught baptism must be employed immediately after birth while others are not baptized until a child is fully aware of his sin, and the sins he or she inherited through our first parents. There is much confusion among the Christians about Baptism. But the Scriptures still state:

"THERE IS ONE BODY, AND ONE SPIRIT, EVEN AS YE ARE CALLED IN ONE HOPE OF YOUR CALLING; ONE LORD, ONE FAITH, ONE BAPTISM, ONE GOD AND FATHER OF ALL, WHO IS ABOVE ALL, AND THROUGH ALL, AND IN YOU ALL." Ephesians 4:4-6.

Let's take a look at the two main variations of Baptism practiced today in both Christian and pagan religions. In the Sun Worship of the Mexicans, they not only baptized their babies at infancy, but performed exorcism. The Mexican midwife would usually perform the sacrament. The midwife facing the west sprinkled water on the infant, then would pronounce these words: "O my child, take and receive the water of the Lord of the world, which is our life, which is given for the increasing and renewing of our body. It is to wash and to purify. I pray that these Heavenly Drops may enter into your body, and dwell there; that they may destroy and remove from you all the evil and sin which was given you before the beginning of the world, since all of us are under its power. . . ." She then washed the body of the child with water, and spoke in this manner: "Whencesoever thou comest, thou that art hurtful to this child, leave him and depart from him, for he now liveth anew, and is born anew; now he is purified and cleansed afresh, and our mother CHALCHIVITLYCUE (GODDESS OF WATER) bringeth him into the world." Having thus prayed, the midwife took the child in both hands, and, lifting him towards heaven, said "O Lord, thou seest here this creature, whom thou hast sent into the world, this place of sorrow, suffering, and penitence. Grant him, O Lord, thy gifts and inspiration, for thou are the great God, and with thee is the great goddess."[16]

In Bible truth, a person is not Baptized until he or she hears the Gospel, repents and confesses his or her sins to God and claims the forgiveness promised by the death of Christ, and made possible by His giving His life as a sacrifice for our past sins. Belief, Repentance, and Baptism is the first step in becoming a Christian. However, how can a child (an infant) understand when there is no knowledge about good and evil in the first month or two of a little one's life?

The commandment from the Author of our Faith told the disciples to preach the Gospel first, then Baptize.

"And he said unto them, Go ye into all the world, and preach the gospel to every creature. He that believeth and is baptized shall be saved; but he that believeth not shall be damned." Mark 16:15,16. Infant Baptism cannot be found in the scriptures, but can be found on the pages of Sun Worship. Baptism found in the Bible is an ordinance commemorating the Death, Burial, and Ressurrection of Christ. The sinner gives a public demonstration of his faith, that he no longer wants to follow "the course of this world, according to the prince of the air, the spirit that now worketh in the children of disobedience." Ephesians 2:2.

After a sinner has heard from the Gospel the saving power of Christ crucified and the sinner's sins are exposed, then a sincere person will want to make his peace with God. Baptism is a public display that denounces Satan as god of this world and that the sinner has chosen Christ as his Lord and Saviour.

"FOR AS MANY OF YOU AS HAVE BEEN BAPTIZED INTO CHRIST HAVE PUT ON CHRIST." Galatians 3:27. "KNOW YE NOT, THAT SO MANY OF US AS WERE BAPTIZED INTO JESUS CHRIST WERE BAPTIZED INTO HIS DEATH? THEREFORE, AS WE ARE BURIED WITH HIM BY BAPTISM INTO DEATH: THAT LIKE AS CHRIST WAS RAISED UP FROM THE DEAD BY THE GLORY OF THE FATHER, EVEN SO WE ALSO SHOULD WALK IN THE NEWNESS OF LIFE." Romans 6:3,4.

In Bible Baptism, we not only publicly denounce Satan, but also die to our old ways. "Knowing this, that our old man is crucified with him, that the body of sin might be destroyed, that henceforth we should not serve sin. For he that is dead is freed from sin. Now if we be dead with Christ, we believe that we shall also live with him. Knowing that Christ being raised from the dead dieth no more; death hath no more dominion over him. For that he died, he died unto sin once: but in that he liveth, he

---

[16] See *The Two Babylons*, by Alexander Hislop, p. 133.

liveth unto God. Likewise, reckon ye also yourselves to be dead indeed unto sin, but alive unto God through Jesus Christ our Lord." Romans 6:6,7,8-11.

As the Scripture states in Ephesians 4:5, there is only one Baptism, and that is by Total Immersion, as Jesus was Baptized by John the Baptist. "AND JESUS, WHEN HE WAS BAPTIZED, WENT UP STRAIGHT OUT OF THE WATER: AND LO, THE HEAVENS WERE OPENED UNTO HIM, AND HE SAW THE SPIRIT OF GOD DESCENDING LIKE A DOVE, AND LIGHTING UPON HIM: AND LO A VOICE FROM HEAVEN, SAYING, THIS IS MY BELOVED SON, IN WHOM I AM WELL PLEASED." Matthew 3:16,17.

Baptism is a sacrament that Jesus the founder of the Faith commanded.

"VERILY, VERILY, I SAY UNTO THEE, EXCEPT A MAN BE BORN OF WATER AND OF THE SPIRIT, HE CANNOT ENTER INTO THE KINGDOM OF GOD. THAT WHICH IS BORN OF THE FLESH IS FLESH; AND THAT WHICH IS BORN OF THE SPIRIT IS SPIRIT. MARVEL NOT THAT I SAID UNTO THEE, YE MUST BE BORN AGAIN. THE WIND BLOWETH WHERE IT LISTETH, AND THOU HEAREST THE SOUND THEREOF, BUT CANST NOT TELL WHENCE IT COMETH, AND WHITHER IT GOETH: SO IS EVERY ONE THAT IS BORN OF THE SPIRIT." John 3:5-8.

The word Christian originally meant a follower of Christ. Jesus the Leader and founder of our Faith was Baptized by John the Baptist, by Immersion. "HE THAT SAITH HE ABIDETH IN HIM OUGHT HIMSELF ALSO SO TO WALK, EVEN AS HE WALKED." I John 2:6.

To be Baptized By Immersion is a symbol of Christ's Death, Burial, and Resurrection. As we partake of Bible Baptism, we also die, are buried in a watery grave, and afterwards are risen in Christ as a new person. To be splashed on the head with holy water, or a sign of the cross drawn on the forehead of a sinner is not Bible Baptism. This practice of baptism loses the whole spiritual meaning for being baptized. A sinner must become aware of his sinful life, believe as the eunuch, that Jesus is the Son of God and suffered on our behalf for our sins, then "Thou Mayest." Acts 8:37, (be baptized).

There is no understanding between right and wrong in infancy. How can a baby confess its sin? How can a baby believe in Jesus with all its heart? Holy water sprinkling is another mystery, found in the "WINE OF HER FORNICATION;" which in Divine Language means: another doctrine of "MYSTERY, BABYLON THE GREAT, THE MOTHER OF HARLOTS AND ABOMINATIONS OF THE EARTH." Revelation 17:2,5.

Nimrod, according to pagan philosophy, who was worshipped as the son of Semiramis, as well as her husband, did cause the whole world to worship the Sun, Moon, and the East Star (Venus). As we have seen throughout this chapter, they were the original pagan trio of the Great Idolatrous Babylonian system of Baal Worship. Every pagan nation borrows its religion from the first civilized city after the flood. In the Scriptures they were:

NIMROD	SEMIRAMIS	TAMMUZ
The Sun God	The Queen of Heaven	The Son of the Sun
Baal	Ashtoroth	The Pagan Messiah
I Kings 16:30-33	Judges 2:13	Ezekiel 8:14

Satan, as stated at the beginning of this book, had men worshipping the sun, the moon, stars, graven images of men, animals, birds, trees, insects, frogs, rocks, humans, etc. . . , everything did the pagan worship except the Creator, who created these things. However, there are multitudes of spiritual lessons to be learned which reveal God's plan for man in the created things of this world. While the ignorant pagan stood in awe at the sun's power to nourish the earth, and how everything in nature which has breath, at sunrise, seemed to turn, and depended on the sun's power for health and growth, he saw only the outward displays of God's love. The pagan studied how some flowers after the sun disappeared from the sky would close up to protect themselves from the cold darkness of the night. At night the beautiful songs of the birds would be hushed. At night, there is no promise of the presence of the sun, the day star.

However, at dawn, the morning star, the light bearer, showed the promise of another day. People who are without Christ are like the flowers who sit in darkness, and close in on themselves, with no hope for the future.

"BUT UNTO YOU THAT FEAR MY NAME SHALL THE SUN OF RIGHTEOUSNESS ARISE WITH HEALING IN HIS WINGS; AND YE SHALL GO FORTH, AND GROW UP AS CALVES OF THE STALL. WHEREBY THE DAYSPRING FROM ON HIGH HATH VISITED US, TO GIVE LIGHT TO THEM THAT SIT IN DARKNESS AND IN THE SHADOW OF DEATH, TO GUIDE OUR FEET INTO THE WAY OF PEACE. WE HAVE ALSO A MORE SURE WORD OF PROPHECY: WHEREUNTO YE DO WELL THAT YE TAKE HEED, AS UNTO A LIGHT THAT SHINETH IN A DARK PLACE, UNTIL THE DAY DAWN, AND THE DAY STAR ARISE IN YOUR HEARTS." Malachi 4:2; Luke 1:78, 79; II Peter 1:19.

Just as the moon, the lesser light of the night has no light of its own, but is a reflection of the sun, so will an evil person who has no righteousness, and no power to do good reflect the righteousness of Christ, if he turns to Him. This does not happen at once to a repented sinner, as the sun doesn't shine all at once. Just as the sun gradually rises at dawn, so will the sinner reflect the righteousness of the SON OF RIGHTEOUSNESS.

In the darkness of paganism, Nimrod throughout the world was worshipped as the great hope for the world, through a multitude of names. He has been worshipped as both son and husband of Semiramis. The son of the Sun home was the MORNING STAR, or EAST STAR, or BETTER KNOWN TODAY AS VENUS. In Bible truth, Satan will be destroyed by Christ forever after Jesus brings the New Jerusalem down to earth. Revelation 20:1-20.

The final destruction of the serpent, Satan's symbol, was foretold to our first parents, Adam and Eve at Eden: "AND THE LORD GOD SAID UNTO THE SERPENT, BECAUSE THOU HAST DONE THIS, THOU ART CURSED ABOVE ALL CATTLE, AND ABOVE EVERY BEAST OF THE FIELD: UPON THY BELLY SHALT THOU GO, AND DUST SHALT THOU EAT ALL THE DAYS OF THY LIFE; AND I WILL PUT ENMITY BETWEEN THEE AND THE WOMAN, AND BETWEEN THY SEED AND HER SEED; IT SHALL BRUISE THY HEAD, AND THOU SHALT BRUISE HIS HEEL." Genesis 3:14,15.

The Seed of Adam who is destined to bruise the serpent's head, and who, in doing so, was to have his own heel bruised. The sons and daughters of our first parents handed this promise down from generation to generation. The Patriarchs of the Bible along with Noah's sons were well acquainted with the promise of a Redeemer who would bruise the serpent's head. Let the reader remember, the whole human race came from Adam and Eve. The first family before the flood sacrificed a lamb that pointed to the Real Lamb of God to come later. Genesis 4:1-4.

The bruising of the heel of the Deliverer implied His death, for the curse of death could only be removed from the world, by the Sinless One, Jesus Christ.

At the Tower of Babel, God scattered man throughout the world, and this ancient promise of a Redeemer went with them. The Great Counterfeiter borrowed his doctrines that made up our Archenemy's religion, from the ancient Patriarchs of God. Nimrod and Semiramis were just human instruments satan used to pervert the True Faith, and cause deceit and destruction to the human race. To show this to be the truth, there is hardly a people or kindred on earth in whose pagan system of sun, moon,

The Egyptian god Horus and the Indian messiah Krishna crushing the head of the serpent. Courtesy of Loizeaux Brothers, Neptune, N.J.

and star worship, that does not have the promise of a Messiah and the final destruction of the Evil One.

The Greek Apollo would slay the serpent Pytho, and Hercules strangle serpents while yet in his cradle. In Egypt, India, Scandinavia and Mexico, there is the promise borrowed from Eden. In Mexico the serpent was crushed by the great spirit TEOTL. The Egyptian God Horus is pictured as piercing the head of a serpent with a spear. Krishna the incarnate of Vishnu is pictured crushing the head of Calyia the serpent, with his foot. In Scandinavia, Thor was said to have bruised the head of the great serpent with his mace.[1]

Before the birth of the real incarnate of God, the Seed that will bruise the serpent's head, the real Bright and Morning Star, the real God-Man, was to make His appearance on the behalf of man. Satan's messiah had already been preached and worshipped throughout the world, counterfeiting the religious rites passed down to God's people by the Patriarchs. Satan tried to destroy the True Faith by false gods, and when the written word was given, Satan hoped the learned men of the world would look to Christ as just another pagan messiah. When the Greatest Advent in man's history came into the world for the salvation of the human race: "HE IS DESPISED AND REJECTED OF MEN; A MAN OF SORROWS, AND ACQUAINTED WITH GRIEF: AND WE HID AS IT WERE OUR FACES FROM HIM; HE WAS DESPISED, AND WE ESTEEMED HIM

---

[1] See *The Two Babylons*, by Alexander Hislop, p. 60.

NOT. SURELY HE HATH BORNE OUR GRIEFS AND CARRIED OUR SORROWS: YET WE DID ESTEEM HIM STRICKEN, SMITTEN OF GOD, AND AFFLICTED. BUT HE WAS WOUNDED FOR OUR TRANSGRESSIONS, HE WAS BRUISED FOR OUR INIQUITIES: THE CHASTISEMENT OF OUR PEACE WAS UPON HIM; AND WITH HIS STRIPES WE ARE HEALED." Isaiah 53:3-5.

In the ancient world, Satan deceived millions with the darkness of pagan Sun worship. In these modern days Satan has taken on a brighter look, it's called Christianity. Instead of using the name Baal, which means Lord or Master, he is coming in the name of Jesus.

"BUT WHEN YE SHALL SEE THE ABOMINATION OF DESOLATION, SPOKEN OF BY DANIEL THE PROPHET, STANDING WHERE IT OUGHT NOT, (LET HIM THAT READETH UNDERSTAND) THEN LET THEM THAT BE IN JUDA FLEE TO THE MOUNTAINS: AND LET HIM THAT IS ON THE HOUSETOP NOT GO DOWN INTO THE HOUSE, NEITHER ENTER THEREIN, TO TAKE ANY THING OUT OF HIS HOUSE. AND LET HIM THAT IS IN THE FIELD NOT TURN BACK AGAIN FOR TO TAKE UP HIS GARMENT. BUT WOE TO THEM THAT GIVE SUCK IN THOSE DAYS." Mark 13:14-17.

One thousand years before the first advent of our Lord, David likened the people of God to Sheep, and our Lord to a GOOD SHEPHERD. David was a shepherd as a boy, who protected his sheep from the evil beasts around them. David, just a boy, killed a lion and a bear that took a lamb out of his flock. See I Samuel 17:34-37. David knew as the shepherd of the field protected his sheep from the evils of the world, so does the GOOD SHEPHERD in HEAVEN watch over His Flock. Just as the shepherd of the field could call his sheep by name, and his sheep knowing his voice would follow, so will the people of the Lord's Flock hear His voice from the Scriptures and do the things which He commands us. One millennium before God became a Man in Christ, David wrote:

"THE LORD IS MY SHEPHERD; I SHALL NOT WANT. HE MAKETH ME TO LIE DOWN IN GREEN PASTURES: HE LEADETH ME BESIDE THE STILL WATERS. HE RESTORETH MY SOUL: HE LEADETH ME IN THE PATHS OF RIGHTEOUSNESS FOR HIS NAME'S SAKE. YEA, THOUGH I WALK THROUGH THE VALLEY OF THE SHADOW OF DEATH, I WILL FEAR NO EVIL: FOR THOU ART WITH ME: THY ROD AND THY STAFF THEY COMFORT ME. THOU PREPAREST A TABLE BEFORE ME IN THE PRESENCE OF MINE ENEMIES: THOU ANOINTEST MY HEAD WITH OIL; MY CUP RUNNETH OVER. SURELY

GOODNESS AND MERCY SHALL FOLLOW ME ALL THE DAYS OF MY LIFE: AND I WILL DWELL IN THE HOUSE OF THE LORD FOREVER." Psalm 23.

At a later time, Jesus said:

"I AM THE GOOD SHEPHERD, AND KNOW MY SHEEP, AND AM KNOWN OF MINE. MY SHEEP HEAR MY VOICE, AND I KNOW THEM, AND THEY FOLLOW ME." John 10:14,27.

In these final days of earth's history, there are multitudes of Christian Churches, pastors, priests, Bible instructors, laymen, using television, radio, magazines, newspapers, and tracts proclaiming the Gospel of Christ; however, there is much religious confusion. But if the seeker would forget about what churches have to say, and find the Lord of the Bible will for him, and seek to do His will: "Then shall ye return, and discern between the righteous and the wicked, between him that serveth God and him that serveth him not." Malachi 3:18.

"THUS SAITH THE LORD THE KING OF ISRAEL, AND HIS REDEEMER THE LORD OF HOSTS; I AM THE FIRST, AND I AM THE LAST, AND BESIDE ME THERE IS NO GOD. AND, BEHOLD, I COME QUICKLY, AND MY REWARD IS WITH ME, TO GIVE EVERY MAN ACCORDING AS HIS WORK SHALL BE. I AM ALPHA AND OMEGA, THE BEGINNING AND THE END, THE FIRST AND THE LAST. I JESUS HAVE SENT MINE ANGEL TO TESTIFY UNTO YOU THESE THINGS IN THE CHURCHES. I AM THE ROOT AND THE OFFSPRING OF DAVID, AND THE BRIGHT AND MORNING STAR. AND THE SPIRIT AND THE BRIDE SAY, COME. . . . AND WHOSOEVER WILL, LET HIM TAKE THE WATER OF LIFE FREELY." Isaiah 44:6; Revelation 22:12,13,16,17.

World Kingdoms Foretold

The four beasts of Daniel's vision (Daniel 7:1-7), which symbolized four ruling Kingdoms of the Old World that would rise in succession.

CHAPTER III

World Kingdoms Foretold

Two of the hardest books to understand in the Bible are the books of Daniel and Revelation. These two books have revealed most of fulfilled history, that was foretold, centuries before it happened. Jewish prophecy is mostly in symbols and types. It was foretold in the book of Daniel that four great monarchies were to rise up and that each would become a world ruling power over all the known civilized world. In the book of Daniel, the second and seventh chapters are where we will study our Lord's great prophecy of world history that has been 100% accurate!

To prove these prophecies we need to know our history, for there were only four kingdoms in history that were Old World conquerors. These four nations were pagan sun, moon, and star worshippers, and each had its version of the system of Baal as its religion. The Lord uses BEASTS to describe the character of each kingdom. Here is the vision:

"IN THE FIRST YEAR OF BELSHAZZAR KING OF BABYLON DANIEL HAD A DREAM AND VISIONS OF HIS HEAD UPON HIS BED: THEN HE WROTE THE DREAM, AND TOLD THE SUM OF THE MATTERS. DANIEL SPAKE AND SAID, I SAW IN MY VISION BY NIGHT, AND, BEHOLD, THE FOUR WINDS OF HEAVEN STROVE UPON THE GREAT SEA. AND FOUR GREAT BEASTS CAME UP FROM THE SEA, DIVERSE ONE FROM ANOTHER. THE FIRST WAS LIKE A LION, AND HAD EAGLE'S WINGS: I BEHELD TILL THE WINGS THEREOF WERE PLUCKED, AND IT WAS LIFTED UP FROM THE EARTH, AND MADE STAND UPON THE FEET AS A MAN, AND A MAN'S HEART WAS GIVEN TO IT. AND BEHOLD ANOTHER BEAST, A SECOND, LIKE TO A BEAR, AND IT RAISED UP ITSELF ON ONE SIDE, AND IT HAD THREE RIBS IN THE MOUTH OF IT BETWEEN THE TEETH OF IT; AND THEY SAID THUS UNTO IT, ARISE, DEVOUR MUCH FLESH. AFTER THIS I BEHELD, AND LO ANOTHER, LIKE A LEOPARD, WHICH HAD UPON THE BACK OF IT FOUR WINGS OF A FOWL; THE BEAST HAD ALSO FOUR HEADS; AND DOMINION WAS GIVEN TO IT. AFTER THIS I SAW IN THE NIGHT VISIONS, AND BEHOLD A FOURTH

BEAST, DREADFUL AND TERRIBLE, AND STRONG EXCEEDINGLY; AND IT HAD GREAT IRON TEETH: IT DEVOURED AND BRAKE IN PIECES, AND STAMPED THE RESIDUE WITH THE FEET OF IT: AND IT WAS DIVERSE FROM ALL THE BEASTS THAT WERE BEFORE IT; AND IT HAD TEN HORNS." Daniel 7:1-7. Now, let's go back and study Daniel 7:1-7 more closely. There are six symbols in these verses we should study very carefully. Just as the countries of the world today are represented by symbols, such as the eagle for the United States and the Bear for Russia, so has the Lord used symbols to represent these four prophetic empires. But in verse two, Daniel saw that four winds of heaven strove upon the great sea. These symbols will explain themselves if we search God's word for their meaning. The FOUR WINDS of HEAVEN represent strife, war and commotion, as in Jeremiah 25:31, 32; 49:36,37.

"A noise shall come even to the ends of the earth; for the Lord hath a controversy with the nations, he will plead with all flesh; he will give them that are wicked to the sword, saith the Lord. Thus saith the Lord of hosts, Behold, evil shall go forth from nation to nation, and a great whirlwind shall be raised up from the coasts of the earth. And upon Elam will I bring THE FOUR WINDS from the four quarters of heaven, and will scatter them toward all those winds; and there shall be no nation whither the outcasts of Elam shall not come. For I will cause Elam to be dismayed before their enemies, and before them that seek their life: and I will bring evil upon them, even my fierce anger, saith the Lord; and I will send the sword after them, till I have consumed them."

Here are two Scriptures that interpret what wind represents in prophecy. As you read, they mean strife and war. Verse two of Daniel the seventh chapter also uses the term GREAT SEA in this prophecy. In Numbers 34:6, the Mediterranean was called the GREAT SEA. The great sea is a symbol of multitudes of peoples. In prophecy, waters are a symbol of people, as in: Isaiah 8:7,8; Revelation 17:15.

"Now therefore, behold, the Lord bringeth up upon them the waters of the river, strong and many, even the king of Assyria, and all his glory: and he shall come up over all his channels, and go over all his banks: And he shall pass through Judah; he shall overflow and go over, he shall reach even to the neck; and the stretching out of his wings shall fill the breadth of the land, O Immanuel. And he saith unto me, the waters which thou sawest, where the whore sitteth, are peoples, and multitudes, and nations, and tongues."

The four beasts will rise out of a great sea of people, nations, and tongues. Now, let's look at the beasts and their symbol meanings:

1. The first was like a lion, and had eagle's wings. (Daniel 7:4)

2. The second was a bear, and it had three ribs in its teeth. (Daniel 7:5)
3. The third was a leopard, which had four wings and four heads. (Daniel 7:6)
4. The fourth beast was dreadful, terrible, strong exceedingly; had great iron teeth: it was diverse from all the beasts, and it had ten horns. (Daniel 7:7)

In order to help us understand this vision of Daniel's four beasts, let us find out the symbolic meaning of beasts. We will be shown this in Daniel 7:17:

"THESE GREAT BEASTS, WHICH ARE FOUR, ARE FOUR KINGS, WHICH SHALL ARISE OUT OF THE EARTH."

Here is the key which unlocks the truth about these beasts. They represent "Four Kings" and a king must have a Kingdom to reign over, so these "Four Kingdoms" would arise out of the old world and each would become a world-ruling power in succession. Who was the first beast, a lion with eagle wings? Go to your encyclopedias and look up Babylon. It was Babylon that first conquered the whole known world from Daniel's time. King Nebuchadnezzar was ruler of Babylon from 605 B.C. to 562 B.C.[1] It was the armies of King Nebuchadnezzar that destroyed Jerusalem and took captives of the Israelites, along with Daniel the prophet, back to Babylon. (Daniel 1:1). Daniel was just a teenager when he was taken captive. It was in Babylon that astrology sprang up after the flood. Babylon in ancient times was called the "Land of the Chaldeans," Ezekiel 12:13; the Land of Shinar, Zechariah 5:11; the Lady of Kingdoms, Isaiah 47:5; Sheshach, Jeremiah 25:12,26; Land of Merathaim, Jeremiah 50:1,21; and the Desert of the Sea, Isaiah 21:1, 9. We read about the destruction of Jerusalem and its burning, and the destruction of the temple of the Lord in II Kings the 24th and 25th chapters.

The destruction of Jerusalem was fortold by Jeremiah the prophet in Jeremiah 21:3-10. In Jeremiah 27:2-8, the Lord foretold through the prophet that all nations would serve the King of Babylon. The Lord used Babylon to punish the old world for their wickedness, Jeremiah 51:7. Micah, another prophet of God who lived during the reigns of King Jotham, King Ahaz, and King Hezekiah foretold both the captivity of Judah and the restoration of the Jews from Babylon.

"Be in pain, and labour to bring forth, O daughter of Zion, like a woman in travail: for now shalt thou go forth out of the city, and thou shalt dwell in the field, and thou shalt go even to Babylon; there shalt

---

[1] See *Collier's Encyclopedia, Vol. 3,* p. 426.

thou be delivered; there the Lord shall redeem thee from the hand of thine enemies. Now also many nations are gathered against thee, that say, Let her be defiled, and let our eye look upon Zion. But they know not the thoughts of the Lord, neither understand they his counsel: for he shall gather them as the sheaves into the floor.'' Micah 4:10-12.

Isaiah the prophet lived in the time of these kings of Judah and foretold the restoration of the Babylonian captivity of the Jews, about a century before it happened. Isaiah was a prophet in Judah around 750-690 B.C., and Jeremiah was a prophet of Judah around 660 B.C.; Daniel was taken captive by King Nebuchadnezzar around 604 B.C. In

The Lion with eagle wings, symbolizing Babylon under King Nebuchadnezzar. The Neo-Babylonian Empire was from 605 B.C. to 539 B.C.

Jeremiah 29:10, it was foretold that the captivity of the Jews would last "70 years;"

"For thus saith the Lord, that after seventy years be accomplished at Babylon I will visit you, and perform my good word toward you, in causing you to return to this place."

In Micah 5:6, the Lord calls Mesopotamia "The Land of Nimrod," and Babylon was the greatest artifical wonder of the ancient world. Babylon was noted for the famous gate of Ishtar, dedicated to the Queen of Heaven. Also for the Hanging Gardens built by King Nebuchadnezzar for his Queen. Babylon was located about 55 miles south of modern Baghdad. The modern "Birs-Nimrud" (anciently the temple of Nebo at Borsippa), and Babil, near Hillah, have both been taken for the site of the Tower of Babel.[2]

History records that Nebuchadnezzar's reign was over the most glorious kingdom in history; however, it was one of the shortest lived empires, for a bear was to rise up and devour it. One of the symbols of ancient Babylon was a lion with eagle wings.

The wings of the lion represent swiftness, as in Deuteronomy 28:49:

"The Lord shall bring a nation against thee from far, from the end of the earth, as swift as the eagle flieth; a nation whose tongue thou shalt not understand:" It was foretold that Babylon would be overthrown by another kingdom and never to be inhabited again as it was. Isaiah foretold this in Isaiah 13:17-22:

"Behold, I will stir up the Medes against them, which shall not regard silver; and as for gold, they shall not delight in it. Their bows also shall dash the young men to pieces; and they shall have no pity on the fruit of the womb; their eye shall not spare children. And Babylon, the glory of kingdoms, the beauty of the Chaldees excellency, shall be as when God overthrew Sodom and Gomorrah. It shall NEVER BE INHABITED, NEITHER SHALL IT BE DWELT IN FROM GENERATION TO GENERATION, NEITHER SHALL THE ARABIAN PITCH TENT THERE; neither shall the shepherds make their fold there. But wild beasts of the desert shall lie there; and their houses shall be full of doleful creatures; and owls shall dwell there, and satyrs shall dance there. And the wild beasts of the islands shall cry in their desolate houses, and dragons in their pleasant palaces: and her time is near to come, and her days shall not be prolonged."

Alexander the Great (356 B.C.-323 B.C.), whom we will study more of shortly, wanted to rebuild a temple to Bel in Babylon, and make

---

[2] See Youngs *Analytical Concordance to the Bible*, p. 66.

Babylon today, the Gate of Ishtar looking south from the procession street. Courtesy of the Oriental Institute.

Babylon the capital of his empire. When Alexander the Great, the greatest conqueror the world has ever known, approached within the sight of Babylon on his first visit, he was warned by some Star-Gazers not to enter therein. His reply was: "THE BEST SEER HE WHO GUESSETH WELL," and Alexander entered the city at the head of his army. Alexander hoped to establish a regular trade route from the Indus to the Tigris and Euphrates, and then to the canals which connected the Nile with the Red Sea. Babylon had not completely reached its prophetic doom in the time of Alexander. Alexander destined Babylon to be his capital, and he wanted Babylon to become a naval station and a center of maritime commerce. On an early day in June, 323 B.C., a friend named Medius carried Alexander off to spend the rest of the night in a bout of

A reconstruction of Babylon, showing the Gate of Ishtar in the foreground. Courtesy of the Oriental Institute.

hard drinking. On the 28th day of June, Alexander died. The man who was to make Babylon again into a glorious city, fell as a victim of its curse.[3]

Over two thousand years later, Austin Henry Layard entered Babylon in 1850. "Babylon," said Layard, "had a sense of mystery and dread hung over its crumbling heaps of brick and sand." His workmen refused to set up camp near the abandoned ruins, and not a blade of grass would grow in the peculiar soil. Layard collected a good many small objects at Babylon but accomplished little else.[4]

Satan's seat was in Babylon, and it was he who actually gave it its splendor, not its past kings and queens. Just as God uses people so does Satan. In Isaiah 14:12-15,22-27 we read:

[3] See *A History of Greece,* by J. B. Bury, pp. 803-806.
[4] See *Road to Nineveh,* by Nora Benjamin Kubie, p. 272.

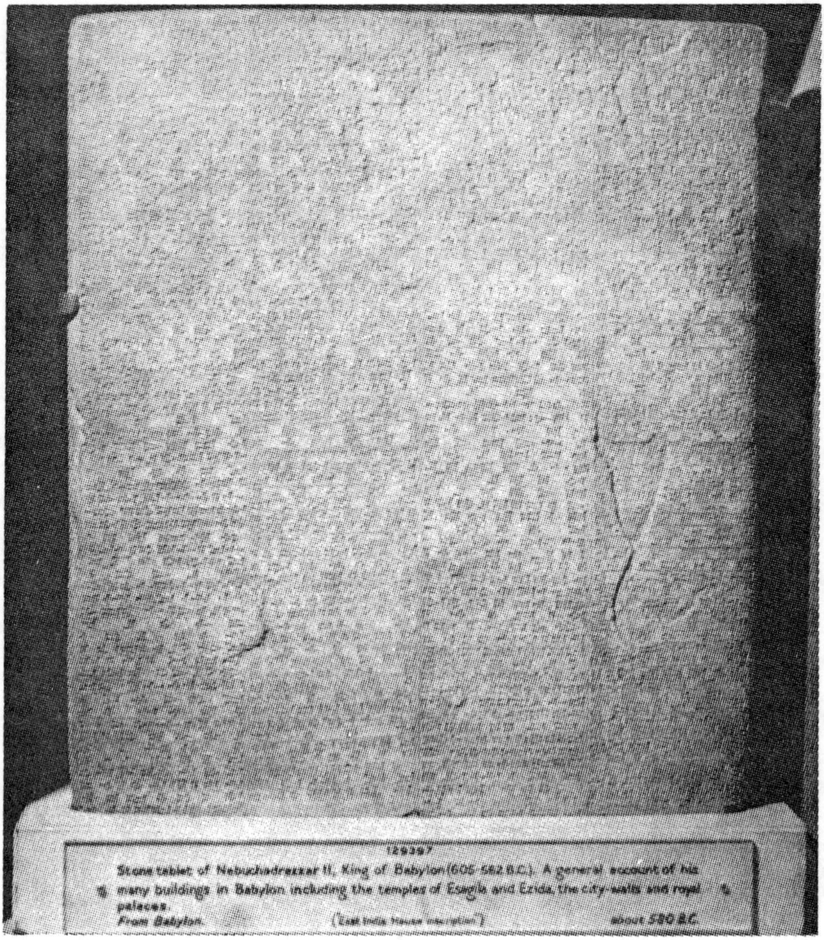

Stone tablet of Nebuchadnezzar. This tablet describes a general account of his many buildings in Babylon including the temples of Esagila and Ezida, the city walls and royal palaces. Courtesy of the British Museum.

"HOW ART THOU FALLEN FROM HEAVEN, O LUCIFER, SON OF THE MORNING! HOW ART THOU CUT DOWN TO THE GROUND, WHICH DIDST WEAKEN THE NATIONS! FOR THOU HAST SAID IN THINE HEART, I WILL ASCEND INTO HEAVEN, I WILL EXALT MY THRONE ABOVE THE STARS OF GOD: I WILL SIT ALSO UPON THE MOUNT OF THE CONGREGATION, IN THE SIDES OF THE NORTH: I WILL ASCEND ABOVE THE HEIGHTS OF THE CLOUDS: I WILL BE LIKE THE MOST HIGH. YET THOU SHALT BE BROUGHT DOWN TO

The Bear with three ribs between its teeth. This is a symbol of the Medo-Persian Empire from 538 B.C. to 331 B.C. The ribs represent the three provinces Babylon was divided into: Babylonia, Lydia, and Egypt.

HELL, TO THE SIDES OF THE PIT. FOR I WILL RISE UP AGAINST THEM, SAITH THE LORD OF HOSTS, AND CUT OFF FROM BABYLON THE NAME AND REMNANT, AND SON, AND NEPHEW, SAITH THE LORD. I WILL ALSO MAKE IT A POSSESSION FOR THE BITTERN, AND POOLS OF WATER: AND I WILL SWEEP IT WITH THE BESOM OF DESTRUCTION, SAITH THE LORD OF HOSTS. THE LORD OF HOSTS HATH SWORN, SAYING, SURELY AS I HAVE THOUGHT, SO SHALL IT COME TO PASS; AND AS I HAVE PURPOSED, SO SHALL IT STAND: THAT I WILL BREAK THE ASSYRIAN IN MY LAND, AND UPON MY MOUNTAINS TREAD HIM UNDER FOOT: THEN SHALL HIS YOKE DEPART FROM OFF THEM, AND HIS BURDEN DEPART FROM OFF THEIR SHOULDERS. THIS IS THE PURPOSE THAT IS PURPOSED UPON THE WHOLE EARTH: AND THIS IS THE HAND THAT IS

Cylinder of Cyrus the Great of Persia, which describes the fall of Babylon. Courtesy of the British Museum.

STRETCHED OUT UPON ALL NATIONS. FOR THE LORD OF HOSTS HATH PURPOSED, AND WHO SHALL DISANNUL IT? AND HIS HAND IS STRETCHED OUT, AND WHO SHALL TURN IT BACK?"

The besom of destruction which began to sweep away Babylon's existence is foretold in Daniel 7:5:

"And behold another beast, a second, like to a bear, and it raised up itself on one side, and it had three ribs in the mouth of it between the teeth of it: and they said thus unto it, Arise, devour much flesh."

History records that the Medo-Persian Empire took over the Babylonian Empire when Nabonidus, the last of the Neo-Babylonian rulers, left his son Belshazzar to reign in his absence. In 538 B.C., Cyrus the Persian ruler took over the city of Babylon without a struggle. The Medo-Persian Empire is recorded in historical records and in the Bible as the kingdom which freed the Jews from their Babylonian captivity.

More than a century before the birth of Cyrus, the Persian, Isaiah the prophet foretold even the name "Cyrus" would be the one who would free the Israelites, and even the manner in which he would do it. In Isaiah 45:1-3 we read:

"Thus saith the Lord to his anointed, to Cyrus, whose right hand I have holden, to subdue nations before him; and I will loose the loins of kings, to open before him THE TWO LEAVED GATES; AND THE GATES SHALL NOT BE SHUT; I will go before thee, and make the crooked places straight: I will break in pieces the gates of brass, and cut in sunder the bars of iron: And I will give thee the treasure of darkness, and hidden riches of secret places, that thou mayest know that I, the Lord, which call thee by thy name, am the God of Israel."

And that is just what happened over a century later. The Persians entered into the city of Babylon by turning away the waters of the Euphrates that ran through Babylon. The gates by the canal that ran through Babylon were carelessly left open, and the Persian army caught the Babylonians unawares and took the city without a fight.

During this time, the last Neo-Babylonian king was Nabunaid, or in Greek, Nabonidus. There was much unrest in Babylon during his reign, because Nabonidus wanted to replace Marduk, the chief head of the Babylonian pantheon of gods in this era of Babylon history, with Sin, the moon god. This of course brought disapproval by the clergy of Marduk. Nabonidus' most cherished dream was to rebuild the temple of Sin in Harran. Nabonidus tells us in one of his cuneiform texts that Marduk appeared to him in a dream and ordered him to rebuild E.hul.hul in Harran. The region of land was under the control of the Medes, a rival of the Persians at this era of time. Cyrus the Persian combined forces with Nabonidus, and took the city.[5]

Ten years of military campaigns gave Cyrus an empire larger than anything the world at that time had ever witnessed, expanding his empire from the Aegean to the Pamirs, a distance of almost three thousand miles. Cyrus, once an ally, now turned his armies toward Babylon. During this time Nabonidus was in Arabia. He had left the government of Babylon in the care of his son Belshazzar (Daniel 5:1-31). The subsequent events are described in detail in the Nabonidus Chronicle; it reads as follows:

"In the month of Tashritu (September-October), when Cyrus attacked the army of Akkad in Opis on the Tigris, the inhabitants of Akkad revolted, but he (Nabonidus) massacred the confused inhabitants.

The fifteenth day, Sippar was seized without a battle. Nabonidus fled. The sixteenth day, Gubaru, the governor of Gutium, and the army of Cyrus entered Babylon without a battle. Afterwards, Nabonidus was arrested in Babylon when he returned (there.)[6]

In *Daniel and the Revelation,* by Uriah Smith, Smith gives historical accounts of Cyrus' military strategy used against the Babylonians: "In their feeling of security lay the source of their danger. Cyrus resolved to accomplish by stratagem what he could not effect by force. Learning of the approach of an annual festival in which the whole city would be

---

[5] See *Ancient Iraq,* by Georges Roux, p. 320.

[6] *Ibid.,* p. 321.

given up to mirth and revelry, he fixed upon that day as the time to carry his purpose into execution. There was no entrance for him into that city unless he could find it where the river Euphrates entered and emerged as it passed under the walls. He resolved to make the channel of the river his highway into the stronghold of his enemy. To do this, the water must be turned aside from its channel through the city. For this purpose, on the evening of the feast day above referred to, he detailed one body of soldiers to turn the river at a given hour into a large artifical lake a short distance above the city; another to take their station at the point where the river entered the city; and a third to take a position fifteen miles below, where the river emerged from the city. The two latter bodies were instructed to enter the channel as soon as they found the river fordable, and in the darkness of the night explore their way beneath the walls, and press on to the palace of the king where they were to surprise and kill the guards, and capture or slay the king. When the water was turned into the lake, the river soon became shallow enough to ford, and the soldiers followed its channel into the heart of the city Babylon.

"But all this would have been in vain, had not the whole city given itself over on that eventful night to the most abandoned carelessness and presumption, a state of things upon which Cyrus calculated largely for the carrying out of his purpose. On each side of the river through the entire length of the city were walls of great height, and of equal thickness with the outer walls. In these walls were huge gates of brass, which, when closed and guarded, debarred all entrance from the river bed to any of the streets that crossed the river. Had the gates been closed at this time, the soldiers of Cyrus might have marched into the city along the river bed, and then marched out again, for all that they would have been able to accomplish toward the subjugation of the place.

"But in the drunken revelry of that fatal night, these river gates were left open, as had been foretold by the prophet Isaiah years before in these words: 'Thus saith the Lord to His anointed, to Cyrus, whose right hand I have holden, to subdue nations before him; and I will loose the loins of kings, to open before him the two-leaved gates; and the gates shall not be shut.' Isaiah 45:1. The entrance of the Persian soldiers was not perceived. Many a cheek would have paled with terror, had the sudden going down of the river been noticed, and its fearful import understood. Many a tongue would have spread wild alarm through the city, had the dark forms of armed foes been seen stealthily treading their way to the citadel of their supposed security. But no one noticed the sudden subsidence of the waters of the river; no one saw the entrance of the Persian warriors; no one took care that the gates should be closed and guarded; no one cared for aught but to see how deeply and recklessly he could plunge into the wild debauch. That night's dissipation cost the Babylonians their kingdom and their freedom.'' *Daniel and the Revelation,* by Uriah Smith, pp. 45-48. Review and Herald Publishing Association, Washington, D.C., revised in 1944, by the Southern Publishing Association, (by permission).

While Cyrus was making his way under the walls of Babylon, Daniel the prophet was with Belshazzar, whom Nabonidus the king, left in charge of his affairs and was acting king. Daniel the 5th chapter, records the event:

''Belshazzar the king made a great feast to a thousand of his lords, and drank wine before the thousand. Belshazzar, whiles he tasted the wine, commanded to bring the golden and silver vessels which his father Nebuchadnezzar had taken out of the temple which was in Jerusalem; that the king, and his princes, his wives, and his concubines, might drink therein. Then they brought the golden vessels that were taken out of the temple of the house of God which was at Jerusalem; and the king, and his princes, his wives, and his concubines, drank in them. They drank wine, and praised the gods of gold, and of silver, of brass, of iron, of wood, and of stone. In the same hour came forth fingers of a man's hand, and wrote over against the candlestick upon the plaster of the wall of the king's palace: and the king saw the part of the hand that wrote. Then the king's countenance was changed, and his thoughts troubled him, so that the joints of his loins were loosed, and his knees smote one against another. The king cried aloud to bring in the astrologers, the Chaldeans, and the soothsayers. And the king spake, and said to the wise men of Babylon, Whosoever shall read this writing, and shew me the interpretation thereof, shall be clothed with scarlet, and have a chain of gold about his neck, and shall be the third ruler in the kingdom. Then came in all the king's wise men: but they could not read the writing, nor make known to the king the interpretation thereof. Then was king Belshazzar greatly troubled, and his countenance was changed in him, and his lords were astonied. Now the queen, by reason of the words of the king and his lords, came into the banquet house: and the queen spake and said, O king, live for ever: let not thy thoughts trouble thee, nor let thy countenance be changed: There is a man in thy kindgdom in whom is the spirit of the holy gods; and in the days of thy father light and understanding and wisdom, like the wisdom of gods, was found in him; whom the king Nebuchadnezzar thy father, the king, I say, thy father, made master of the magicians, astrologers, Chaldeans, and soothsayers; Forasmuch as an excellent spirit, and knowledge, and understanding, interpreting of dreams, and shewing of hard sentences, and dissolving of doubts, were found in the same Daniel, whom the king named Belteshazzar: now let

Daniel be called, and he will shew the interpretation. Then was Daniel brought in before the king. And the king spake and said to Daniel, Art thou that Daniel, which art of the children of the captivity of Judah, whom the king my father brought out of Jewry? I have even heard of thee, that the spirit of the gods is in thee, and that light and understanding and excellent wisdom is found in thee. And now the wise men, the astrologers, have been brought in before me, that they should read this writing, and make known unto me the interpretation thereof: but they could not shew the interpretation of the thing: And I have heard of thee, that thou canst make interpretations, and dissolve doubts: now if thou canst read the writing, and make known to me the interpretation thereof, thou shalt be clothed with scarlet, and have a chain of gold about thy neck, and shalt be the third ruler in the kingdom. Then Daniel answered and said before the king, Let thy gifts be to thyself, and give thy rewards to another; yet I will read the writing unto the king, and make known to him the interpretation. O thou king, the most high God gave Nebuchadnezzar thy father a kingdom, a majesty, and glory, and honour: And for the majesty that he gave him, all people, nations, and languages, trembled and feared before him: whom he would he slew; and whom he would he kept alive; and whom he would he set up; and whom he would he put down. But when his heart was lifted up, and his mind hardened in pride, he was deposed from his kingly throne, and they took his glory from him: And he was driven from the sons of men; and his heart was made like the beasts, and his dwelling was with the wild asses: they fed him with grass like oxen, and his body was wet with the dew of heaven; till he knew that the most high God ruled in the kingdom of men, and that he appointed over it whosoever he will. And thou his son, O Belshazzar hast not humbled thine heart, though thou knewest all this; But hast lifted up thyself against the Lord of heaven; and they have brought the vessels of his house before thee, and thou, and thy lords, thy wives, and thy concubines, have drunk wine in them; and thou hast praised the gods of silver, and gold, of brass, iron, wood, and stone, which see not nor hear, nor know: and the God in whose hand thy breath is, and whose are all thy ways, hast thou not glorified: Then was the part of the hand sent from him; and this writing was written. And this is the writing that was written, ME-NE, ME-NE, TE-KEL, U-PHAR-SIN. This is the interpretation of the thing: ME-NE; God hath numbered thy kingdom, and finished it. TE-KEL; Thou art weighed in the balances, and art found wanting. PE-RES; Thy kingdom is divided, and given to the Medes and Persians. Then commanded Belshazzar, and they clothed Daniel with scarlet, and put a chain of gold about his neck, and made a proclamation concerning him, that he should be the third ruler in the kingdom. In that night was

Belshazzar the king of the Chaldeans slain. And Darius the Median took the kingdom, being about threescore and two years old."

Verses 2 and 11 from Daniel 2, say that Belshazzar's father was Nebuchadnezzar. However, in those days any paternal male ancestor was called "Father." Nebuchadnezzar was in reality his grandfather. Verses 5:31; 6:1,2; say, that Darius was allowed to rule Babylon. Other historians say it was Cyrus' son Cambyses. But another historian named Ptrideaux said the following:

"Darius the Mede, that is Cyaxares, the uncle of Cyrus, took the kingdom for Cyrus allowed him the title of all his conquests as long as he lived." See Humphrey Ptrideaux, *The Old and New Testament Connected in the History of the Jews,* Vol. I, p. 137.

Cyrus at the time of Babylon's fall was a pagan, and worshipped Ahura Mazda (the Persian chief Sky God). Like King Nebuchadnezzar, Cyrus did not see his calling at first. However, later after Daniel was delivered from the lion's den (Daniel 6), Cyrus said: (He is the God), which is in Jerusalem. Ezra 1:3.

The "Bear" symbolized as Persia (Daniel 7:5), never became the glorious kingdom Babylon was. The three ribs in the teeth of the bear represent the provinces Babylon was divided into, (Babylon, Lydia, and Egypt). Nimrod's capital of idolatry had reached its prophetic time table. Its fall was also foretold in Jeremiah 51:8.

"Babylon is suddenly fallen and destroyed: howl for her; take balm for her pain, if so be she may be healed."

Just as living lambs were used for a sacrifice and foreshadowed Christ's death on the cross, so was Babylon of old just a shadow of the spiritual Babylon of Revelation the 17th and 18th chapters. We will investigate this truth later. The Medo-Persian Empire was from 538 B.C. to 331 B.C.

"After this I beheld, and lo another, like a leopard, which had upon the back of it four wings of a fowl; the beast had also four heads; and dominion was given to it." Daniel 7:6.

Who could this third world empire be? None other than Alexander the Great and his Grecian Empire. At the death of his father Philip II, the Macedonian king in 336 B.C., Alexander fell heir to the throne, however, not without opposition. Alexander was menaced with enemies on all sides at first, but later he was chosen supreme general of the divided Greek states. In the year 334 B.C., Alexander crossed over into Asia Minor with an army of thirty-five thousand Macedonians and Greeks. Between May and June Alexander and his army fought the Persians at the battle of Granicus. Alexander himself was in the thickest of the fight, dealing wounds and receiving blows. After a sharp melee on the steep banks, the Persians were broken and put to flight. Only losing a few of his men, Alexander cleared out of his way the only army which was to oppose his progress in Asia Minor, and conquered Lydia, one of the providences Cyrus took from the Babylonians just over 200 years earlier.[1] In two years Alexander conquered the Western third of the Persian Empire. Then in 331 B.C., Alexander marched his army into Mesopotamia. There the Persian King Darius III, waited for him. After a clash with the advancing army of Alexander, Darius turned his chariot, deserted his army and fled for his life. Darius fled to the highlands of Media, but Alexander did not pursue after the King of Persia, but turned his army towards the wall of Babylon. Alexander, expecting a fight with the Babylonians, marched his army in full array against the city, but was met with a welcome instead of adversity. After this Alexander spent eight years fighting with the Persian army in other parts of the known world, but the battle at Arbela, 331 B.C., was Alexander's most decisive battle against the Persians. Here is where Alexander found the King of Persia's chariot, his shield, and his bow. From here is where Darius fled for his life and the fall of the Persian Empire.[2]

As we saw earlier, Alexander returned to Babylon later, and died there of a drunken fever. The leopard-like beast was a fitting symbol for the Kingdom of Greece. Never has the world since Alexander the Great seen a conqueror as the Macedonian King. The first beast of the four that Daniel saw in his vision was a lion with eagle wings which was the prophetic symbol of Babylon. In the vision the lion only had two wings, but the leopard with four heads had four wings, showing this kingdom would be twice as swift in conquering the known world than Babylon. The four heads of the beast represent the four kingdoms Alexander's kingdom was divided into after the death of the conqueror. Alexander had four generals under him at the time of his death. They were Lysimachus, Cassander, Ptolemy, and Seleucus. These four generals argued among themselves who would become heir of Alexander's throne, and feeling no one was greater than the other, divided the kingdom into four parts. In *Daniel and the Revelation* we read the following:

"The Grecian Empire did not go to Alexander's sons. Within a few years after his death, all his posterity had fallen victim to the jealousy and ambition of his leading generals, who tore the kingdom into four parts. How short is the transit from the highest pinnacle of earthly glory to the lowest depths of oblivion and death! Alexander's four leading generals Cassander, Lysimachus, Seleucus, and Ptolemy—took posses-

[1] See *A History of Greece*, by J. B. Bury, pp. 737-740.
[2] See *A History of Greece*, by J. B. Bury, p. 764.

The Four Winged and Four Headed Leopard Beast of Daniel 7:6. The four wings represented the swiftness in conquering the known world. It had two more wings than the Lion (Babylon), and it was twice as fast in conquering. This symbolized the Empire of Alexander the Great. The four heads represented the four generals that divided the Grecian Empire into four nations.

sion of the empire. After the death of Antigonus (301 B.C.), the four confederate princes divided his dominions between them; and hereby the whole empire of Alexander became parted, and settled into four kingdoms. Ptolemy had Egypt, Libya, Arabia, Coele Syria, and Palestine, Cassander, Macedon and Greece; Lysimachus, Thrace, Bithynia, and some other of the provinces beyond the Hellespont and the Bosphorus; and Seleucus all the rest.[3]

"After this I saw in the night visions, and behold a fourth beast, dreadful and terrible, and strong exceedingly; and it had great iron teeth: it devoured and brake in pieces, and stamped the residue with the feet of it: and it was diverse from all the beasts that were before it; and it had ten horns." Daniel 7:7.

Here we are to the fourth beast of Daniel's vision of Daniel 7:1-8. This beast was different from all the beasts before it. Its huge size shows us that this kingdom would be even larger than the three kingdoms before it. What empire is it that any school child who is old enough to learn history will answer? It existed between 168 B.C. to 476 A.D.; it persecuted the Jewish nation, Christ was crucified under its control; it destroyed the second temple in Jerusalem in 70 A.D.; the Emperors threw Christians to lions as they looked on it as sport; the Emperors were worshipped as gods; it also was known as Saturian land, the Land of Mystery; it invented short iron swords that broke its enemies; its Empire was divided into two territories—Western and Eastern—the Western part is known today as Europe; who could it be but the Roman Empire? In the battle of Pydna in 168 B.C., the Romans won a complete victory over Perseus of Macedonia.[4] Greece was divided after Rome destroyed the Macedonians. Rome then turned to the other Greek states and conquered them. It did this by promising the people who joined its movement, that they would be rewarded after victory and that those who didn't would be punished.

All the old world came under the iron hand of the Roman Empire, and like a huge prehistoric beast, anything that got in its way, was trampled underfoot. This pagan kingdom has left its influence with us today with the names of the week and the names of the months which are used in our calendar. The architecture of most government buildings in our Nation's Capital is borrowed from Roman designs, which were borrowed from the Greeks. Our official titles and sayings are many times written in Latin. Look on the back of a dollar bill. You will see the great seal of the United States. Under the pyramid is written in Latin, NOVUS ORDO SECLORUM, which means: A New Order For The Ages. Over top of the

[3] See *Daniel and The Revelation,* by Uriah Smith, pp. 234,235.

[4] See *A History of Rome to A.D. 565,* by Arthur E. R. Boak, William G. Sinnigen, p. 133.

pyramid is written in Latin ANNUIT COPETIS, which means: He (God) has favored our undertakings. On the other side of the seal is an eagle, the symbol of the United States, with a long ribbon in its beak. Inscribed on it is, E PLURIBUS UNUM, which means: One Out Of Many. The foundation of the pyramid has Roman numerals MDCCLXXVI, which adds up to 1776, the year of our Declaration of Independence. Roman numerals are very much used in our numbering system today.

We should keep an eagle eye on this numerical system for the Lord has warned his servants the Antichrist's Number is 666, and those who are deceived into receiving it shall drink the wrath of God. Revelation 13:17,18.

The book of Revelation reveals that the Antichrist is both a political power and a man, and in the last days the whole world and its nations will come under his control, including the United States. Except for a small remnant of God's people who have searched the Scriptures and have found what the meaning of the 666, the "Mark of the Beast," and the image of the beast really means, and how to avoid it, all will be lost. Many professed religious authorities pass over this warning as unimportant, and believe that we should just worry about our relationship with Christ and our salvation, but Jesus is the one who gave us this warning, and He says:

"BLESSED IS HE THAT READETH, AND THEY THAT HEAR THE WORDS OF THIS PROPHECY, AND KEEP THOSE THINGS WHICH ARE WRITTEN THEREIN: FOR THE TIME IS AT HAND." Revelation 1:3.

Most pastors teach their congregations not to worry about receiving the "Mark" or "Number," or about worshipping his image because this is after the rapture of the saints by Christ, and only those who are left behind will have to go through this Great Tribulation period, not the saints. This false doctrine is just one of the many which will lead people to the wide gate; ". . . for wide is the gate, and broad is the way, that leadeth to destruction, and many there be which go in thereat: Because strait is the gate, and narrow is the way, which leadeth unto life, and few there be that find it." Matthew 7:13,14.

Another reason many pastors do not want to discuss the Antichrist is because they have no knowledge about it. And when men stand for the truth about this coming horror, those who lack understanding, start hurling words at them like, heretic, communist or some other derogatory statements. Like Elijah when he made his stand for truth, those who stand for the real truth about the Gospel will find themselves a very small minority. Jesus Himself warned if all would speak well of those who preached,that this was a sure sign of a false teacher. "WOE UNTO YOU,

WHEN ALL MEN SHALL SPEAK WELL OF YOU! FOR SO DID THEIR FATHERS TO THE FALSE PROPHETS." Luke 6:26.

In the days of Israel's apostasy from the Word of God, the false prophets used Scriptures mingled with tradition to soften the strong rebukes of the Scriptures that exposed their wickedness. The straight preaching of the Word of God is always a rebuke to the hearer. For the more the character of God is revealed to the hearer, the more the hearer sees his shame. Because this brings on a terrible sense of guilt, some abhor hearing God's Word. They only want to hear the things that sound good to them found in the Scriptures: "WHICH SAY TO THE SEERS, SEE NOT; AND TO THE PROPHETS, PROPHESY NOT UNTO US RIGHT THINGS, SPEAK UNTO US SMOOTH THINGS, PROPHESY DECEITS." Isaiah 30:10.

To follow in Christ's footsteps we must call sin by its name. The scriptures reveal all have sinned and have come short of the glory of God. We need to confess our sins, pray for forgiveness and power to resist the temptations of the devil. This is a struggle that everyone must go through, regardless of how righteous we might seem to be in man's sight. Some try to hide their wickedness from the public eye, but Christ said in Matthew 10:26,27:

"Fear them not therefore: for there is nothing covered, that shall not be revealed; and hid, that shall not be known. What I tell you in darkness, that speak ye in the light: and what ye hear in the ear, that preach ye upon the housetops."

In the next chapter we will study the prophecies and history of the Antichrist that the Lord revealed through his prophet Daniel and the apostles of the New Testament. Just as sure as Daniel was 100% accurate in foretelling the four world ruling Empires which were:

1. BABYLON — 605-539 B.C. — THE LION
2. MEDO-PERSIA — 539-331 B.C. — THE BEAR
3. GRECIAN EMPIRE — 331-168 B.C. — THE LEOPARD
4. ROMAN EMPIRE — 168 B.C. - 476 A.D. — THE DRAGON,

so has Daniel foretold with 100% accuracy the kingdom and work of the ANTICHRIST. And we will shout it from the housetops, not to point and condemn those who have been deceived in following this movement of Satan's behind the public's eye, but to expose it for what it represents and that those who are in it might see the truth and come out of it. For, surely, the Lord still has his people within it.

There have been many theories and speculations about the Antichrist, and who it could be. But, the prophecies of the seventh chapter of Daniel will not leave any room for doubt for those who have ears to hear what the Spirit is saying unto the Churches. The prophecies of the Antichrist of both Daniel and the book of Revelation reveal there are two periods in the great deceptions of the Antichrist. First, Satan through his spirit has conditioned the world into an apostasy from the pure teaching of the Gospel, to human tradition, pagan festivals and pagan rites that lead the heart away from God. This is also history. This terrible deception has not come to us all at once, but little by little down through the centuries from the time of the apostles. Paul said in II Thessalonians that it would start after his departure:

"For I know this, that after my departing shall grievous wolves enter in among you, not sparing the flock. Also of your own selves shall men arise, speaking perverse things, to draw away disciples after them. Therefore watch, and remember, that by the space of three years I ceased not to warn every one night and day with tears. For the Mystery of Iniquity doth already work: only he who now letteth will let, until he be taken out of the way." Acts 20:29-31; II Thessalonians 2:7.

The apostle John also knew about the spirit of the Antichrist movement in his day:

"And this is the spirit of Antichrist, whereof ye have heard that it should come; and even now already is it in the world." I John 4:3.

Let us take the attitude of Solomon when he humbled himself to the Almighty and said:

"I am but a little child: I know not how to go out or to come in." I Kings 3:7. Solomon knew his lack of discernment of judging between good and evil and knew how helpless he was without God. As it was with Solomon, let us ask God for an understanding heart, that we not only save ourselves from this great deception of Satan's but also those who hear us. To those who see their spiritual poverty comes the promise:

"BLESSED ARE THE POOR IN SPIRIT: FOR THEIRS IS THE KINGDOM OF HEAVEN." Matthew 5:3.

CHAPTER IV

The Antichrist and His Number 666

"And they worshipped the dragon which gave power unto the beast: and they worshipped the beast, saying, Who is like unto the beast? Who is able to make war with him? And there was given unto him a mouth speaking great things and blasphemies; and power was given unto him to continue forty and two months. And he opened his mouth in blasphemy against God, to blaspheme his name, and his tabernacle, and them that dwell in heaven. And it was given unto him to make war with the saints, and to overcome them: and power was given him over all kindreds, and tongues, and nations. And all that dwell upon the earth shall worship him, whose names are not written in the book of life of the Lamb slain from the foundation of the world. If any man have an ear, let him hear. Here is wisdom. Let him that hath understanding count the number of the beast: for it is the number of a man; and his number is six hundred threescore and six." Revelation 13:4-9,18.

To understand this passage of prophecy we need to go back to Daniel the seventh chapter, and compare prophetic symbols. John gives the Antichrist as a beast and also a Man, Revelation 13:18. Daniel 7:17,24, says a beast is a symbol of a kingdom. There are several titles Satan's movement is given in the Scriptures:

1. Antichrist — I John 4:1-3
2. The Mystery of Iniquity — II Thessalonians 2:7
3. Babylon the Great, The Mother of Harlots — Revelation 17:5
4. Baalim — Judges 2:11
5. Little Horn — Daniel 7:8,24,25
6. Man of Sin, Son of Perdition — II Thessalonians 2:3
7. Beast 666 — Revelation 13:18

But the reader may say, "How can we understand these prophetic symbols?" The Bible prophecies are full of comfort and joy to those who make a sincere effort to seek God and to know the truth. Just as a person prepares his life with an academic education that will fit him for a place of employment, so is a servant of the Lord to search the Scriptures which will prepare him to live in the Heavenly Kingdom of God. This is how our faith will grow. How can a person believe in something he knows nothing about?

"So then faith cometh by hearing, and hearing by the word of God." Romans 10:17. "Incline your ear, and come unto me: hear, and your soul shall live; and I will make an everlasting covenant with you, even the sure mercies of David." Isaiah 55:3.

Prophecy is foretelling events before they happen. God gave the gift of prophecy to prove to the world that there is a Lord in Heaven who knows the outcome of this horrible world we live in. He has presented a blueprint of the future in symbols so that all who are sincere in knowing the truth, can search the Scriptures for truth. The sad part is that the prophecies reveal only that a small remnant will be saved; it will not be the majority. This is very important to know and realize. These last days we live in will become just like the last days before the flood.

However, not one soul shall perish who repents and is found doing God's will. As sure as Christ was God manifested in the flesh, so will Christ lead us through the narrow path that leads to eternal life. Rely not on the teaching of man. Let the Lord be your teacher, trust not in any man. Put your trust in Jesus, for all men are subject to error, no matter what office they hold:

"THUS SAITH THE LORD; CURSED BE THE MAN THAT TRUSTETH IN MAN, AND MAKETH FLESH HIS ARM, AND WHOSE HEART DEPARTETH FROM THE LORD." Jeremiah 17:5.

The Lord has said there is none good, no not one. Follow after the footsteps of Christ, not after man. If we desire to be Christians, we should desire to do the things Christ says. However, there are today multitudes of Christian denominations who say, "We have the truth!" While others say, "No they don't, we have the truth." As a child can see, there is much religious confusion in the world. Let us seek what Christ says before the Catholic and Protestant churches were heard of. The Bible and only the Bible is to be the standard of measuring truth; let us prove all things by comparing Scripture with Scripture and Spiritual things with Spiritual things. We should test all doctrines with Scripture. As there are multitudes of Christian Churches, there are multitudes of doctrines and faiths, but the Scriptures say there is one faith (Ephesians 4:5). Let us study the Scriptures. "That we henceforth be no more children, tossed to and fro, and carried about with every wind of doctrine, by the sleight of men, and cunning craftiness, whereby they lie in wait to deceive;" Ephesians 4:14.

Satan is the founder of religious confusion. However, Christ has given us the "Spirit of Prophecy" to help us avoid Satan's falsehoods and snares. Before the Roman Catholic or Protestant Churches came into history, the Lord foretold every phase in the work of the Antichrist. The prophet Daniel reveals more of the first phase, while the book of Revelation reveals both the first and second periods of the deception. These prophecies would not be completely understood says Daniel 12:4, until the time of the end.

The starting point of the first phase of the Antichrist begins at the fourth beast, that Daniel foretold would rise up after the Grecian Empire and would conquer the whole known world. As history recorded, it was the Roman Empire, 168 B.C. to 476 A.D., that fits perfectly in this time slot. Remember, Daniel lived in the time of King Nebuchadnezzar of Babylon and saw the Medo-Persians take over the Babylonian Empire. Daniel was in his last years when Cyrus the King of Persia took Babylon. Daniel had died many centuries before the Roman Empire, but his written Word given by Divine Inspiration is still working for our behalf.

Most theologians will agree that the four beasts represented in symbols are the Babylonians, Medo-Persians, and the Grecian and Roman Empires. But what they miss is the "TEN HORNS" of the fourth beast:

"THUS HE SAID, THE FOURTH BEAST SHALL BE THE FOURTH KINGDOM UPON EARTH, WHICH SHALL BE DIVERSE FROM ALL KINGDOMS, AND SHALL DEVOUR THE WHOLE EARTH, AND SHALL TREAD IT DOWN, AND BREAK IT IN PIECES. AND THE TEN HORNS OUT OF THIS KINGDOM ARE TEN KINGS THAT SHALL ARISE; AND ANOTHER SHALL RISE AFTER THEM; AND HE SHALL BE DIVERSE FROM THE FIRST, AND HE SHALL SUBDUE THREE KINGS." Daniel 7:23,24.

After the "Fourth Beast" (Rome) was to fall, "Ten Nations" would arise out of the Fourth Beast (Rome). Daniel uses horns as symbols of nations (Daniel 7:23). Does history record "Ten Kingdoms," after the fall of the Roman Empire, that arose from its ruins? Just as sure as Daniel lived, so did "Ten Nations" arise out of the Roman Empire. They were:

1. Anglo-Saxons
2. Franks
3. Alemanni
4. Lombards
5. Ostrogoths
6. Visogoths
7. Burgundians
8. Vandals
9. Suevi
10. Heruli

These nations originated in the great barbarian tribes that came down from the North and Africa and destroyed the Roman Empire. The Goths,

The Fourth Beast with Ten Horns and the Little Horn whose look was more stout than his fellows. Daniel 7:7, 8, 20, 24, 25. The fourth beast is a symbol of the Roman Empire from 168 B.C. to 476 A.D. The Ten Horns are symbols of the Ten Nations that arose up after the Roman Empire fell in 476 A.D. The Little Horn whose look was more stout than his fellows is the Papacy from 538 A.D. to 1798 A.D., when it ruled the old world under a religious dictatorship of its Popes.

Huns, Heruli and Vandals were the first invaders to sack Rome, and all had a part in causing the Roman Empire to fall in 476 A.D.

History books are filled with stories of the fall of pagan Rome, and also the history of the European countries today. But still another "LITTLE HORN" was to rise up out of "TEN NATIONS" (HORNS) and destroy three of the first ten horns. Daniel 7:8:

"I CONSIDERED THE HORNS, AND BEHOLD, THERE CAME UP AMONG THEM ANOTHER LITTLE HORN, BEFORE WHOM THERE WERE THREE OF THE FIRST HORNS PLUCKED UP BY THE ROOTS: AND, BEHOLD, IN THIS HORN WERE EYES LIKE THE EYES OF MAN, AND A MOUTH SPEAKING GREAT THINGS."

A "HORN," as Daniel 7:24 clearly points out, is a kingdom, not a person. Some theologians, both Christian and Jewish, have interpreted this as being a historical tyrant. Many have applied it to Titus, the general who destroyed Jerusalem in 70 A.D., or Antiochus I Epiphanes of Syria who set up an image of Zeus, that looked like him, in the temple of Jerusalem. Others have applied the "LITTLE HORN" of Daniel 7:24, 25, to Mohammed. But let us consider that a horn represents a "KINGDOM" not a person, as Daniel explains, and we will not err in the symbolic term applied here, as plucking up three horns, Daniel 7:8,24.

"AND THE TEN HORNS OUT OF THIS KINGDOM ARE TEN KINGS THAT SHALL ARISE: AND ANOTHER SHALL RISE AFTER THEM; AND HE SHALL BE DIVERSE FROM THE FIRST, AND HE SHALL SUBDUE THREE KINGS. AND HE SHALL SPEAK GREAT WORDS AGAINST THE MOST HIGH, AND SHALL WEAR OUT THE SAINTS OF THE MOST HIGH, AND THINK TO CHANGE TIMES AND LAWS: AND THEY SHALL BE GIVEN INTO HIS HAND UNTIL A TIME AND TIMES AND THE DIVIDING OF TIME." Daniel 7:24,25.

This "LITTLE HORN'S" first act, according to Daniel, would be to destroy "THREE OF THE TEN NATIONS" that arose out of the fall of the Roman Empire. Does history record "THREE KINGDOMS" destroyed or plucked up as Daniel described? Just as Christ arose from the dead, so were THREE of these KINGDOMS destroyed as the term applies.

The Roman Empire after its fall was divided into Ten Gothic nations. This is a historical fact. Seven of these ten nations are with us today, but under different names, and are in the Western part of the Old Roman Empire. They are listed as part of the world that is called Europe. After Christianity was accepted in most of the known countries and after the persecutions by Roman emperors; a new and different kingdom arose among these TEN KINGDOMS and destroyed the nations of the Heruli in

493 A.D., the Vandals in 534 A.D., and the last of the three, the Ostrogoths. Who is the LITTLE HORN THAT PLUCKED UP BY THE ROOTS (Daniel 7:8) the Heruli, Vandals and the Ostrogoths? History says the Roman Catholic Church employed armies to pull up by the roots these three Arian Nations. After Zeno the emperor of the east, who was a friend of the pope, drove out Odoacer, the King of the Heruli in 493 A.D., a few years later Emperor Justinian entered the Vandal and Gothic wars. In 533 A.D., Justinian made a decree that established the pope as the head of all Christian Churches.[1] The Vandals and the Ostrogoths who did not accept the Deity of Christ, or the authority of the pope, fought holy wars with Roman Catholics. Although the Ostrogoths, the last of the three kingdoms foretold by Daniel, were completely destroyed in 554 A.D.[2], it was in 538 A.D., that the Ostrogoths lost the decisive battle that eventually drove them out of Italy. And from 538 A.D., began the Middle Ages and the religious dictatorship of the papacy. Not only did this date 538 A.D., mark the time of the supremacy of the Roman Catholic Church as head of the Christian Church, but also the "Corrector of Heretics." Daniel gives the symbol of the Antichrist as a LITTLE HORN while John the penman of Revelation gives the symbol as a BEAST. Both are symbols of the same kingdom whose invisible head is SATAN. Not only will this kingdom be branded with the number 666, but the MAN who rules this kingdom will also have this number: "HERE IS WISDOM. LET HIM THAT HATH UNDERSTANDING COUNT THE NUMBER OF THE BEAST; FOR IT IS THE NUMBER OF A MAN; AND HIS NUMBER IS SIX HUNDRED THREESCORE AND SIX." Revelation 13:18.

Many believed in the past and still do, that Nero was the Antichrist; if you take his name in Greek, and translate it into Hebrew letters and give the numerical equivalents in the following manner it will add to 666.[3]

ר	ס	ק	ו	י	ר	נ		
200	60	100	50	6	200	50	=	666

The system of the pagan worship of Saturn, which is the equivalent of Baalim, is spelled S T U R in Aramaic. This comes to 666 in Aramaic numerical values:[4]

S	T	U	R		
200	60	400	6	=	666

[1] See *The Prophetic Faith of Our Fathers*, by Le Roy E. Froom, pp. 593,594.
[2] See *Encyclopedia Americana*, Vol. 13, American Corp., 1979, p. 115.
[3] See *The Interpreters Bible*, Abingdon Press, Vol. 12, p. 466.
[4] See *The Two Babylons*, by Alexander Hislop, p. 269.

The Beast of Revelation 13.

The early Romans worshipped the Sun God under a name that identifies with Saturn. In Alexander Hislop's, *The Two Babylons,* we read the following:

"Saturn and Lateinos are synonymous, having precisely the same meaning, and belonging equally to the same god. The reader cannot have forgotten the lines of Virgil, which showed that Lateinos, to the Romans or Latin race traced back their lineage, was represented with a glory around his head, to show that he was a child of the sun." *The Two Babylons,* by Alexander Hislop, p. 270.

Here we begin to see how Satan uses not only religion to deceive, but also the "ARTS," for the reader only has to open a book about the Middle Ages, and he will find paintings of Jesus, like the pagan sun gods, with a glory of a sun disk or beams around our Lord's head.

To understand how the mysterious number of doom (666), is applied to the LITTLE HORN (PAPACY) AND THE BEAST OF REVELATION 13:18, we must look at the two controlling powers, or the two INVISIBLE HEADS. Here is the ancient Greek name for SATAN in transliterations, with its numeral values:*

T	E	I	T	A	N	
300	5	10	300	1	50	= 666

Here is the name JESUS in Greek transliterations with its numeral values:

I	Ē	S	O	U	S	
10	8	200	70	400	200	= 888

The name Jesus above adds up to the number 888. Seven (7) is the perfect number in the Bible, and the Scriptures show the name JESUS is above perfection. Satan's number is 666 and comes short of 777, so will his power to work miracles come short and those who are being used by him to perform them. In Daniel 7:25, we read the following:

"AND HE SHALL SPEAK GREAT WORDS AGAINST THE MOST HIGH, AND SHALL WEAR OUT THE SAINTS OF THE MOST HIGH, AND THINK TO CHANGE TIMES AND LAWS: AND THEY SHALL BE GIVEN INTO HIS HAND UNTIL A TIME AND TIMES AND THE DIVIDING OF TIME."

After the LITTLE HORN would subdue the THREE KINGS, Daniel shows four more acts the little horn would perform. We will take each act separately, using the publications of the Roman Catholic Church, comparing world history with each of Daniel's four points, to show how the papacy has fulfilled this description the prophet saw.

"AND HE SHALL SPEAK GREAT WORDS AGAINST THE MOST HIGH." TO SPEAK GREAT WORDS AGAINST THE MOST HIGH MEANS TO BLASPHEME THE LORD. John in Revelation, before the Catholic Church came into history, said:

---

* See *The Two Babylons,* Alexander Hislop, pp. 276, 277.

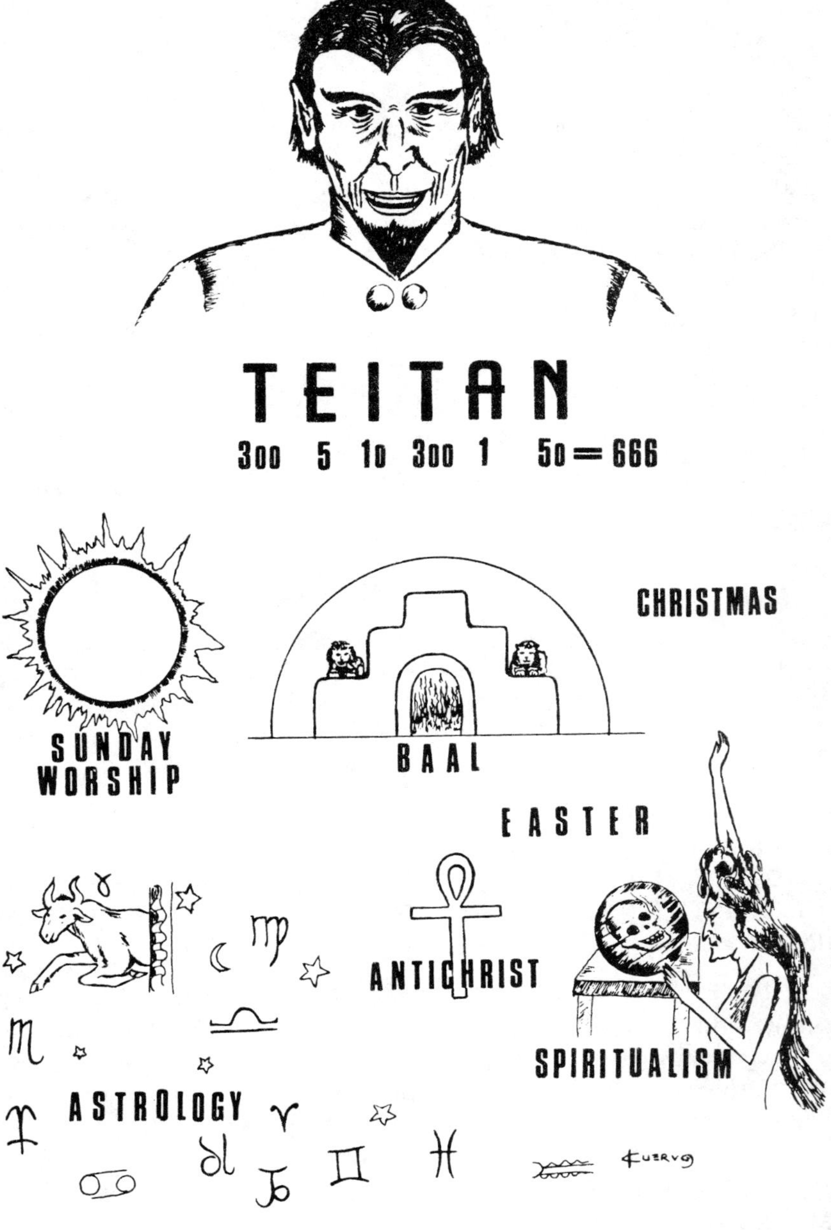

The Chaldean TEITAN (Satan) in Greek transliterations, with numerical values. The invisible head of the Mystery of Iniquity. 2 Thessalonians 2:7.

IĒSOUS (Jesus) in Greek transliterations, the Creator of the World and the invisible head of the Mystery of Godliness. I Timothy 3:16.

"AND THERE WAS GIVEN UNTO HIM A MOUTH SPEAKING GREAT THINGS AND BLASPHEMIES; AND POWER WAS GIVEN UNTO HIM TO CONTINUE FORTY AND TWO MONTHS. AND HE OPENED HIS MOUTH IN BLASPHEMY AGAINST GOD, TO BLASPHEME HIS NAME, AND HIS TABERNACLE, AND THEM THAT DWELL IN HEAVEN." Revelation 13:5,6.

If you remember, the reason the Jews crucified Jesus was because they accused him of blasphemy. The Jews publicly pronounced that Jesus of Nazareth committed blasphemy against God because Jesus used the Old Testament names which applied to Jehovah, such as the title, "I Am," Exodus 3:13-15. Jesus claimed to be the great, "I Am." John 8:58,59.

"Jesus said unto them, Verily, verily, I say unto you, Before Abraham was, I Am. Then took they up stones to cast at him: but Jesus hid himself, and went out of the temple, going through the midst of them, and so passed by."

However, when the Creator of the universe, the second Being of the Holy Trinity was interjected into the history of the world, he was despised and rejected. And Jesus said in John 5:43:

"I AM COME IN MY FATHER'S NAME, AND YE RECEIVE ME NOT: IF ANOTHER SHALL COME IN HIS OWN HAME, HIM YE WILL RECEIVE."

As stated before, Satan himself will come as a man and personate Christ. He will do this just before the Real Jesus appears in the air to meet His people. But before this can happen, the people of the world will be in a condition to believe a false system of Christianity. The Lord has given His people an unmistakable clue. It would be branded with its founder's number 666. Here in Greek, with its transliterations and numeral values, is where Satan's seat is today HĒ LATINĒ BASILEIA, WHICH MEANS THE LATIN KINGDOM.

H	Ē	L	A	T	I	N	Ē	
0	8	30	1	300	10	50	8	
B	A	S	I	L	E	I	A[1]	
2	1	200	10	30	5	10	1	= 666

Here is the Little Horn's Church in Greek with its numeral values, ITALIKA EKKLĒSIA, WHICH MEANS ITALIAN CHURCH.

[1] See *Unfolding the Revelation,* by Roy A. Anderson, p. 130.

I	T	A	L	I	K	A		
10	300	1	30	10	20	1		
E	K	K	L	Ē	S	I	A[2]	
5	20	20	30	8	200	10	1	= 666

Here in Greek transliterations is the kingdom's language, LATENINOS, which means, LATIN SPEAKING OR LATIN MAN.

L	A	T	E	I	N	O	S[3]	
30	1	300	5	10	50	70	200	= 666

Here in Latin is an offical name for the POPE with the numerical value of the Roman Numerals found in the name.

V	I	C	A	R	I	U	S
5	1	100	0	0	1	5	0

F	I	L	I	I		D	E	I[4]	
0	1	50	1	1		500	0	1	= 666

Vicarius Filii Dei is Latin for "VICAR OF THE SON OF GOD," and from a publication written by Catholic authorities, we read the following:

"The title of the Pope of Rome is *vicarius filii dei* and if you take the letters of his title which represent Latin numerals (Printed large) and add them together they come to 666." *Our Sunday Visitor,* Nov. 15, 1914.

The word "POPE" means papa, in Latin. Translated into English it means "Father." In *A New Catechism: Catholic Faith for Adults,* we read the following about the office of the Pope:

"The unifying function of the Pope entails an important task as teacher. As head of the Infallible College of Bishops, he possesses Infallability in a special measure. He is the beacon. This does not mean that he can proclaim dogmas apart from the church. He can only declare what the Church Universal believes. He takes counsel with all the Catholic Bishops, particularly with the synod of bishops instituted since the second Vatican Council. But since union with the Pope is the touchstone for belonging to the unity, an utterance of the Pope is certainly full of the truth of God's spirit, at least when he affirms explicitly (which happens very rarely) that he is speaking Infallibly and binding all Christians." *A New Catechism: Catholic Faith for Adults:* Translated from the Dutch by Kerin Smyth, London, Burns & Oates: New York, Herder and Herder, 1967, page 368.

---

[2] *Ibid,* p. 130.
[3] *Ibid,* p. 131.
[4] *Ibid,* p. 133.

The papacy claims the office of the pope possesses infallibility. In other words they claim the pope cannot err in anything according to the Scriptures. The *Vicarius Filii Dei* is without fault, and the words he speaks are binding on all Christians, according to the papacy. But where in the Word of God can we find any statement that Jesus, the founder of Christianity, commanded a spiritual ruler or a substitute in His place to rule over His people? Where in the Word of God did Jesus set up a hierarchy of Archbishops, Cardinals, Priests, and a Sisterhood of Nuns? Where in the Word of God can we find the exaltation of the Virgin Mary as the Mother of God? Where in the Word of God can we find a commandment from Jesus for women to consecrate their virginity to God, and men as well as women forbidden to marry? Where in the Word of God is the sacrament of the 40 days of lent? Where in the Word of God is the Observance of Good Friday and the making of Hot Cross Buns? Where in the Word of God is the Festival of Christmas commanded to be observed December 25th? Where in the Word of God is the Festival of Easter to be celebrated? Where in the Word of God are the repetitious prayers of the Rosary? Where in the Word of God is the Auricular Confession? Where in the Word of God did Jesus command that the Holy Sabbath Day, the seventh day of the week, be changed to the day of the pagan Sun God Baal? Where in the Word of God can we find the power of the priests to change a wafer into the real flesh and the wine into the blood of Jesus? These and other doctrines of the Roman Catholic Church, handed down to many Protestants, we will study and compare with the Scriptures.

But first, we want to express our feeling toward the people who make up the Catholic Church. We do not have any hatred toward any member of the Roman Catholic Church, not even the Pope himself. We are against the system, not the people of the Catholic faith. We believe that the foundation to all Christian doctrine is found written in the Holy Scriptures. We believe all Christians should follow in the steps of our Leader, Jesus Christ. We believe the books of the Bible were given before the Roman Catholic Church or a Protestant Church came into being, and the Lord gave them to be a guide which will lead to eternal life with our Saviour Jesus Christ. We believe by reading the Word of God that a person is transformed from strength to strength, from glory to glory, in the image of Christ. We believe knowledge of the truth produces faith and will give correction to the ways of error. We believe at present the Lord has His people in all faiths but will seperate all people of the world into two bands; those that do the will of God and those who do not. We believe that there is a last day message to the people of the modern world and after this message there is no other. The door of eternal life will be shut and those who have rejected and obeyed not the Gospel will lose their salvation. We believe the last day message is found in the three angels messages of Revelation 14:6-13:

"AND I SAW ANOTHER ANGEL FLY IN THE MIDST OF HEAVEN, HAVING THE EVERLASTING GOSPEL TO PREACH UNTO THEM THAT DWELL ON THE EARTH, AND TO EVERY NATION, AND KINDRED, AND TONGUE, AND PEOPLE, SAYING WITH A LOUD VOICE, FEAR GOD, AND GIVE GLORY TO HIM; FOR THE HOUR OF HIS JUDGMENT IS COME: AND WORSHIP HIM THAT MADE HEAVEN, AND EARTH, AND THE SEA, AND THE FOUNTAINS OF WATERS. AND THERE FOLLOWED ANOTHER ANGEL, SAYING, BABYLON IS FALLEN, IS FALLEN, THAT GREAT CITY, BECAUSE SHE MADE ALL NATIONS DRINK OF THE WINE OF THE WRATH OF HER FORNICATION. AND THE THIRD ANGEL FOLLOWED THEM, SAYING WITH A LOUD VOICE, IF ANY MAN WORSHIP THE BEAST AND HIS IMAGE, AND RECEIVE HIS MARK IN HIS FOREHEAD, OR IN HIS HAND, THE SAME SHALL DRINK OF THE WINE OF THE WRATH OF GOD, WHICH IS POURED OUT WITHOUT MIXTURE INTO THE CUP OF HIS INDIGNATION; AND HE SHALL BE TORMENTED WITH FIRE AND BRIMSTONE IN THE PRESENCE OF THE HOLY ANGELS AND IN THE PRESENCE OF THE LAMB: AND THE SMOKE OF THEIR TORMENT ASCENDETH UP FOR EVER AND EVER: AND THEY HAVE NO REST DAY NOR NIGHT, WHO WORSHIP THE BEAST AND HIS IMAGE, AND WHOSOEVER RECEIVETH THE MARK OF HIS NAME. HERE IS THE PATIENCE OF THE SAINTS: HERE ARE THEY THAT KEEP THE COMMANDMENTS OF GOD, AND THE FAITH OF JESUS. AND I HEARD A VOICE FROM HEAVEN SAYING UNTO ME, WRITE, BLESSED ARE THE DEAD WHICH DIE IN THE LORD FROM HENCEFORTH: YEA, SAITH THE SPIRIT, THAT THEY MAY REST FROM THEIR LABOURS; AND THEIR WORKS DO FOLLOW THEM.

We believe when this message is understood the seeker's discernment between truth and falsehood shall be open and some, whether pastor, priest, or layman, when they find themselves in error, will say:

"IT IS OF THE LORD'S MERCIES THAT WE ARE NOT CONSUMED, BECAUSE HIS COMPASSIONS FAIL NOT. LET US SEARCH AND TRY OUR WAYS, AND TURN AGAIN TO THE LORD." Lamentations 3:22, 40.

We believe those who will receive the MARK OF THE BEAST OR THE NUMBER OF HIS NAME will be those whom Paul describes in II Thessalonians 2:10-12:

"BECAUSE THEY RECEIVED NOT THE LOVE OF THE TRUTH, THAT THEY MIGHT BE SAVED. AND FOR THIS CAUSE GOD SHALL SEND THEM STRONG DELUSION, THAT THEY SHOULD BELIEVE A LIE: THAT THEY ALL MIGHT BE DAMNED WHO BELIEVED NOT THE TRUTH, BUT HAD PLEASURE IN UNRIGHTEOUSNESS."

One of the early names for the Pope was PONTIFEX MAXIMUS. This in Latin means Supreme Pontifex. It was the name for the pagan chief Prince of Rome long before The Roman Catholic Church became history.[1] The Pope has had a number of titles down through the centuries. Here are two in Latin with their meanings:

DUX CLERI — which means Captain of the Clergy, and
LUDOVICUS — which means the Chief Vicar of the Court of Rome.

Here are these titles of the Pope with numerical values for the Roman numerals:

D	U	X	C	L	E	R	I[2]	
500	5	10	100	50	0	0	1	= 666

L	U	D	O	V	I	C	U	S[3]	
50	5	500	0	5	1	100	5	0	= 666

From the words of the Papacy, we read these shocking facts from *The World of the Vatican:*

"In certain respects the Pope himself appears to be the lineal descendant of the Caesars. A good deal of the cherished terminology of the Roman Catholic Church antedates the Christian era. For example, the title of Pontifex Maximus, or Supreme Pontiff, which originally meant "Bridge Builder" but now simply denotes the Pope, was used to describe the office of the head of pagan cults centuries before the Emperor Constantine recognized Christianity as a legal religion. Julius Caesar, among other notables, was a Roman Pontiff. So were Lepidus and Augustus. The expression "Roman Curia" which today means the Church's headquarters in the Eternal City, originated in the early days of Rome. It then meant an assembly of tribes; later, during the Republic it became a virtual synonym for the Roman Senate. The term "Diocese," meaning today the territory under a bishop's jurisdiction, was originally an administrative unit devised by the Emperor Diocletian, who was, incidentally, noted for his persecution of Christians." *The World of the Vatican,* by Robert Neville, Harper & Row, Publishers, New York and Evanston, page 10.

---

[1] See *The Oxford Dictionary of the Christian Church,* p. 1089.
[2] See *The Prophetic Faith of Our Fathers,* Vol. II, By Le Roy E. Froom, p. 77.
[3] *Ibid.,* Vol. III, p. 242.

Speaking about the high priest of Janus in Rome, Alexander Hislop shows the reader where the Catholic Church received the name "CARDINAL." From Hislop's *The Two Babylons* we read:

"In the worship of Janus in Rome, the high priest had the title of *jus vertendi cardinis,* which meant the power of turning the hinge or opening and shutting. The pagan High Priest had a College of Councilors who helped him in temporal matters as well as religious matters. They were called "Cardinals" the priests of the "hinge."[1]

The backbone of the Roman Catholic Church is the authority of the Pope. They claim their authority was handed down from the apostle Peter. They use Matthew 16:16-19:

"And Simon Peter answered and said, Thou art the Christ, the Son of the living God. And Jesus answered and said unto him, Blessed art thou, Simon Barjona: for flesh and blood hath not revealed it unto thee, but my Father which is in heaven. And I say also unto thee, That thou art Peter, and upon this rock I will build my church; and the gates of hell shall not prevail against it. And I will give unto thee the keys of the kingdom of heaven: and whatsoever thou shalt bind on earth shall be bound in heaven: and whatsoever thou shalt loose on earth shall be loosed in heaven."

This passage of Scripture is the foundation of the Great Roman Catholic Church Hierarchy. The whole foundation of Vatican City is laid upon this passage of Scripture. Did Christ set up a religious dictatorship as the Roman Catholic Church claims? Let us first investigate the papacy's own words and then compare them with the commandments of our Lord Jesus Christ. From the book *Vatican Council II,* we read the following:

"The Pope, as supreme pastor of the Church, may exercise his power at any time, as he sees fit, by reason of the demands of his office."[2] From the book, *Christ Among Us: A Modern Presentation of the Catholic Faith,* we read the following:

"Infallibility is expressed by the Pope when teaching *ex cathedra,* that is, under these conditions: when he teaches as the visible head of the Church, to all Catholics, on a matter of religion or morality, intending to use his full authority and give an unchangeable decision. Infallibility refers only to the Pope's power or charism of correctly teaching Christ's revelation to mankind. In personal belief or morality, in science, politics, etc., the Pope can be wrong. He can sin, and make mistakes — and many have in governing the Church." *Christ Among Us: a Modern*

---

[1] See *The Two Babylons,* by Alexander Hislop, pp. 210,211.

[2] See *Vatican Council II,* General Editor Austin Flannery, O.P., p. 426.

Presentation of the Catholic Faith, by Anthony Wilhelm, Paulist Press, New York, Paramus, Toronto, p. 148.

The papacy claims the pope possesses Infallibility when he teaches as the visible head of the Church, and he has full authority and has power to give an unchangeable decision. They claim to have this power because the pope is the successor of Peter. But the truth can be found by searching the Scriptures to see if Peter, the apostle had any power to hand down.

However, before we investigate this, let's take a look at the word "POPE," for it too, is a contradiction to the Scriptures. Jesus the founder and finisher of the Christian faith says:

"AND CALL NO MAN YOUR FATHER UPON THE EARTH: FOR ONE IS YOUR FATHER, WHICH IS IN HEAVEN." Matthew 23:9.

The word "POPE" means "Father," and as the reader probably already knows, thè Catholic priests are called "FATHERS." This is only the beginning, there are just about as many contradictions to the Scriptures, as the Roman Catholic Church has men who call themselves FATHERS." Paul who foretold this "Mystery of Iniquity," said in II Thessalonians 2:4:

"WHO OPPOSETH AND EXALTETH HIMSELF ABOVE ALL THAT IS CALLED GOD, OR THAT IS WORSHIPPED; SO THAT HE AS GOD SITTETH IN THE TEMPLE OF GOD, SHEWING HIMSELF THAT HE IS GOD."

This Scripture has a "twofold meaning." The present pope is not the Antichrist, but just a shadow of the real one to come. Satan, as we stated earlier will come as a man and personate Christ.

Let us go on to see how the papacy — "SPEAKS GREAT WORDS AGAINST THE MOST HIGH." Daniel 7:25. The papacy also says that all the names that were applied to Christ, apply to the pope! Here from their own publications: "A MOUTH SPEAKING GREAT THINGS AND BLASPHEMIES;" (Revelation 13:5).

"The Pope is of so great dignity and so exalted that he is not a mere man, but as it were GOD, AND THE VICAR OF GOD." "The Pope by reason of the excellence of his supreme dignity is called bishop of bishops." "He is also called ordinary of ordinaries." "He is likewise the DIVINE MONARCH AND SUPREME EMPEROR, AND KING OF KINGS." "HENCE THE POPE IS CROWNED WITH A TRIPLE CROWN, AS KING OF HEAVEN AND OF EARTH AND OF THE LOWER REGIONS." — Lucius Ferraris, *Prompta Bibliotheca,* Vol. 6, art. "Papa" II.

Nonetheless, Jesus says: "FOR WHOSOEVER EXALTETH HIMSELF SHALL BE ABASED; AND HE THAT HUMBLETH HIMSELF SHALL BE EXALTED." Luke 14:11

The papacy claims the office of the Pope IS SO EXALTED that he is called the DIVINE MONARCH and SUPREME EMPEROR and KING OF KINGS.

However, the Bible says: "That thou keep this commandment without spot, unrebukeable, until the appearing of our Lord Jesus Christ: Which in his times he shall shew, who is THE BLESSED AND ONLY POTENTATE, THE KING OF KINGS, AND LORD OF LORDS." I Timothy 6:14, 15

What a contrast is the life of the meek and lowly One, who had no place to lay His head. Paul said in Philippians that even Jesus did not seek to exalt Himself or gain reputation.

"Let this mind be in you, which was also in Christ Jesus: Who, being in the form of God, thought it not robbery to be equal with God: But made himself of no reputation, and took upon him the form of a servant, and was made in the likeness of men: And being found in fashion as a man, he humbled himself, and became obedient unto death, even the death of the cross. Wherefore God also hath highly exalted him, and given him a name which is above every name." Philippians 2:5-9

Nevertheless, the papacy says: "We hold upon this earth the place of God Almighty." -- Pope Leo XIII, in an encyclical letter dated June 29, 1894, *The Great Encyclical Letters of Leo XIII*, p. 304

Speaking about the Pope, the blasphemous words of the papacy: "THOU ART THE SHEPHERD, THOU ART THE PHYSICIAN, THOU ART THE DIRECTOR, THOU ART THE HUSBANDMAN; FINALLY, THOU ART ANOTHER GOD ON EARTH." -- From *The Oration of Christopher Marcellus (R.C.) in the 4th session of the 5th Lateran Council, 1512 (an address to the Pope); History of the Councils*, Labbe and Conssart, vol. 24, col. 109

Our Lord taught humbleness in His daily life while He was here on earth. Did He contradict His teachings and command that there should be a Divine Monarch, a man who is a sinner and needs forgiveness for his sins like all people, a man subject to the same temptations and evils we are, to rule not only the religious life of people, but claim to have power to be a Lord over the private lives of people, as well?

Listen to the advice of the Saviour: "But Jesus called them to him, and said unto them, Ye know that they which are accounted to rule over the Gentiles exercise lordship over them; and their great ones exercise authority upon them. But so shall IT NOT BE AMONG YOU: BUT WHOSOEVER WILL BE GREAT AMONG YOU, SHALL BE YOUR MINISTER: And whosoever of you will be the chiefest, shall be servant of all. For even the Son of man came not to be ministered unto, but to minister, and to give his life a ransom for many.'' Mark 10:42-45.

Our Lord who is the Originator of all truth, taught the opposite from the papacy claims, because the invisible head of the papacy is just the opposite. Let us see what Peter has to say about being Lord over God's people. Did Peter think he was the Prince of the Apostles, the Chief Shepherd, the Holy Father, the Vicar of Christ, or any of the other multitude of exalted names the papacy applies to the pope? Here is Peter's own word, before this claim by the papacy about the power of the pope came into history: ''The elders which are among you I exhort, who am also an elder, and a witness of the sufferings of Christ, and also a partaker of the glory that shall be revealed:'' I Peter 5:1.

Peter told his brethren that he was just an ''ELDER'' in the Church as they were, not a Divine Monarch. Peter goes on to say: ''FEED THE FLOCK OF GOD WHICH IS AMONG YOU, TAKING THE OVERSIGHT THEREOF, NOT BY CONSTRAINT, BUT WILLINGLY; NOT FOR FILTHY LUCRE, BUT OF A READY MIND; NEITHER AS BEING LORDS OVER GOD'S HERITAGE, BUT BEING ENSAMPLES TO THE FLOCK.'' I Peter 5:2,3.

Peter plainly told his brethren to feed the flock, not by constraint or being Lords over God's heritage, but by being examples to them. What a contrast again do we see in the difference of the commandments of the papacy and the commandments of the Lord and the counsel of his apostles. They are opposite from each other. Christ says to DENY OURSELVES, that meant everybody including the apostles. God is not a respecter of persons (James 2:9).

Jesus said in Matthew 16:24: ''Then said Jesus unto His disciples, If any man will come after me, let him deny himself, and take up his cross, and follow me.''

Jesus taught all to deny themselves, not to exalt themselves. Self exaltation is from the spirit of the Father of pride working in the hearts of men. For that very reason, was Satan's fall; see Isaiah 14:12-15.

The papacy and the pope claim to have infallibility which only the Godhead has. They claim they have direct authority to manage private lives of people and governmental matters, which only belongs to God. Once again, here are the papacy's own words found in the book, *The Roman Catholic Church:*

''The powers of the Pope are defined in canon law in words taken from the first Vatican Council as 'the Supreme and full power or jurisdiction over the Universal Church both in matters of faith and morals and in matters of discipline and government.' This power is qualified as genuinely episcopal, ordinary, and immediate over each and every Church as well as over each and every pastor and believer, independent of any human authority." Quoted from *The Roman Catholic Church*, by John L. McKenzie, Image Books, edition 1971, by special arrangement with Holt, Rinehart and Winston, Inc., p. 39

Let us now examine another great error of the Roman Catholic Church. They say that the Lord gave Peter the keys of heaven which gives his successor, the Pope, also the right to open and shut the blessings from heaven. From *New Catholic Encyclopedia*, we read the following:

"In the light of canonical and extracanonical parallels, it seems certain that Mt. 16.19a, means not that St. Peter is to be gatekeeper of heaven, but that Christ will confer on him vicarious authority over his household on Earth, that is, over the Church that he promises to build on him as on a rock. For it is on Earth that Peter will exercise his power of binding and loosing (Mt. 16.19bc). The keys that Christ will give to Peter are the kingdom of heaven, in the sense that Peter's authoritative decisions will bind men in conscience; on their acceptance of his teaching of the gospel and his direction in the way of salvation will depend their entrance into the kingdom of God." *New Catholic Encyclopedia*, New York, McGraw Hill, 1967, p. 172

Let's go back to Matthew 16:18, 19. The Lord said to Peter -- "and upon this rock I will build my church." Christ was not referring to Peter as the papacy claims. Peter is not the rock that is the foundation of the Church; Christ is. The symbolic term "ROCK" has been applied to Christ throughout the entire Bible. Peter himself said Christ was the chief corner stone to the Church:

"Wherefore also it is contained in the Scripture, Behold, I lay in Sion a chief corner stone, elect, precious: and he that believeth on him shall not be confounded. Unto you therefore which believe he is precious: but unto them which be disobedient, the stone which the builders disallowed, the same is made the head of the corner, And a stone of stumbling, and a rock of offence, even to them which stumble at the word, being disobedient: whereunto also they were appointed." I Peter 2:6-8

"And whosoever shall fall on this stone shall be broken: but on whomsoever it shall fall, it will grind him to powder. For other foundation can no man lay than that is laid, which is Jesus Christ." Matthew 21:44; I Corinthians 3:11

If the apostle Peter was told by Christ that he was to be the prince of the apostles and awarded the keys that open and shut Heaven, and that he had infallibility, how is it Paul did not think so, for the apostle Paul rebuked Peter openly in Galatians 2:11-14? As for infallibility, out of all the apostles, it was Peter who seemed to make the most mistakes. It was

The pagan priest-king Pharaoh of Egypt being carried to the temple of his god. Notice the fan to your left and how the pagan Pharaoh was carried on a portable throne to pay a visit to his god. This same observance is held for the *Vicarius Filii Dei* (The Pope). See opposite page. Courtesy of Loizeaux Brothers, Neptune, N.J.

Peter whom the Lord rebuked most strongly in the same chapter the papacy uses to defend their authority. In Matthew 16:23, we read the following:

"But he turned, and said unto Peter, Get thee behind me, Satan: thou art an offence unto me: for thou savourest not the things that be of God, but those that be of men."

Christ said to Peter in Matthew 16:19, that he would give him the keys of the kingdom of Heaven; and what he would bind on Earth would be bound in Heaven and what he would loose on Earth would be loosed in Heaven. What is the meaning of the keys of the Kingdom of Heaven? They are the Old and New Testaments; not ecclesiastical power. It is the Holy Scriptures that open the doors of Eternal Life. Jesus gave us a good example of shutting up the Kingdom of Heaven when he rebuked the Pharisees for not preaching the Word of God. Matthew 23:13,15.

"For ye shut up the kingdom of heaven against men: for ye neither go in yourselves, neither suffer ye them that are entering to go in. Woe unto you, scribes and Pharisees, hypocrites! for ye compass sea and land to make one proselyte, and when he is made, ye make him twofold more the child of hell than yourselves."

Here again we can observe the striking contrast between the Meek and Lowly Jesus of Nazareth and the PROUD popes of Rome. Jesus said in Matthew 23:9 that we are not to call any man our father when addressing the spiritual things of God. The name "*pope*" means "*father.*" There is only ONE FATHER and He is in Heaven, not at Vatican City.

History says the Roman Catholic Church did this also. In the Dark Ages the ordinary people were commanded not to have a Bible in their possession. From *The Great Controversy,* by Ellen G. White, we read the following quotes from the Roman Catholic Church:

"Efforts to Suppress, and Destroy the Bible. — The Council of Toulouse, which met about the time of the crusade the Albigenses, ruled: 'We prohibit laymen possessing copies of the Old and New Testaments. . . . We forbid them most severely to have the above books in the popular vernacular.' The lords of the districts shall carefully seek out the heretics in dwellings, hovels, and forests, and even their underground retreats shall be entirely wiped out." *Concil. Tolosanum, Pope Gregory IX,* Anno. chr. 1229. Canons 14. This Council sat at the time of the crusade against the Albigenses.

"This pest (The Bible) had taken such an extension that some people had appointed priests of their own, and even some evangelists who distorted and destroyed the truth of the gospel and made new gospels for their own purpose . . . (they know that) the preaching and explanation of the Bible is absolutely forbidden to the lay members." — *Acts of Inquisition,* Philip van Limborch, *History of the Inquisition,* Chapter 8. Quoted from *The Great Controversy,* by Ellen G. White, Pacific Press Publishing Association, Mountain View, Calif. pp. 604,605.

Not to preach the Word of God as it is found unmixed with human theory is a woe to religious leaders, and professed Christians. The commandment is:

"Go ye therefore, and teach all nations, baptizing them in the name of the Father, and of the Son, and of the Holy Ghost: Teaching them to observe all things whatsoever I have commanded you: and, lo, I am with you alway, even unto the end of the world. Amen." Matthew 28:19,20. "And this gospel of the kingdom shall be preached in all the world for a witness unto all nations; and then shall the end come." Matthew 24:14.

What was the biggest reason that the Jews were blinded in their rejection of Jesus as the true Messiah that was to come? Jesus said in Matthew 22:29: "Jesus answered and said unto them, YE DO ERR, NOT KNOWING THE SCRIPTURES, NOR THE POWER OF GOD." It was because of a lack of knowledge of the Scriptures that many of the Jews were lost. All through the New Testament we read how Jesus rebuked the Pharisees by using the Holy Scriptures to back up his admonishments. Every deed Christ did in his life was foretold in the Scriptures. The Holy Scriptures were given to us that we might believe that Jesus is the Christ and He has power to save the human race from destroying itself while Satan our adversary supplies the temptations. When the Jews rejected Christ and His teachings, He said:

"Do not think that I will accuse you to the Father: there is one that accuseth you, even Moses, in whom ye trust. For had ye believed Moses, ye would have believed me: for he wrote of me. But if ye believe not his writings, how shall ye believe my words?" John 5:45-47.

Just as the Jews erred in the Scriptures with their own traditions borrowed from paganism, so has the papacy. Not only she, but her daughters the Protestants, which she begot. Here are some very shocking and sad words quoted by a Catholic writer. In the book *The Papacy,* we read the following:

"Our separate brethren start from the principle that the Scriptures alone are the source alike of all truth and all authority within the Church. In our view this unqualified Biblicism goes beyond the Bible. Nowhere in the Bible is it said that the Bible is the sole means chosen by Jesus Christ for the transmission of truth and His authority. Unqualified Biblicism is not Biblical." *The Papacy,* Wladimir D' Ormesson, Hawthorn Books, Publishers, New York, 1959 Translated.

Here is another reason why the Roman Catholic Church is being used by the master of deception. In *The Catholic Encyclopedia* we read the following Tradition:

"IN A SPECIAL SENSE, THERE IS BUT ONE SOURCE OF REVEALED TRUTH AND THIS SOURCE IS DIVINE TRADITION. By this is meant the body of revealed truth handed down from the Apostles through the ages and contained in the doctrine, teaching, and practice of the Catholic Church. As defined by the Council of Trent (SESS. IV, EB46), this includes both the Scriptures and the unwritten or oral tradition. It is the Church in her living magisterium, THE HOLDER OF TRADITION, which gives life to the Scriptures." *The Catholic Encyclopedia,* by Robert C. Broderick, Thomas Nelson, Inc., Publishers, Nashville, New York, p. 581. 1976.

The Roman Catholic Church openly admits that it does not believe the Holy Scriptures are the only infallible guide for the Christian. She places human theory and tradition as the divine channel that makes up the insufficient plan found in the Bible. But again we find this, the opposite teaching from Christ. For the Author of the Scripture says:

"SEARCH THE SCRIPTURES; FOR IN THEM YE THINK YE HAVE ETERNAL LIFE: AND THEY ARE THEY WHICH TESTIFY OF ME." John 5:39.

"STUDY TO SHEW THYSELF APPROVED UNTO GOD, A WORKMAN THAT NEEDETH NOT TO BE ASHAMED, RIGHTLY DIVIDING THE WORD OF TRUTH." II Timothy 2:15.

"FOR WHATSOEVER THINGS WERE WRITTEN AFORETIME WERE

WRITTEN FOR OUR LEARNING, THAT WE THROUGH PATIENCE AND COMFORT OF THE SCRIPTURES MIGHT HAVE HOPE." Romans 15:4.

"NOW ALL THESE THINGS HAPPENED UNTO THEM FOR ENSAMPLES: AND THEY ARE WRITTEN FOR OUR ADMONITION, UPON WHOM THE ENDS OF THE WORLD ARE COME." I Corinthians 10:11.

"ALL SCRIPTURE IS GIVEN BY INSPIRATION OF GOD, AND IS PROFITABLE FOR DOCTRINE, FOR REPROOF, FOR CORRECTION, FOR INSTRUCTION IN RIGHTEOUSNESS." II Timothy 3:16.

"TAKE HEED UNTO THYSELF AND UNTO THE DOCTRINE; CONTINUE IN THEM: FOR IN DOING THIS THOU SHALT BOTH SAVE THYSELF, AND THEM THAT HEAR THEE." I Timothy 4:16.

Again we see the error of those who claim to have Infallibility. The Holy Scriptures offer hope in believing and proving them. The Holy Scriptures teach us correction in wrong doing and also teach us righteousness. By reading the Scriptures our ignorance is exposed and we become repentant, and wise in the way that leads to salvation. The Scriptures, which were given by divine inspiration, expose the movement and subtle works of our adversary. The Scriptures teach us how to overcome him. Jesus claimed to be the Author of the Scriptures and bids us to study them. They are a powerful source of receiving the Holy Spirit. Jesus promised us that the Holy Spirit would bring all things to our remembrance. The Lord has spoken to us, not the Vicar of Christ, the Bishop of Rome, the Holy See, or whatever exalted name the Papacy uses. The Holy Spirit is Christ's representative here on earth. He is God on earth, not a weak sinful man. The Comforter is Christ's teacher of Spiritual things:

"EVEN THE SPIRIT OF TRUTH; WHOM THE WORLD CANNOT RECEIVE, BECAUSE IT SEETH HIM NOT, NEITHER KNOWETH HIM: BUT YE KNOW HIM; FOR HE DWELLETH WITH YOU, AND SHALL BE IN YOU." John 14:17.

"NEVERTHELESS I TELL YOU THE TRUTH; IT IS EXPEDIENT FOR YOU THAT I GO AWAY: FOR IF I GO NOT AWAY, THE COMFORTER WILL NOT COME UNTO YOU; BUT IF I DEPART, I WILL SEND HIM UNTO YOU. AND WHEN HE IS COME, HE WILL REPROVE THE WORLD OF SIN, AND OF RIGHTEOUSNESS, AND OF JUDGMENT." John 16:7,8.

Jesus clearly stated here that the Comforter is Christ's Vicar here on earth until He comes again. It is the Holy Spirit we are to obey, not the Bishop of Rome. "AND GRIEVE NOT THE HOLY SPIRIT OF GOD, WHEREBY YE ARE SEALED UNTO THE DAY OF REDEMPTION." Ephesians 4:30.

Let's take another look at the Papacy's claim to the Keys of Peter, which the Pope has, according to the Papacy. The keys in which, the papacy says, is ecclesiastical power to shut Heaven's blessings, is not an invention of the Catholic Church, but of Baal worship. In *The Two Babylons* we read:

"The College of Cardinals, with the Pope at its head, is just the counter part of the Pagan College of Pontiffs, with its PONTIFEX MAXIMUS or Sovereign Pontiff, which has existed in Rome from the earliest times, and which is known to have been framed on the model of the grand original Council of Pontiffs at Babylon. The Pope now pretends to supremacy in the church as the successor of Peter, to whom it is alleged that our Lord exclusively committed the keys of the kingdom of Heaven. But here is the important fact, that till the Pope was invested with the title, which for a thousand years had had attached to it the power of the keys of Janus and Cybele, no such claim to pre-eminence, or anything approaching to it, was ever publicly made on his part, on the ground of his being the possessor of the keys bestowed on Peter. Very early indeed, did the Bishops of Rome show a proud and ambitious spirit: but, for the first three centuries, their claim for superior honor was founded simply on the dignity of their See, as being that of the imperial city, the capital of the Roman world. When, however, the seat of the empire was removed to the east, and Constantinople threatened to eclipse Rome, some new ground for maintaining the dignity of the bishop of Rome must be sought. That new ground was found when, about 378, the Pope fell heir to the two keys that were the symbols of two well-known pagan divinities in Rome. Janus bore a key, and Cybele bore a key: and these are the two keys that the Pope emblazons on his arms as the ensigns of his spiritual authority." Quoted from *The Two Babylons,* Alexander Hislop, pp. 206,207 A.H. Loizeaux Brothers, Neptune, N.J. (by permission).

The power of the keys of the papacy, is just another counterfeit of the Gospel of Christ and its roots are from Baalim. It is Christ who opens and shuts the windows and doors of Heaven, not this so-called Holy Father:

"HE THAT HATH AN EAR, LET HIM HEAR WHAT THE SPIRIT SAITH UNTO THE CHURCHES. AND TO THE ANGEL OF THE CHURCH IN PHILADELPHIA WRITE; THESE THINGS SAITH HE THAT IS HOLY, HE THAT IS TRUE, HE THAT HATH THE KEY OF DAVID, HE THAT

OPENETH, AND NO MAN SHUTTETH; AND SHUTTETH, AND NO MAN OPENETH;'' Revelation 3:6,7.

As the priest kings of Sun Worship pretended to be the incarnate of the Sun God, so does the VICARIUS FILII DEI (POPE) pretend to be the incarnate of Christ. Since we have proved with the Scriptures, Baalim, and with the papacy's own words that the office of the Pope is Anti-christ, let us now move on and investigate his clergy.

After the sacrifice of the real Lamb of God, who was Jesus Christ who taketh away the sins of the world, was completed, the ceremonial law of the system of the temple services was done away with. The Jews were under the sacrificial law and the moral law which is summed up in the Ten Commandments. The Old Covenant of the priesthood in the ceremonial law was not needed after the sacrifice of Jesus. The priesthood was just a shadow here on earth of what was to come later when Christ would be resurrected and enter the Heavenly sanctuary:

''But Christ being come an high priest of good things to come, by a greater and more perfect tabernacle, not made with hands, that is to say, not of this building; Neither by the blood of goats and calves, but by his own blood he entered in once into the holy place, having obtained eternal redemption for us. Which hope we have as an anchor of the soul, both sure and stedfast, and which entered into that within the veil; Whither the forerunner is for us entered, even Jesus, made an high priest for ever after the order of Melchisedec.'' Hebrew 9:11,12; 6:19,20.

The Roman Church claims to intercede for the sins of the people through their Bishop of Rome and his clergy. But Christ is the Mediator between God and man according to the Scriptures. Christ is our advocate who pleads for our behalf for the sins we have committed against God, not a weak sinful man such as ourselves. God has said there is none good, no not one. Should we confess our sins to a man who is subject to the same passions and evils to which we are tempted? God Forbid:

''FOR THERE IS ONE GOD, AND ONE MEDIATOR BETWEEN GOD AND MEN, THE MAN CHRIST JESUS;'' I Timothy 2:5.

''WHEREFORE HE IS ABLE ALSO TO SAVE THEM TO THE UTTERMOST THAT COME UNTO GOD BY HIM, SEEING HE EVER LIVETH TO MAKE INTERCESSION FOR THEM. FOR SUCH A HIGH PRIEST BECAME US, WHO IS HOLY, HARMLESS, UNDEFILED, SEPARATE FROM SINNERS, AND MADE HIGHER THAN THE HEAVENS; WHO NEEDETH NOT DAILY, AS THOSE HIGH PRIESTS, TO OFFER UP SACRIFICE, FIRST FOR HIS OWN SINS, AND THEN FOR THE PEOPLE'S: FOR THIS HE DID ONCE, WHEN HE OFFERED UP HIMSELF. FOR THE LAW MAKETH MEN HIGH PRIESTS WHICH HAVE

INFIRMITY; BUT THE WORD OF THE OATH, WHICH WAS SINCE THE LAW, MAKETH THE SON WHO IS CONSECRATED FOR EVERMORE." Hebrews 7:25-28.

The early sanctuary of the Jews was patterned after the Heavenly Temple of the Most High. Until Christ came, the priesthood with the ceremonial rites of the Jews were a temporary earthly system of forgiveness of sins, where the high priest was a figure of the real High Priest to come, as the sacrifical lamb was a figure of the Real Lamb of God, Jesus Christ.

"NOW OF THE THINGS WHICH WE HAVE SPOKEN THIS IS THE SUM: WE HAVE SUCH A HIGH PRIEST, WHO IS SET ON THE RIGHT HAND OF THE THRONE OF THE MAJESTY IN THE HEAVENS; A MINISTER OF THE SANCTUARY, AND OF THE TRUE TABERNACLE, WHICH THE LORD PITCHED, AND NOT MAN. WHO SERVE UNTO THE EXAMPLE AND SHADOW OF HEAVENLY THINGS, AS MOSES WAS ADMONISHED OF GOD WHEN HE WAS ABOUT TO MAKE THE TABERNACLE: FOR, SEE, SAITH HE, THAT THOU MAKE ALL THINGS ACCORDING TO THE PATTERN SHEWED TO THEE IN THE MOUNT." Hebrews 8:1,2,5.

Our Intercessor sits by the throne in Heaven, not in Vatican City, Rome. In the book, *The Wine of Roman Babylon,* Mary E. Walsh, who was once a Roman Catholic herself, quotes from a Roman Catholic publication about the office of the Roman Catholic priest and one of his duties during the Eucharist (MASS):

"Marvelous dignity of the priests! exclaims St. Augustine: In the hands, as in the womb of the blessed Virgin Mary, the Son of God becomes incarnate. . . . Behold the power of the priest! It is more than creating the world. Someone said, Does St. Philomena, then, obey the cure of ARS? Certainly, she may well obey him, since God OBEYS HIM. The blessed Virgin cannot make her divine son descend into the host. A PRIEST CAN, HOWEVER SIMPLE HE MAY BE." H. Convert, *Eucharistic Medications* (Extracts from the writings of the blessed J. M. Vianney), pp. 111,112. Quoted in *The Wine of Roman Babylon,* Mary E. Walsh, The Southern Publishing Association, Nashville, Tenn., p. 62.

The blasphemous claim that a priest can change a wafer into the flesh and the wine into the blood of Jesus Christ, is the same doctrine taught by the Mother of Harlots, before she took on the name Christian. As we saw in the first chapter, the pagan high priests and kings impersonated their deities by pretending they were Baal's incarnate, who had power to turn the round disk wafer into their chief god. The Roman Catholic priest

Here is a photo of Pope Paul VI giving a mass in St. Peter's Basilica. Notice the round disk wafer. Usually this wafer will have the initials I. H. S. on it. In Egyptian Sun worship, this wafer, shaped in the form of the sun represented the body of the dead and risen sun god. The initials were the initials for the Egyptian Trinity (Isis, Horus, Seb); that is—the Mother, the Child, and the Father of Gods. Courtesy of the Religious News Service.

also claims to have power to do this. Again, from the book, *The Wine of Roman Babylon,* we read the following:

"Seek where you will, through heaven and earth, and you will find one created being who can forgive the sinner, who can free him from the chains of hell, that extraordinary being is the priest, the Roman Catholic priest. Who can forgive sins except God? was the question which the Pharisees sneeringly asked. 'Who can forgive sins?' is the question which the Pharisees of the present day also ask, and I answer there is a man on earth that can forgive sins, and that man is the (Roman) Catholic priest. Yes, beloved brethren, the priest not only declares that the sinner is forgiven, but he really forgives him. The priest raises his hand, he pronounces the word of absolution, and in an instant, quick as a flash of light the chains of hell are burst asunder, and the sinner becomes a child of God. So great is the power of the priest that the judgments of Heaven ARE SUBJECT TO HIS DECISION." Michael Muller, *The Catholic Priest,* pp. 78, 79—Quoted in *The Wine of Roman Babylon,* by Mary E. Walsh, Southern Publishing Association, Nashville, Tenn., p. 45.

Mark 2:7-10, is where the papacy quoted, "WHO CAN FORGIVE SINS, BUT GOD?" Jesus said in verse 10: "BUT THAT YE MAY KNOW

THAT THE SON OF MAN HATH POWER ON EARTH TO FORGIVE SINS."

Jesus has power to forgive sins because Christ was God manifested in the flesh. The same God that pronounced a curse on Adam and Eve, is the same Jesus who forgives sin through His shedding of His own blood:

"IN WHOM WE HAVE REDEMPTION THROUGH HIS BLOOD, THE FORGIVENESS OF SINS, ACCORDING TO THE RICHES OF HIS GRACE;" Ephesians 1:7.

Not only does the Papacy claim the priests have power to forgive sins, but they tell our Lord what to do. From *Daniel and the Revelation,* we read:

"We ask if the power represented by this symbol has fulfilled this part of the prophecy. In comments on Daniel 7:25, we saw clearly from the evidence submitted that he had spoken 'great words' against the God of Heaven. Now observe what is said regarding the claim of the priesthood to forgive sins:

"THE PRIEST HOLDS THE PLACE OF THE SAVIOR HIMSELF, WHEN, BY SAYING *'Ego te absolvo'* (I THEE ABSOLVE), He absolves from sin. . . . To pardon a single sin requires all the omnipotence of God. . . . But what only God can do by HIS omnipotence, the priest can also do by saying *'Ego te absolvo a peccatis tuis.'*. . . Innocent III has written : 'Indeed, it is not too much to say that in view of the sublimity of their offices the priests are so many gods!' "

Note still further the blasphemous utterances of this power:

"But our wonder should be far greater when we find that in obedience to the words of His priests — HOC EST CORPUS MEUM (This is My body) God Himself descends on the altar, that he comes wherever they call Him, and as often as they call Him, and places Himself in their hands, even though they should be His enemies. And after having come, He remains, entirely at their disposal; they move Him as they please, from one place to another: they may if they wish, shut Him up in the tabernacle, or expose Him on the altar, or carry Him outside the church: they may, if they choose, eat His flesh, and give Him for food of others. 'Oh, how very great is their power,' says, St. Laurence Justinian, speaking of priests. 'A word falls from their lips and the body of Christ is there substantially formed from the matter of bread, and the Incarnate Word descended from heaven is found really present on the table of the altar!' " Alphonsus de Liguori, *Dignity and Duties of Priests,* pp. 34-36,26,27,32,33, Quoted in *Daniel and the Revelation* by Uriah Smith, Southern Publishing Association, Nashville, Tenn., 1944.

What is so amazing about the boldness of the blasphemous claims of the Roman Church is that they too know the priesthood of the Roman Catholic Church is not found in the Bible. Here from the book, *The Roman Catholic Church,* we read the following:

"In the Roman Ecclesiastical Structure, one descends from the Roman Pontiff, the bishop of the entire Roman Church, to the ordinaries, the Bishops of local dioceses, to the priests, the immediate point of contact between the sacred personnel and the laity." LIKE THE EPISCOPACY, THE PRIESTHOOD AS WE KNOW IT DOES NOT APPEAR IN THE NEW TESTAMENT! *The Roman Catholic Church,* John L. McKenzie, S.F. 1st ed., New York, Holt, Rinehart and Winston, 1969, p. 96.

Now, let us study another important part of the Roman Catholic Church that has its roots from Sun Worship and not from the Bible. It is the Sisterhood of Nuns. In the book *Vatican Council II,* is a list of norms regulating papal enclosure of Nuns. Space or interest does not allow quoting all of them, but here are a couple of them:

"1. The enclosure reserved for the Nuns totally dedicated to contemplation (Perfectae Caritatis, n. 16) is called papal since the norms which govern it must be sanctioned by apostolic authority, even though they are established by particular law, by which are fitly expressed the characteristics proper to each Institute.

"3. The area of the convent subject to the law of enclosure must be circumscribed in such a way that material separation be ensured (Ecclesiae Sanctae, II, n. 31) that is, all coming in and going out must be thereby rendered impossible (e. g., by a wall or some other effective means, such as a fence of planks or heavy iron mesh, or a thick and firmly rooted hedge). Only through doors kept regularly locked may one enter or leave the enclosure." *Vatican Council II,* Austin Flannery, O. P. Costello Publishing Company, Northport, New York, 1975, pp. 671, 672.

Just as the Vestal Virgins or the other Virgins of the Sun were shut up in a house for women, as we have read, so are these poor young women of the Catholic Church. In *The Two Babylons,* we can find the origin of the word "NUN."

"The term Nun itself is a Chaldean word. Ninus, the son in Chaldee is either Nin or Non. Now, the feminine of Non, a Son, is Nonna, a 'daughter,' which is just the Popish canonical name for a 'Nun,' and Nonnus, in like manner, was in early times the designation for a monk in the east." (Gieseler, Vol. 2, p. 14, Note) — Quoted in *The Two Babylons,* Alexander Hislop, A. H. Loizeaux Brothers, Neptune, N.J., p. 223.

There is no commandment whatsoever from the Lord for the position of the Pope or his clergy. Neither is there the slightest hint that men as well as women practice Celibacy. On the contrary we read in the Scriptures the opposite:

"I SAY THEREFORE TO THE UNMARRIED AND WIDOWS, IT IS GOOD FOR THEM IF THEY ABIDE EVEN AS I. BUT IF THEY CANNOT CONTAIN, LET THEM MARRY: FOR IT IS BETTER TO MARRY THAN TO BURN." I Corinthians 7:8,9.

"THIS IS A TRUE SAYING, IF A MAN DESIRE THE OFFICE OF A BISHOP, HE DESIRETH A GOOD WORK. A BISHOP THEN MUST BE BLAMELESS, AND THE HUSBAND OF ONE WIFE, VIGILANT, SOBER, OF GOOD BEHAVIOUR, GIVEN TO HOSPITALITY, APT TO TEACH;" I Timothy 3:1,2.

Now let's study one of the biggest falsehoods of the Roman Catholic Church. In *A New Catechism: Catholic Faith for Adults,* we read the following:

"On the one hand we believe that Jesus is the Son of God, but once we have acknowledged this, we feel able to push it aside in all further consideration of Jesus. We go on to consider Him as a Rabbi who lived two thousand years ago. We speak of Him as a great man. We do not really see in His human life the person of the Son of God, the radiance of the eternal light.

To counteract this tendency, the Council of Ephesus proclaimed in 431 A.D., that in spite of the difference between divine and human nature, there is one person in Christ. We find God in the man Jesus. To express forcibly this mystery of Christ, the Council gave Mary the title of THEOTOKOS, Mother of God." *A New Catechism: Catholic Faith for Adults,* The Seabury Press, New York, N.Y., 1969, p. 80.

Again, from *A New Catechism: Catholic Faith for Adults,* we read the following:

"It is truth that Mary was free from the guilt of original sin. She was conceived Immaculate. Living in a sinful world, she shared the pain of the world, but not its wickedness. She is our sister in suffering, but not in evil." *A New Catechism: Catholic Faith for Adults,* the Seabury Press, New York, N.Y., 1969, p. 268.

From *The Catholic Encyclopedia,* 1975, we read:

"Assumption of the Blessed Virgin Mary: The doctrine of the taking up the body and soul of the Mother of God into heaven after her death was an early teaching of the fathers and of special interest to all Christians. Tradition and theological reasoning show that the privilege of the Assumption was revealed implicitly. On Nov. 1, 1950, Pope Pius

XII declared the Assumption of the Blessed Mother of God a doctrine of faith. The solemnity is celebrated on Aug. 15, and is a holy day of obligation." *The Catholic Encyclopedia,* (1975), by Robert C. Broderick, Thomas Nelson, Inc., Publishers, Nashville, New York, 1976, p. 56.

The Roman Catholic Church tries to make the world believe that Mary, the mother of Jesus, was free from spot or stain; spotlessly clean, free from original sin. They teach that Mary is the mother of God and even call her by one of the ancient names, "The Queen of Heaven," known as the pagan Mother Goddess. From *The Catholic Encyclopedia,* (1957 ed.) we read the following:

"REGINA COELI — Literally from the Latin 'QUEEN OF HEAVEN,' this title is accorded the BLESSED VIRGIN MARY; it is also the title of a poem composed in the twelfth century and the verse of a traditional hymn of the Easter season." *The Catholic Encyclopedia,* Thomas Nelson, Inc., Publishers, New York, Nashville, 1976, p. 518.

Again we have another belief taught in the Roman Catholic Church about Mary. In *Christ Among Us: A Modern Presentation of The Catholic Faith,* we read the following:

"We believe in Mary's Assumption, that she was taken into heaven body and soul at the end of her earthly life. Here again Mary imitated her Son who was taken to heaven when his work was finished. What happened to her is meant to encourage us — as she was taken to heaven and glorified, we have the assurance that one day we also will be. She was taken in a special way because it was not fitting that the body from which God the Son had taken his human body should undergo corruption." *Christ Among Us: A Modern Presentation of the Catholic Faith,* by Anthony Wilhelm, Paulist Press, New York, Paramus, Toronto, 1975, p. 368.

The Roman Catholic Church says Mary was conceived in her mother's womb without the stain of original sin, (Immaculate Conception). But the Bible says:

"If we say that we have not sinned, we make him a liar, and his word is not in us. They are 'ALL' gone out of the way, they are together become unprofitable; . . . THERE IS NONE THAT DOETH GOOD, NO, NOT ONE. FOR 'ALL' HAVE SINNED, AND COME SHORT OF THE GLORY OF GOD." I John 1:10, Romans 3:12,23.

If Mary was sinless as the Catholic Church says, why didn't Mary think so? For she showed in Luke 1:46,47 she too needed a Saviour:

"AND MARY SAID, MY SOUL DOTH MAGNIFY THE LORD, AND MY SPIRIT HATH REJOICED IN GOD MY SAVIOR."

A graven image of the queen of heaven and her son; now worshipped as the Virgin Mary and Jesus. The scriptures clearly condemn making any graven images. "Thou shalt not make unto thee any graven image." Exodus 20:4. Courtesy of the Louvre.

The Roman Catholic Church claims Mary was taken up to heaven like Jesus and she plays a great role in God's plan of Salvation. In *The Wine of Roman Babylon,* Mary E. Walsh, quotes from a Catholic publication. It reads as follows:

"O, Mary, we poor sinners know no other refuge than thee, for THOU ART OUR ONLY HOPE, AND ON THEE WE RELY FOR OUR SALVATION. THOU ART OUR ONLY ADVOCATE WITH JESUS CHRIST: TO THEE WE ALL TURN OURSELVES." Alfonsus M. de Liguori, *The Glories of Mary* (Revised by Robert A. Coffin), p. 96, — Quoted from *The Wine of Roman Babylon,* Mary E. Walsh, p. 129, the Southern Publishing Association, Nashville, Tenn.

The Roman Catholic Church says Mary acts as an ADVOCATE, HELPER, BENEFACTRESS, AND MEDIATRIX. In *Vatican Council II,* we read the following:

"62. This motherhood of Mary in the order of grace continues uninterrupted from the consent which she loyally gave at the Annunciation and which she sustained without wavering beneath the cross, until the eternal fulfillment of all the elect. Taken up to heaven she did not lay aside this saving office but by her manifold intercession continues to bring us the gifts of Eternal Salvation. By her maternal charity, she cares for the brethren of her Son, who still journey on earth surrounded by dangers and difficulties, until they are led into their blessed home. Therefore the Blessed Virgin is invoked in the Church under the titles of ADVOCATE, HELPER, BENEFACTRESS, AND MEDIATRIX. THIS, HOWEVER, IS SO UNDERSTOOD THAT IT NEITHER TAKES AWAY ANYTHING FROM NOR ADDS ANYTHING TO THE DIGNITY AND EFFICACY OF CHRIST THE ONE MEDIATOR." *Vatican Council II,* General Editor, Austin Flannery, O.P., Costello Publishing Company, Northport, New York, 1975, p. 419.

The Roman Catholic Church says Mary is a co-worker with Christ in the Salvation of souls. But Jesus says:

". . . I AM THE WAY, THE TRUTH, AND THE LIFE: NO MAN COMETH UNTO THE FATHER, BUT BY ME." John 14:6.

Peter the apostle to Jesus from whom the Catholic Church claim they receive their authority, said in Acts 4:12:

"NEITHER IS THERE SALVATION IN ANY OTHER: FOR THERE IS NONE OTHER NAME UNDER HEAVEN GIVEN AMONG MEN, WHEREBY WE MUST BE SAVED."

The Roman Catholic Church teaches the dead do not die but become spirits after death. This belief as we saw earlier, in chapter two, is called

Immortality of the soul. Man becoming spirits after the death of a human was the most cherished pagan belief. Just as the pagan believed in the burning place of torment (HELL FIRE), Limbo (purgatory) and a place for the good spirits to go (Paradise), so does the Mother of Harlots teach this. They teach, however, Mary the mother of Jesus went to Heaven both in body and soul. She, according to the Roman Catholic Church, comforts those who are in a state of Limbo (purgatory). This is a state where the dead go for purification. In *The Wine of Roman Babylon,* Mary E. Walsh quotes from *The Glories of Mary,* a Catholic publication we referred to earlier. The following states that Mary appeared to a certain Saint of the Roman Catholic Church:

"The divine mother once addressed these words to Saint Bridget. I am the mother of all souls in purgatory: for all the pains that they have deserved for their sins are every hour, as long as they remain there, in some way mitigated by my prayers. The compassionate mother even condescends to go herself occasionally into that holy prison, to visit and comfort her suffering children. Saint Bonaventure, applying to Mary the words of Ecclesiasticus, I have penetrated into the bottom of the deep, says, 'The deep, that is, purgatory, to receive by my presence the holy souls detained there. O, how courteous and benign is the most blessed virgin,' says Saint Vincent Ferrer, 'to those who suffer in purgatory! Through her they constantly receive comfort and refreshment . . .' The mere name of Mary, that name of hope and salvation, and which is frequently invoked by her beloved children in their prison, is a great source of comfort to them; 'for,' says, Novarinus, 'that loving mother no sooner hears them call upon her than she offers her prayers to God, and these prayers, as a heavenly dew, immediately refresh them in their burning pains.' " Alfonsus M. de Liguori. *The Glories of Mary,* pp. 206,207, quoted in *The Wine of Roman Babylon,* pp. 161,162, Southern Publishing Association, Nashville, Tenn.

To help the reader understand the above, here is the definition of purgatory according to the Roman Catholic Church. In *The Catholic Encyclopedia* we read the following:

"Purgatory — The souls of those who have died in the state of grace suffer for a time a purging that prepares them to enter heaven and appear in the presence of the beatific vision. The purpose of purgatory is to cleanse one of imperfection, venial sins, and faults, and to remit or do away with the temporal punishment due to mortal sins that have been forgiven in the Sacrament of Penance. It is an intermediate state in which the departed souls can atone for unforgiven sins before receiving their final reward." *The Catholic Encyclopedia,* by Robert C. Broderick, Thomas Nelson, Inc., Publishers, Nashville, New York, 1976, p. 502.

Like the pagans of Sun Worship, the Roman Church holds a festival for dead. In ancient times and in these modern times, it is called ALL SOULS DAY and this is the origin of Halloween. Again from *The Catholic Encyclopedia,* we read the following:

"All Souls Day is a day of solemn prayer for all the departed souls, which the Church observes on Nov. 2. the day in the calendar is a solemnity (transferable to Nov. 3) and was initially instituted for celebration on the day after All Saints Day by St. Odilo in A.D. 998. By a decree of Aug. 10, 1915, issued by Pope Benedict XV, a priest is granted the privilege of saying three Masses on this day: one for all the faithful departed, one for the intention of the Holy Father, and one for his particular intention." *The Catholic Encyclopedia,* by Robert C. Broderick, Thomas Nelson, Inc., Publishers, Nashville, New York, 1976, p. 30.

Not only does the Roman Catholic Church hold festivals to honor the departed spirits of loved ones, but it claims to have within the church, members who claim to receive messages from the dead. Instead of calling this practice of the occult NECROMANCY, THE ROMAN CATHOLIC CHURCH CALLS IT MYSTICISM. AND INSTEAD OF CALLING THE PEOPLE WHO PERFORM THIS ABOMINATION (MEDIUMS), THEY ARE CALLED "MYSTICS." From *The Roman Catholic Church,* we read the following:

"Most MYSTICS experience one or several apparitions of Jesus Christ. Teresa of Avila believed that sensible apparitions are a lower, introductory form of mysticism which leads one to a higher nonsensible perception of divine reality. When the mystics claim to have received information from Jesus himself about details of his life, especially detailed accounts of his passion, criticism demands a very reserved attitude. Some mystical accounts of the passion are so far out of line with known historical facts that they are simply incredible. In other cases, the Mystic may receive a message for the Church or some of its officers. The message may direct that a new devotion be instituted: thus the institution of the festival of Corpus Christi, the devotions of the Sacred Heart, the Rosary, the scapular, and several others are credited to mystical revelations. The message may deal with the problems of the church. Catherine of Siena, the counselor of popes, was a mystic; no one has ever questioned the soundness of her utterances. Some celebrated mystics, such as Teresa of Avila and John of the Cross, had no message for anyone and founded no new devotions. Apparitions as we have seen, have also been frequent; one may mention Lourdes, Guadalupe, and Fatima among the better known. These revelations all dealt with the institution of new devotions. Marian apparitions are even more characteristically Roman Catholic than Christocentric apparitions. Both types are often mentioned in connection with the foundation of new religious orders." *The Roman Catholic Church,* John L. McKenzie, S. J. 1st ed., New York, Holt, Rinehart and Winston, 1969, pp. 235,236.

The "MYSTICS" of the Roman Catholic Church have and are claimed to have seen and received messages from Jesus, Mary and dead saints, as they clearly boast about. But, reader, be not deceived by this falsehood, for they are not receiving messages from Jesus of the Bible, or dead saints, but doctrines of "DEVILS."

"FOR IN DEATH THERE IS NO REMEMBRANCE OF THEE, IN THE GRAVE WHO SHALL GIVE THEE THANKS?" Psalm 6:5.

"WILT THOU SHEW WONDERS TO THE DEAD? SHALL THE DEAD ARISE AND PRAISE THEE? SELAH. SHALL THY LOVING KINDNESS BE DECLARED IN THE GRAVE? OR THY FAITHFULNESS IN DESTRUCTION? SHALL THY WONDERS BE KNOWN IN THE DARK? AND THY RIGHTEOUSNESS IN THE LAND OF FORGETFULNESS?" Psalm 88:10-12.

"FOR THE LIVING KNOW THAT THEY SHALL DIE: BUT THE DEAD KNOW NOT ANYTHING, NEITHER HAVE ANY MORE A REWARD; FOR THE MEMORY OF THEM IS FORGOTTEN." Ecclesiastes 9:5.

"THE DEAD PRAISE NOT THE LORD, NEITHER ANY THAT GO DOWN INTO SILENCE." Psalm 115:17.

"SO MAN LIETH DOWN, AND RISETH NOT: TILL THE HEAVENS BE NO MORE, THEY SHALL NOT AWAKE, NOR BE RAISED OUT OF THEIR SLEEP. HIS SONS COME TO HONOUR, AND HE KNOWETH IT NOT; AND THEY ARE BROUGHT LOW, BUT HE PERCEIVETH IT NOT OF THEM." Job 14:12,21.

The dead according to the Scriptures do not send messages to the living, "for there is no work, nor device, nor knowledge, nor wisdom, in the grave, whither thou goest." Ecclesiastes 9:10. In the Bible, spirits that communicate with the living were called Familiar Spirits. Modern witchcraft calls them spirit guides.

"There SHALL NOT be found among you any one that maketh his son or daughter to pass through fire, or that useth DIVINATION, or an OBSERVER OF TIMES or an ENCHANTER, or a WITCH, or a CHARMER (HYPNOTIST), or a CONSULTER WITH FAMILIAR SPIRITS (SPIRIT GUIDES) or a WIZARD, or a NECROMANCER (MAGICIAN,

SORCERER, SOOTHSAYER, PSYCHIC). FOR ALL THAT DO THESE THINGS ARE AN ABOMINATION UNTO THE LORD: AND BECAUSE OF THESE ABOMINATIONS THE LORD THY GOD DOTH DRIVE THEM OUT FROM BEFORE THEE." Deuteronomy 18:10-12.

Modern day PSYCHICS, ASTROLOGERS, MYSTICS, and SOOTHSAYERS, etc., usually profess to believe in God. However, at the same time claim to receive messages and vibrations from the supernatural. The dead do not talk to us. These so-called vibrations that psychics receive and the spirit mediums can produce are not messages from God and are not spirits of dead loved ones. They are from Satan himself and his evil angels. Many have and many will be approached by spirits of devils in personating Jesus, some saint, dead relatives or departed friends. But those who have placed themselves on God's side have the promise: "THE ANGEL OF THE LORD ENCAMPETH ROUND ABOUT THEM THAT FEAR HIM, AND DELIVERETH THEM." Psalm 34:7.

There are Spirits of Angels of God and there are Spirits of Devils which are Satan's Angels:

"BLESS THE LORD, YE HIS ANGELS, THAT EXCEL IN STRENGTH, THAT DO HIS COMMANDMENTS, HEARKENING UNTO THE VOICE OF HIS WORD. WHO MAKETH HIS ANGELS SPIRITS; HIS MINISTERS A FLAMING FIRE:" Psalm 103:20; 104:4.

Those who have made their peace with God and seek to obey His Word as it is found in the Bible, are placing themselves under the protection of Jesus and His Holy Angels. Those who are claiming to receive messages from the spirit world, are placing themselves to be controlled and used by the worst tyrant in history. Those who seek their counsel shall also receive their reward. It is the lack of interest in studying the Scriptures that leads the ignorant in believing these deceptions. But the claims of the spiritualist can easily be proven false, when a brother or sister makes the Bible his infallible guide. Deception is not all falsehood. If deception were all falsehood it would be spotted in a moment. Satan must do some good and mix some truth or he will not deceive. While the Roman Catholic Church uses the name Christian and appears to be doing some good in the world, it at the same time leads its followers to ". . . GIVING HEED TO SEDUCING SPIRITS, AND DOCTRINES OF DEVILS;" I Timothy 4:1.

The next doctrine that we shall investigate, taught in the Catholic Church, (which they say was given in a message to a Mystic), is the use of the Rosary. In the book *A New Catechism: Catholic Faith for Adults*, we read the following:

"A very simple and common way to create a space of peace is to recite set prayers. We must not despise this form of prayer. In a busy life, fixed forms can be a help and an inspiration, as when we say the Our Father and the Hail Mary to ourselves. The sign of the cross before and after are like two doors, between which we are free for God." *A New Catechism: Catholic Faith for Adults,* translated by Kervin Smyth, The Seabury Press, 1969, p. 314.

From *The Catholic Encyclopedia* we read the following:

Rosary: "This is the name of both a devotion and the chain of beads used for counting the prayers. As a devotion, the Rosary arose in the fifteenth century and became very popular. It was begun by a Dominican preacher, Alan de Rupe (D. 1475), in northern France and Flanders. Belief that the devotion was revealed to St. Dominic was based chiefly on a report of a vision of de Rupe. The devotion is directed to the Blessed Mother and has been highly indulgenced by the Church. The Rosary has three parts. It consists of an initial prayer, the Apostles' Creed, followed by the Our Father and three Hail Marys, and a Glory be to the Father, which are said beginning on the crucifix and continued on the pendant portion of the chain of beads. There follow fifteen decades or groups of ten beads separated by a single bead. Each decade consists of the recitation of the Our Father, ten Hail Marys, and concludes with one Glory be to the Father. The devotion is for private or public use. While saying the prayers of each decade, the person praying is to meditate on the mysteries of the Rosary, fifteen in all (cf. Mysteries of the Rosary). *The Catholic Encyclopedia,* by Robert C. Broderick, Thomas Nelson, Inc., Publishers, Nashville, New York, 1976, p. 529.

The Lord, as we clearly saw in Matthew 6:5-8, in the first chapter, forbids us to pray in a repetitious manner, for it is the way the heathen worshipped and prayed to their idols. The Catholic Church says this devotion was introduced in the fifteenth century by a vision, however, this heathen devotion can be traced to the ancient Sun Worshippers. In *The Two Babylons,* we read the following:

"Every one knows how thoroughly Romanist is the use of the Rosary; and how the devotees of Rome mechanically tell their prayers upon their beads. The Rosary, however, is no invention of the Papacy. It is of the highest antiquity, and almost universally found in Pagan nations. The Rosary was used as a sacred instrument among the ancient Mexicans. It is commonly employed among the Brahmins of Hindustan; and in the Hindu sacred books reference is made to it again and again. Thus, in an account of the death of Sati the wife of Shiva, we find the Rosary introduced: 'On hearing of this event, Shiva fainted from grief; then, having recovered, he hastened to the banks of the river of heaven, where he beheld lying the body of his beloved Sati, arrayed in white garments, HOLDING A ROSARY IN HER HAND, AND GLOWING WITH SPLENDOR, BRIGHT AS BURNISHED GOLD.' In Tibet it has been used from time immemorial and among all the millions in the East that adhere to the Buddhist faith. The following from Sir John F. Davis, will show how it is employed in China: 'From the Tartar religion of the Lamas, the Rosary of 108 beads has become a part of the ceremonial dress attached to the nine grades of official rank. It consists of a necklace of stones and coral, nearly as large as a pigeon's egg, descending to the waist, and distinguished by various beads, according to the quality of the wearer. There is a small Rosary of eighteen beads, of inferior size, with which the bonzes count their prayers and ejaculations exactly as in the Romish ritual. The laity in China sometimes wear this at the wrist, perfumed with musk, and give it the name of Heang-choo, or fragrant beads.' In Asiatic Greece the Rosary was commonly used, as may be seen from the image of the Ephesian Diana. In Pagan Rome the same appears to have been the case. The necklaces which the Roman ladies wore were not merely ornamental bands about the neck, but hung down the breast, just as the modern Rosaries do; and the name by which they were called indicates the use to which they were applied (MONILE), the ordinary word for necklace, can have no other meaning than that of a REMEMBRANCER." *The Two Babylons,* Alexander Hislop, 2nd ed., 1959, Loizeaux Brothers, Neptune, New Jersey, pp. 187,188, (by permission).

But what is so ironic about the Rosary is that Mary is not living according to the Scriptures, for the dead know not anything and the Roman Catholic Church teaches its members to pray to her. From *The Catholic Encyclopedia* we read the following:

"AVE MARIA—literally 'HAIL MARY,' Ave Maria is the title of the familiar two part prayer: 'Hail Mary, full of grace, the Lord is with thee; blessed art thou among all women, and blessed is the fruit of thy womb, Jesus. Holy Mary, Mother of God, pray for us sinners now and at the hour of our death.' " *The Catholic Encyclopedia,* by Robert C. Broderick, Thomas Nelson, Inc., Publishers, Nashville, New York, 1976, pp. 59,60.

But Jesus says: "FOR HE IS NOT A GOD OF THE DEAD, BUT OF THE LIVING: FOR ALL LIVE UNTO HIM." Luke 20:38.

As Semiramis the original "Queen of Heaven," the mother of gods worship was a myth, so is it with the worship of the Virgin Mary, whom they call today, the Queen of Heaven. Just as the pagans during their New Year's Festivals, baked cakes with a cross on them to honour the Pagan Goddess and her son Tammuz, so do the Roman Catholics have their "HOT CROSS BUNS." From *The American Dictionary*, p. 585, we read the following:

"HOT CROSS BUN — a bun with a cross of frosting on it, eaten chiefly during Lent." *The American College Dictionary*, C. L. Barnhart, Editor-in-Chief, Random House, New York. The L. W. Singer Co., Syracuse.

Jeremiah 7:17-19, describes Israel's apostasy in keeping the custom of honoring the pagan Queen of Heaven by making cakes (HOT CROSS BUNS).

"SEEST THOU NOT WHAT THEY DO IN THE CITIES OF JUDAH AND IN THE STREETS OF JERUSALEM? THE CHILDREN GATHER WOOD, AND THE FATHERS KINDLE THE FIRE, AND THE WOMEN KNEAD THEIR DOUGH, TO MAKE CAKES TO THE QUEEN OF HEAVEN, AND TO POUR OUT DRINK OFFERINGS UNTO OTHER GODS THAT THEY MIGHT PROVOKE ME TO ANGER. DO THEY PROVOKE ME TO ANGER? SAITH THE LORD: DO THEY NOT PROVOKE THEMSELVES TO THE CONFUSION OF THEIR OWN FACES?"

Not only does the Roman Catholic Church observe this heathen custom, but it was the Roman Catholic Church who promoted the pagan festivals, Easter, Christmas, Good Friday, and Sunday sacredness which we will study later. None of these Pagan Festivals were kept at the time of the apostles of Christ. As a matter of fact, they were shunned by both the Jews and Christ's followers.

Like the Israelites in their apostasy, it did not come all at once, but a little at a time, the enemy of the Gospel mingled the unholy practices of Baal worship into the pure worship of God. But Satan will be unmasked "AND THE GLORY OF THE LORD SHALL BE REVEALED, AND ALL FLESH SHALL SEE IT TOGETHER: FOR THE MOUTH OF THE LORD HATH SPOKEN IT." Isaiah 40:5.

Again, another abominable practice, we saw in Baal worship, that Satan leads millions to practice both in the Roman Catholic Church and some Protestant churches is the reference for graven images. From *Vatican Council II*, we read the following:

"SACRED ART AND SACRED FURNISHINGS: 125. The practice of placing sacred IMAGES in churches so that they be venerated by the faithful is to be maintained. Nevertheless their number should be moderate and their relative positions should reflect right order. For otherwise the Christian people may find them incongruous and they may foster devotion of doubtful orthodoxy." *Vatican Council II,* General Editor, Austin Flannery, O.P., Costello Publishing Company, Northport, New York, 1975, p. 35.

If you look in a Bible dictionary or concordance, you will find that any graven-image-making of a deity is idolatry. Idolatry is bowing down to images, worshipping images or sacrificing to images. Even though the Papacy states that they do not worship them, they still reverence them, which is the same as worship. Just as the pagans adorned their idols with clothing, jewels and flowers, so do the Catholics. When God led the Israelites out of Egypt and gave the land of Canaan to the Jews, He ordered them to destroy the images that were standing throughout the land. Many of these images were of Ashtaroth (Judges 2:13), the Queen Of Heaven to the Philistines, Phoenicians, and Zidonians. Today she is worshipped under the name, Virgin Mary.

In the "TEN COMMANDMENTS," the second commandment says:

"THOU SHALT NOT MAKE UNTO THEE ANY GRAVEN IMAGE, OR LIKENESS OF ANYTHING THAT IS IN HEAVEN ABOVE, OR THAT IS IN THE EARTH BENEATH, OR THAT IS IN THE WATER UNDER THE EARTH: THOU SHALT NOT BOW DOWN THYSELF TO THEM, NOR SERVE THEM: FOR I THE LORD THY GOD AM A JEALOUS GOD, VISITING THE INIQUITY OF THE FATHERS UPON THE CHILDREN UNTO THE THIRD AND FOURTH GENERATION OF THEM THAT HATE ME; AND SHEWING MERCY UNTO THOUSANDS OF THEM THAT LOVE ME, AND KEEP MY COMMANDMENTS." Exodus 20:4-6.

If you ever read the Old Testament you will remember that idolatry was the main reason God cast both the northern and southern kingdoms of Israel out of his sight. (Ezekiel 16:1-63). The Israelites not only made idols to Baal, but also idols of Jehovah when professing to serve Him. So does the Roman Catholic Church. This mingling the unholy with the holy is described in Ezekiel 20:39:

"AS FOR YOU, O HOUSE OF ISRAEL, THUS SAITH THE LORD GOD; GO YE, SERVE YE EVERY ONE HIS IDOLS, AND HEREAFTER ALSO, IF YE WILL NOT HEARKEN UNTO ME: BUT POLLUTE YE MY HOLY

NAME NO MORE WITH YOUR GIFTS, AND WITH YOUR IDOLS."

"I AM THE LORD: THAT IS MY NAME: AND MY GLORY WILL I NOT GIVE TO ANOTHER, NEITHER MY PRAISE TO GRAVEN IMAGES." Isaiah 42:8.

"HEAR, O EARTH: BEHOLD, I WILL BRING EVIL UPON THIS PEOPLE, EVEN THE FRUIT OF THEIR THOUGHTS, BECAUSE THEY HAVE NOT HEARKENED UNTO MY WORDS, NOR TO MY LAW, BUT REJECTED IT." Jeremiah 6:19.

Instead of images of Baal, Ashtaroth, and Tammuz, the Roman Catholic Church changed the faces of the idols to Jesus, Mary, and Peter; and instead of the worship of the lesser gods in heaven, the worship of the saints. Here is another doctrine of the Roman Catholic Church that SPEAKS GREAT WORDS AGAINST THE MOST HIGH (Daniel 7:25). From *A New Catechism: Catholic Faith for Adults,* we read the following:

"IT IS ANCIENT CATHOLIC DOCTRINE that Christians baptized outside the community of the Catholic Church really receive baptism. Apart from our common humanity, this is the most profound and solid foundation of the ECUMENICAL MOVEMENT." *A New Catechism: Catholic Faith for Adults,* translated by Kervin Smyth, The Seabury Press, 1969, p. 248.

For the sake of UNITING THE DAUGHTERS (PROTESTANTS) back to their MOTHER CHURCH, (THE PAPACY), she accepts all three forms of Baptism found throughout Christianity. Here from *The Catholic Encyclopedia,* we read the following:

"The Church recognizes three forms of giving valid baptism: Immersion, the lowering of the body into water; Aspersion, the sprinkling of the water; and Infusion, the pouring of the water."

Further on we read: "The Church recognizes as valid baptisms properly performed by non-Catholic ministers. Baptism is conferred conditionally when there is doubt concerning a previous baptism or the dispositions of the person to be baptized. Because baptism is necessary for salvation, anyone may baptize an infant in danger of death, and an ABORTED FETUS, IF ALIVE, SHOULD BE BAPTIZED, OR IF NO SIGN OF LIFE IS PRESENT, THEN THE FETUS SHOULD BE BAPTIZED CONDITIONALLY." *The Catholic Encyclopedia,* by Robert Broderick, Thomas Nelson, Inc., Publishers, Nashville, New York, 1975, p. 65.

As we saw earlier in chapter one, the pagans had infant baptism and practiced a form of communion. The very round disk wafer the Egyptians used in their version of the bread of life, with the letters I.H.S. engraved on it, which means: THE MOTHER, THE CHILD AND THE FATHER OF THE GODS,[1] is used today in the EUCHARIST of the Catholic Church. Only the meaning has been changed. A sacred dish called the "PATEN" HAS THE LETTERS I.H.S. ON IT.[2]

There are many, many other facts to show the reader how this LITTLE HORN of Daniel 7:25, speaks great words against the Most High, to blaspheme His name, and His Tabernacle, but space does not allow this. However, before we investigate how the Roman Catholic Church has fulfilled the second act of Daniel 7:25 — "AND HE SHALL WEAR OUT THE SAINTS OF THE MOST HIGH" — there is just one more doctrine of the Roman Catholic Church which deserves our attention. This papal doctrine is the worst of all her blasphemies. It is the sale of forgiveness of sins through indulgences. From *Vatican Council II,* we read the following:

"The authorities of the Church have two aims in granting indulgences. The first is to help the faithful to expiate their sins. The second is to encourage them to do works of piety, penitence and charity, particularly those which lead to growth in faith and which help the common good.

"Further, if the faithful offer indulgences by way of intercession for the dead they cultivate charity in an excellent way. While they raise their minds in heaven they bring a wiser order into the things of this world." *Vatican Council II,* General Editor, Austin Flannery, O.P., Costello Publishing Company, Northport, New York, 1975, p. 71.

To show the depth of the great atrocities committed against God by the Roman Catholic Church, we will quote from a religious writer who has compiled historical facts about the sale of forgiveness of sins by the Roman Catholic Church. The writer is the late Ellen G. White and her book is *The Great Controversy:*

"The Roman Church had made merchandise of the grace of God. The tables of the money-changers (Matthew 21:12) were set up beside her altars, and the air resounded with shouts of buyers and sellers. Under the plea of raising funds for the erection of St. Peter's Church at Rome, indulgences for sin were publicly offered for sale by the authority of the pope. By the price of a crime a temple was to be built up for God's worship—the cornerstone laid with the wages of iniquity! But the very

---

[1] See *The Two Babylons,* by Alexander Hislop, p. 164.
[2] See *The Catholic Encyclopedia,* p. 458.

means adopted for Rome's aggrandizement provoked the deadliest blow to her power and greatness. It was this that aroused the most determined and successful of the enemies of popery, and led to the battle which shook the papal throne and jostled the triple crown upon the pontiff's head.

"The official appointed to conduct the sale of indulgences in Germany—Tetzel by name—had been convicted of the basest offenses against society and against the law of God; but having escaped the punishment due him for his crimes, he was employed to further the mercenary and unscrupulous projects of the pope. With great effrontery he repeated the tales to deceive an ignorant, credulous, and superstitious people. Had they possessed the word of God they would not have been thus deceived. It was to keep them under the control of the papacy, in order to swell the power and wealth of her ambitious leaders, that the Bible had been withheld from them. (See John C.L. Gieseler, *A Compendium of Ecclesiastical History,* per. 4, sec. 1, par. 5).

"As Tetzel entered a town, a messenger went before him, announcing: The grace of God and of the holy father is at your gates. — D'Aubigne, b. 3, ch. 1. 'And the people welcomed the blasphemous pretender as if he were God Himself come down from heaven to them. The infamous traffic was set up in the church, and Tetzel, ascending the pulpit, extolled the indulgences as the most precious gift of God. He declared that by virtue of his certificates of pardon all the sins which the purchaser should afterward desire to commit would be forgiven him, and that not even repentance is necessary,' — Ibid., b. 3, ch. 1. More than this, he assured his hearers that the indulgences had power to save not only the living but the dead; that the very moment the money should clink against the bottom of his chest the soul in whose behalf it had been paid would escape from purgatory and make its way to heaven. (See K. R. Hagenbach, *History of the Reformation,* vol. 1, p. 96).

"When Simon Magus offered to purchase of the apostles the power to work miracles, Peter answered him: '. . . Thy money perish with thee, because thou hast thought that the gift of God may be purchased with money.' Acts 8:20. But Tetzel's offer was grasped by eager thousands. Gold and silver flowed into his treasury. A salvation that could be bought with money was more easily obtained than that which requires repentance, faith, and diligent effort to resist and overcome sin.

"The doctrine of indulgences had been opposed by men of learning and piety in the Roman Church, and there were many who had no faith in pretensions so contrary to both reason and revelation. No prelate dared lift his voice against this iniquitous traffic; but the minds of men were becoming disturbed and uneasy, and many eagerly inquired if God would not work through some instrumentality for the purification of His church.

"Luther, though still a papist of the straitest sort, was filled with horror at the blasphemous assumptions of the indulgence mongers. Many of his own congregation had purchased certificates of pardon, and they soon began to come to their pastor, confessing their various sins, and expecting absolution, not because they were penitent and wished to reform, but on the ground of the indulgence. Luther refused them absolution, and warned them that unless they should repent and reform their lives, they must perish in their sins. In great perplexity they repaired to Tetzel with the complaint that their confessor had refused his certificates; and some boldly demanded that their money be returned to them. The friar was filled with rage. He uttered the most terrible curses, caused fires to be lighted in the public squares, and declared that he 'had received an order from the pope to burn all heretics who presumed to oppose his most holy indulgences.'— D'Aubigne, b. 3, Ch. 4.

"Luther now entered boldly upon his work as a champion of the truth. His voice was heard from the pulpit in earnest solemn warning. He set before the people the offensive character of sin, and taught them that it is impossible for man, by his own works, to lessen its guilt or evade its punishment. Nothing but repentance toward God and faith in Christ can save the sinner. The grace of Christ cannot be purchased; it is a free gift. He counseled the people not to buy indulgences, but to look in faith to a crucified Redeemer. He related his own painful experience in vainly seeking by humiliation and penance to secure salvation, and assured his hearers that it was by looking away from himself and believing in Christ that he found peace and joy.

"As Tetzel continued his traffic and his impious pretensions, Luther determined upon a more effectual protest against these crying abuses. An occasion soon offered. The castle of Wittenberg possessed many relics, which on certain holy days were exhibited to the people, and full remission of sins was granted to all who then visited the church and made confession. Accordingly, on these days the people in great numbers resorted thither. One of the most important of these occasions, the festival of All Saints, was approaching. On the preceding day, Luther, joining the crowds that were already making their way to the church, posted on its door a paper containing ninety-five propositions against the doctrine of indulgences. He declared his willingness to defend these theses next day at the university, against all who should see fit to attack them.

"His propositions attracted universal attention. They were read and reread, and repeated in every direction. Great excitement was created in the university and in the whole city. By these theses it was shown that the power to grant the pardon of sin, and to remit its penalty, had never been committed to the pope or to any other man. The whole scheme was a farce, -- an artifice to extort money by playing upon the superstitions of the people, -- a device of Satan to destroy the souls of all who should trust to its lying pretensions. It was also clearly shown that the gospel of Christ is the most valuable treasure of the church, and that the grace of God, therein revealed, is freely bestowed upon all who seek it by repentance and faith.

"Luther's theses challenged discussion: but no one dared accept the challenge. The questions which he proposed had in a few days spread through all Germany, and in a few weeks they had sounded throughout Christendom. Many devoted Romanists, who had seen and lamented the terrible iniquity prevailing in the church, but had not known how to arrest its progress, read the propositions with great joy, recognizing in them the voice of God. They felt that the Lord had graciously set His hand to arrest the rapidly swelling tide of corruption that was issuing from the See of Rome. Princes and magistrates secretly rejoiced that a check was to be put upon the arrogant power which denied the right of appeal from its decisions.

"But the sin-loving and superstitious multitudes were terrified as the sophistries that had soothed their fears were swept away. Crafty ecclesiastics, interrupted in their work of sanctioning crime, and seeing their gains endangered, were enraged, and and rallied to uphold their pretensions. The Reformer had bitter accusers to meet. Some charged him with acting hastily from impulse. Others accused him of presumption, declaring that he was not directed of God, but was acting from pride and forwardness. 'Who does not know,' he responded, 'that a man rarely puts forth any new idea without having some appearance of pride, and without being accused of exciting quarrels? . . . Why were Christ and all the martyrs put to death? Because they seemed to be proud contemners of the wisdom of the time, and because they advanced novelties without having first humbly taken counsel of the oracles of the ancient opinions.'

"Again he declared: 'Whatever I do will be done, not by the prudence of men, but by the counsel of God. If the work be of God, who shall stop it? if it be not, who can forward it? Not my will, not theirs, not ours: but Thy will, O holy Father, which art in heaven.' -- *Ibid.*, b. 3, ch. 6

"Though Luther had been moved by the Spirit of God to begin his work, he was not to carry it forward without severe conflicts. The reproaches of his enemies, their misrepresentation of his purposes, and their unjust and malicious reflections upon his character and motives, came in upon him like an overwhelming flood; and they were not without effect. He had felt confident that the leaders of the people, both in the church and in the schools, would gladly unite with him in efforts for reform. Words of encouragement from those in high position had inspired him with joy and hope. Already in anticipation he had seen a brighter day dawning for the church. But encouragement had changed to reproach and condemnation. Many dignitaries, of both church and state were convicted of the truthfulness of his theses; but they soon saw that the acceptance of these truths would involve great changes. To enlighten and reform the people would be virtually to undermine the authority of Rome, to stop thousands of streams now flowing into her treasury, and thus greatly to curtail the extravagance and luxury of the papal leaders. Furthermore, to teach the people to think and act as responsible beings, looking to Christ alone for salvation, would overthrow the pontiff's throne and eventually destroy their own authority. For this reason they refused the knowledge tendered them of God and arrayed themselves against Christ and the truth by their opposition to the man whom He had sent to enlighten them.

"Luther trembled as he looked upon himself— one man opposed to the mightiest powers of earth. He sometimes doubted whether he had indeed been led of God to set himself against the authority of the church. 'Who was I,' he writes, 'to oppose the majesty of the pope, before whom . . . the kings of the earth and the whole world trembled? . . . No one can know what my heart suffered during these first two years, and into what despondency, I may say into what despair, I was sunk.' — Ibid., b. 3, ch. 6. But he was not left to become utterly disheartened. When human support failed, he looked to God alone and learned that he could lean in perfect safety upon that all-powerful arm.

"To a friend of the Reformation Luther wrote: 'We cannot attain to the understanding of Scripture either by study or by intellect. Your first duty is to begin by prayer. Entreat the Lord to grant you, of His great mercy, the true understanding of His word. There is no other interpreter of the word of God than the Author of his word, as He Himself has said, 'They shall be all taught of God.' Hope for nothing from your own labors, from your own understanding: trust solely in God, and in the influence of His Spirit. Believe this on the word of a man who has had experience.' Ibid., b. 3, ch. 7. Here is a lesson of vital importance to those who feel that God has called them to present to others the solemn truths for this time. These truths will stir the enmity of Satan and of men who love the fables that he has devised. In the conflict with the powers of evil there is need of something more than strength of intellect and human wisdom.

"When enemies appealed to custom and tradition, or to the assertions and authority of the pope, Luther met them with the Bible and the Bible only. Here were arguments which they could not answer; therefore the slaves of formalism and superstition clamored for his blood, as the Jews had clamored for the blood of Christ. 'He is a heretic,' cried the Roman zealots. 'It is high treason against the church to allow so horrible a heretic to live one hour longer. Let the scaffold be instantly erected for him!' -- *Ibid.*, b. 3, ch. 9. But Luther did not fall a prey to their fury. God had a work for him to do, and angels of heaven were sent to protect him. Many, however, who had received from Luther the precious light were made the objects of Satan's wrath and for the truth's sake fearlessly suffered torture and death." *The Great Controversy*, Ellen G. White, Pacific Press Publishing Association, Mountain View, California, (by permission from Ellen G. White Estate), pp. 127-142 (114-126 PB)

In the beginning of his efforts to show the falsehood of indulgences, Luther had no thought of leaving the Roman Catholic Church, but to establish a reformation. However, after being rejected as a heretic, he was led by the Lord to examine other papal doctrines. When Luther allowed the Spirit of God to be his interpreter, he was revealed this truth, when he said:

"I despise and attack it, as impious, false . . . . It is Christ Himself who is condemned therein. . . . I rejoice in having to bear such ills for the best of causes. Already I feel greater liberty in my heart; FOR AT LAST I KNOW THAT THE POPE IS ANTICHRIST, AND THAT HIS THRONE IS THAT OF SATAN HIMSELF." (D'Aubigné, b. 6, ch. 9)

Satan's seat is now at Vatican City. The Roman Catholic Church is the LITTLE HORN OF DANIEL 7:25. IT IS THE FIRST BEAST OF REVELATION 13:1. IT IS THE MOTHER OF HARLOTS OF REVELATION 17:5. Here is another identifying mark in her history that proves her to be the Mystery of Iniquity:

"AND I SAW THE WOMAN DRUNKEN WITH THE BLOOD OF THE SAINTS, AND WITH THE BLOOD OF THE MARTYRS OF JESUS: AND WHEN I SAW HER, I WONDERED WITH GREAT ADMIRATION." Revelation 17:6

Now we come to the second point of Daniel's prophecy of the LITTLE HORN. We have seen how the papacy has committed great blasphemy against the Most High; now we will see the murderous character of Satan displayed down through history by these bloody popes. Jesus foretold that His followers would suffer persecution. We read:

"BUT BEFORE ALL THESE, THEY SHALL LAY THEIR HANDS ON YOU, AND PERSECUTE YOU, DELIVERING YOU UP TO THE

SYNAGOGUES, AND INTO PRISONS, BEING BROUGHT BEFORE KINGS AND RULERS FOR MY NAME'S SAKE. YEA, AND ALL THAT WILL LIVE GODLY IN CHRIST JESUS SHALL SUFFER PERSECUTION." Luke 21:12; II Timothy 3:12.

"BLESSED ARE THEY WHICH ARE PERSECUTED FOR RIGHTEOUSNESS SAKE: FOR THEIRS IS THE KINGDOM OF HEAVEN. BLESSED ARE YE, WHEN MEN SHALL REVILE YOU, AND PERSECUTE YOU, AND SHALL SAY ALL MANNER OF EVIL AGAINST YOU FALSELY, FOR MY SAKE. REJOICE, AND BE EXCEEDING GLAD: FOR GREAT IS YOUR REWARD IN HEAVEN: FOR SO PERSECUTED THEY THE PROPHETS WHICH WERE BEFORE YOU." Matthew 5:10-12.

From the beginning, those who stood for the truth have suffered persecution, as Jesus said to the Pharisees, Matthew 23:33-35:

"Ye serpents, ye generation of vipers, how can ye escape the damnation of hell? Wherefore, behold, I send unto you prophets, and wise men, and scribes: and some of them ye shall kill and crucify; and some of them shall ye scourge in your synagogues, and persecute them from city to city: That upon you may come all the righteous blood shed upon the earth, from the blood of righteous Abel unto the blood of Zacharias son of Barachias, whom ye slew between the temple and the altar."

It is the goodness of God that brings an evil doer to repentance, not force. However, the second act of the LITTLE HORN would be to WEAR OUT THE SAINTS OF THE MOST HIGH. In Revelation, the apostle John said:

"AND IT WAS GIVEN UNTO HIM TO MAKE WAR WITH THE SAINTS, AND TO OVERCOME THEM: AND POWER WAS GIVEN HIM OVER ALL KINDREDS, AND TONGUES, AND NATIONS." Revelation 13:7.

Many, many names are listed in the books of heaven who gave their lives for the cause of Christ, taken first by Pagan Rome, then by Papal Rome. Most people who have any knowledge about World War II, have heard the name Hitler, and how he was responsible for mudering multitudes of Jews. This was a hellish act of Satanic power, but few people indeed know that the Roman Catholic Church under its religious dictatorship, murdered more people down through the centuries than any other power on earth. It has been estimated that during the Dark Ages, ONE HUNDRED MILLION people lost their lives when the papacy had control over the known world. In the *Encyclopedia Americana,* we read the following:

"Early Christians combated heresy by peaceful methods: persuasion, moral example, and theological polemic. A change came when Christianity became the official religion of the Roman Empire during the fourth century. The emperors, desperate to preserve the unity of classical civilization by enforcing unity of belief, enacted repressive legislation against heretics. Church authorities did not quickly accept the use of state power for punishment of heresy. The opinion of St. Augustine (354-430), however, was decisive for the middle ages." *Encyclopedia Americana,* Vol. 15, p. 191.

Uriah Smith in his book, *Daniel and the Revelation,* has compiled historical facts about how the Roman Catholic Church MADE WAR WITH THE SAINTS:

"It requires but little historical investigation to prove that Rome, both in the times of antiquity and during the Dark Ages, carried forward a work of destruction against the church of God. Abundant evidences can be given showing that prior to and following the great work of the Reformation, wars, crusades, massacres, inquisitions, and persecutions of all kinds were the methods adopted to compel all to submit to the Roman yoke.

"The story of medieval persecution is a frightful one, and we dread to dwell upon its detail. Yet for a proper understanding of this passage (Daniel 7:25), it is necessary that we recall some of the happenings of these unhappy times. Albert Barnes, in his comment on this passage, remarks:

'Can anyone doubt that this is true of the papacy? The Inquisition, the persecutions of the Waldenses; the ravages of the Duke of Alva; the fires of Smithfield; the tortures at Goa — indeed, the whole history of the papacy may be appealed to in proof that this is applicable to that power. If anything could have worn out the saints of the Most High — could have cut them off from the earth so that evangelical religion would have become extinct, it would have been the persecutions of the papal power. In the year 1208, a crusade was proclaimed by Pope Innocent III, against the Waldenses and Albigenses, in which a million men perished. From the beginning of the order of the Jesuits, in the year 1540, to 1580, nine hundred thousand were destroyed. One hundred and fifty thousand perished by the Inquisition in thirty years. In the Low Countries fifty thousand persons were hanged, beheaded, burned, and buried alive, for the crime of heresy, within the space of thirty-eight years from the edict of Charles V against the Protestants, to the peace of Chateau Cambreses in 1559. Eighteen thousand suffered by the hand of the executioner in the space of five years and a half during the administration of the Duke of Alva. Indeed, the slightest acquaintance with the history of the papacy will convince any one that what is here said of 'making war with the saints' (verse 21), and 'wearing out the saints of the Most High' (verse 25), is strictly applicable to that power, and will accurately describe its history.' Albert Barnes, *Notes on Daniel,* p. 328, comment on Daniel 7:25.

"These facts are confirmed by the testimony of W. E. H. Lecky. He declares:

'That the Church of Rome has shed more innocent blood than any institution that has ever existed among mankind, will be questioned by no Protestant who has a complete knowledge of history. The memorials, indeed, of many of her persecutions are now so scanty that it is impossible to form a complete conception of the multitude of her victims, and it is quite certain that no power of imagination can adequately realize their sufferings. . . . These atrocities were not perpetrated in the brief paroxysms of a reign of terror, or by the hands of obscure sectaries, but were inflicted by a triumphant church, with every circumstance of solemnity and deliberation.' See — William E. H. Lecky, *History of the Rise and Influence of the Spirit of Rationalism in Europe,* Vol. II, pp. 35,37.

"It makes no difference that in numerous instances the victims were turned over to the civil authorities. It was the church that made the decision upon the question of heresy and it then passed the offenders over to the secular court. But in those days the secular power was but the tool in the hands of the church. It was under its control and did its bidding. When the church delivered its prisoners to the executioners to be destroyed, with fiendish mockery it made use of the following formula: 'And we do leave and deliver thee to the secular arm, and to the power of the secular court; but at the same time do most earnestly beseech that court so to moderate its sentence as not to touch thy blood, or to put thy life in danger.' " Michal Geddes, "*A View of the Court of Inquisition in Portugal,*" *Miscellaneous Tracts,* Vol. I, p. 408. See also Philip Limborch, *The History of the Inquisition,* Vol. II, p. 289.

"Then, as intended, the unfortunate victims of popish hate were immediately executed. The testimony of Lepicier is to the point in this connection:

'The civil power can only punish the crime of unbelief in the manner and to the extent that the crime is judicially made known to it by ecclesiastical persons, skilled in the doctrine of the faith. But the church taking cognizance by herself of the crime of unbelief, can by herself decree the sentence of death, yet not execute it; but she hands over the execution of it to the secular arm.' Alexius M. Lepicier, *The Stability and Progress of Dogma,* p. 195.

"The false claims of some Catholics that their church has never killed dissenters, have been flatly denied by one of their own standard writers, Cardinal Bellarmine, who was born in Tuscany in 1542 and who, after his death in 1621, came very near being placed in the calendar of saints on account of his great services in behalf of the church. This man, on one occasion, under the spur of controversy, betrayed himself into an admission of the real facts in the case. Luther having said that the church (meaning the true church) never burned heretics, Bellarmine, understanding it of Roman Catholic Church, made answer:

'This argument proves not the sentiment, but the ignorance or impudence of Luther; for as almost an infinite number were either burned or otherwise put to death, Luther either did not know it, and was therefore ignorant; or if he knew it, he is convicted of impudence and falsehood—for that heretics were often burned by the church, may be proved by adducing a few from many examples.' John Dowling, *The History of Romanism,* p. 547.

"Alfred Baudrillart, rector of the Catholic Institute of Paris, when referring to the attitude of the church toward heresy, remarks:

'When confronted by heresy, she does not content herself with persuasion; arguments of an intellectual and moral order appear to her insufficient, and she has recourse to FORCE, TO CORPORAL PUNISHMENT, TO TORTURE. She creates tribunals like those of the Inquistion, she calls the laws of state to her aid, if necessary she encourages a crusade, or a religious war, and all her 'horror of blood' practically culminates into urging the secular power to shed it, which proceeding is almost more odious — for it is less frank — than shedding it herself.

'Especially did she act thus in the sixteenth century with regard to Protestants. Not content to reform morally, to teach by example, to convert people by eloquent and holy missionaries, she lit in Italy, in the Low Countries, and above all in Spain, the funeral pyres of the Inquisition. In France under Francis I and Henri II, in England under Mary Tudor, she tortured the heretics, while both in France and Germany, during the second half of the sixteenth, and the first half of the seventeenth centuries, if she did not actually begin, at any rate she encouraged and actively aided the religious wars.' Alfred Baudrillant, *The Catholic Church, the Renaissance, and Protestantism,* pp. 182,183.

"In a letter of Pope Martin V (A.D. 1417-1431), are the following instructions to the King of Poland:

'Know that the interest of the Holy See, and those of your crown, make it a duty to exterminate the Hussites. Remember that these impious persons dare proclaim principles of equality; they maintain that all Christians are brethren and that God has not given to privileged men the right to ruling the nations; they hold that Christ came on earth to abolish slavery; they call the people to liberty, that is, to the annihilation of kings and priests! Whilst there is still time, then, turn your forces against Bohemia; burn, massacre, make deserts everywhere, for nothing could be more agreeable to God, or more useful to the cause of kings, than the extermination of the Hussites.' L. M. de Cormenin, *The Public and Private History of the Popes of Rome,* Vol. II, pp. 116,117.

"All this was in harmony with the teaching of the church. Heresy was not to be tolerated, but to be destroyed.

"Pagan Rome persecuted the Christian church relentlessly. It is estimated that three million Christians perished in the first three centuries of the Christian Era. Yet it is said that the primitive Christians prayed for the continuance of imperial Rome, for they knew that when this form of government should cease, another far worse persecuting power would arise, which would literally 'wear out the saints of the Most High,' as this prophecy declares. Pagan Rome could slay the infants, but spare the mothers; but papal Rome slew both the mothers and infants together. No age, no sex, no condition in life, was exempt from her relentless rage." Quoted from *Daniel and the Revelation,* by Uriah Smith, revised by Southern Publishing Association, 1944, Nashville, Tenn., pp. 130-135.

Uriah Smith's statement about the Roman Catholic Church slaying innocent children as well as the mothers, can be confirmed in history with just one glance through the *Fox Book of Martyrs,* by John Fox. If the reader needs more evidence to see how the papacy made war with the saints, pick up a copy of the *Fox Book of Martyrs* at the library and read through pages 43-45, about how the papacy tried to destroy the Berengarians before the age of Luther, about 1000 A.D. Then another reformer named Peter Bruis, whom the Lord gave understanding, wrote a book called ANTICHRIST, which convicted many Catholics that the Church they were in was not Christian. Many of the sincere believers left the Church and became later what was known as the Berengarians. By the year 1140 A.D., many of the deceptions of the papacy were exposed, and many began to leave it. Another man whom the Lord gave understanding was Peter Waldo, or Valdo, a native of Lyons. Known for his piety and learning, he became a strenuous opposer to the Roman Catholic doctrines. Pope Alexander III, excommunicated Waldo and those who believed his rebuke of Romanism. Waldo, and those who took hold of his truth were called the Waldenses. The Waldenses were among the first victims of an order to deal with heretics to come shortly after a new pope took the throne. His name was Pope Innocent III, and he hired learned monks to preach among the Waldenses and tried to change their opinions about Catholicism. However, when the monks could not persuade them Scripturally, other forceful means were employed. An over zealous barbaric monk named Dominic, instituted an order, which, from him, was called the order of Dominican Friars. From these monks came the inquisitors that murdered without any consideration of AGE, SEX, or RANK. Let a person just be accused of an accusation against the Roman Catholic Church, this was sufficient evidence to die at the hands of these barbarians.

In the book *The Great Controversy,* Ellen G. White, tells the courage of the Waldenses during their persecution from the Roman Catholic Church:

"The Waldenses were among the first of the people of Europe to obtain a translation of the Holy Scriptures. Hundreds of years before the Reformation they possessed the Bible in manuscript in their native tongue. They had the truth unadulterated, and this rendered them the special objects of hatred and persecution. They declared the Church of Rome to be the apostate Babylon of the Apocalypse, and at the peril of their lives they stood up to resist her corruptions. While, under the pressure of long-continued persecution, some compromised their faith, little by little yielding its distinctive principles, others held fast the truth. Through ages of darkness and apostasy there were Waldenses who denied the supremacy of Rome, who rejected image worship as idolatry, and who kept the true Sabbath. Under the fiercest tempests of opposition they maintained their faith. Though gashed by the Savoyard spear, and scorched by the Romish fagot, they stood unflinchingly for God's word and His Honor.

"Behind the lofty bulwarks of the mountains — in all ages the refuge of the persecuted and oppressed — the Waldenses found a hiding place. Here the light of truth was kept burning amid the darkness of the Middle Ages. Here, for a thousand years, witnesses for the truth maintained the ancient faith.

"God had provided for His people a sanctuary of awful grandeur, befitting the mighty truths committed to their trust. To those faithful exiles the mountains were an emblem of the immutable righteousness of Jehovah. They pointed their children to the heights towering above them in unchanging majesty, and spoke to them of Him with whom there is no variableness nor shadow of turning, whose word is as enduring as the everlasting hills. God had set fast the mountains and girded them with strength; no arm but that of the Infinite Power could move them out of their place. In like manner He had established His law, the foundation of His government in heaven and upon earth." *The Great Controversy* by Ellen G. White, Pacific Press Publishing Association, Mountain View California, (by permission Ellen G. White Estate), pp 61, 62.

From the Roman Catholic Church — *The Catholic Encyclopedia,* we read their own words:

"Inquisition: 1. Historically, a legal court of the Church, sometimes administered in cooperation with the civil authority, for the investigation and sentencing of persons professing or accused of formal heresy. As such, the inquisitions were first begun in 1233 by Pope Gregory IX, based on the Inquisitorial plan originated by Pope Lucius III. Between 1227 to 1299, French councils had decreed that an 'inquisition' or court consisting of one priest and two laymen should be set up in each parish to check and prevent heresy. Especially in view of the fact that barbarism was not entirely expelled by the Christian impact, this led to abuses that to some degree were in the structure itself and in the crude application of too zealous a form of justice. Some of these abuses were: refusal of legal advisers, acceptance of testimony of heretics and excommunicants, the use of torture, and the denial of natural rights to the accused." *The Catholic Encyclopedia,* by Robert C. Broderick, Thomas Nelson, Inc., Publishers, Nashville, New York, 1975, p. 293.

To hide these monstrous deeds of the papacy, she who claims to be infallible, tries to hide her bloodstained hands in these modern days by changing the name of this order to the Congregation of the Holy Office. And to wipe the slate clean, she simply says, "this is in the past." From *The Roman Catholic Church,* we read the following:

"The Congregation of the Holy Office, formerly known as the Inquisition, has long enjoyed a bad name among Protestants; and this no doubt had something to do with the change of its name to the Congregation of the Faith, a change made by Paul VI in a *motu proprio* of December 6, 1965. The Pope made it clear that by changing the name he intended a change of character as well as of reputation. The Congregation was to do its work by promoting sound doctrine rather than by the detection and condemnation of error. In some degree the evil name of Roman Inquisition throughout history was undeserved; most of the terror associated with the name belonged to regional and diocesan inquisitorial offices. The Spanish Inquisition was not the Roman Inquisition, in spite of the direct and immediate power of the Pope over the churches, pastors, and believers of Spain. In those days, this direct and immediate power was rather effectively filtered through the Spanish monarchy. Visitors to the Castel Sant Angelo (now the property of the Italian government) are shown the dungeons and torture instruments of the medieval and Renaissance papacy; the visitor should not conclude that these facilities were made use of solely by the Roman Inquisition." *The Roman Catholic Church,* by John McKenzie, Image Books, A division of Doubleday & Company, Inc., Garden City, New York, 1969, p 42.

As we saw earlier, the Catholic Church employed the governments of the countries to carry out the murdering of innocent people during the inquisitions. Whether it was done solely by the Roman Church or not, it was caused by the false doctrines of the papacy, and the loyal followers of Christ who saw through this great religious deception, gave up their lives rather than bow to the dictates of the great red dragon; which gave power unto the beast, saying, "Who is like unto the beast? who is able to make war with him?" Revelation 13:4.

"Who shall separate us from the love of Christ? shall tribulation, or distress, or persecution, or famine, or nakedness, or peril, or sword? as it is written, For thy sake we are killed all the day long; we are accounted as sheep for the slaughter. Nay, in all these things we are more than conquerors through him that loved us. For I am persuaded, that neither death, nor life, nor angels, nor principalities, nor powers, nor things present, nor things to come, nor height, nor depth, nor any other creature, shall be able to separate us from the love of God, which is in Christ Jesus our Lord." Romans 8:35-39.

We do not want to go on and on with the terrible slaughter of Protestants down through the centuries by the satanic force, but we wanted to point out just a little of the multitude of murders this Roman Church committed in the name of Jesus. Why is it today we have freedom of religion and the persecutions have stopped? It was because the Roman Catholic Church lost her power to control the world according to her dictates. Her power was taken away and she is helpless in this stage of history. The Pope has trouble within his own church making the Catholics obey him, much less the Protestants. However, this was foretold also. The same spirit that led the inquisitors to murder innocent men, women and children during the Dark Ages is still here, and he is the same yesterday, today and forever. If the Roman Catholic Church was in power today, as it was during the Dark Ages, the same murderous character of Satan would be employed. The Roman Catholic Church has no power to force its religious beliefs on people, but this power will be restored in the last generation. It has been foretold from ancient times and it will come to pass. We will investigate these prophecies later.

In the book of Revelation, which sums up the whole Bible, we find a clear picture for those who understand prophecy about the persecution of God's people by Satan. As pointed out earlier, the Lord uses women as symbols of the true church of Jesus Christ as well as the false church. Revelation, the 17th and 18th chapters, describes Babylon the Great, the Mother of Harlots; and Revelation the 12th chapter describes the Lord's true Church, "a woman clothed with the sun, the moon under her feet and upon her head a crown of twelve stars." Revelation 12:1. The woman of Chapter 12 of Revelation is a direct contrast to the whore of Revelation the 17th chapter. When the apostles established a Christian Church at Rome, the Gospel was presented unmixed with paganism. However, after Paul and Peter were slain for their faith, Satan began his plans to change Christianity into nothing less than Baal worship using the name Christian. This was not to happen all at once as we pointed out earlier, but little by little, until the apostasy of God's word would be as that of the Israelites, in the time of Elijah the prophet. The Israelites were so blinded and degraded by the system of Baal, that they didn't know which of the two systems was the true faith. This is the plan Satan has for us in these modern times. However, there is and always will be a distinction that can be clearly seen between Baal worship and those who honor God as the Creator. This distinction will be brought out in the open for all who call themselves Christians. This too was tucked away by the Roman Catholic Church before the Protestants came into history.

The Bible is God's way to lead man back to a personal relationship with his Maker again and Satan has worked almost 6000 years leading man in another direction. Because the Bible exposes the falsehood of the Roman Catholic Church, it tried everything it could during the Dark Ages to keep the Bible from the ordinary people. The Scriptures are to be made a guide of life and no one is permitted to add or take anything from the Scriptures:

"ADD THOU NOT UNTO HIS WORDS, LEST HE REPROVE THEE, AND THOU BE FOUND A LIAR." Proverbs 30:6.

However, history says that the word of God has been tampered with, and a doctrine of Baalim was put in the place of a doctrine of the Bible.

This doctrine, which the Catholic Church is responsible for changing, will become the most controversial issue in days to come. This doctrine was almost lost sight of during the Dark Ages, but will be brought out into the light for everyone to see. Satan is so bent in this world on trampling under foot this commandment of God, that in the past Satan used men with high authority to enforce laws that would hide its truth. This was foretold, and it is the third ACT or the LITTLE HORN (PAPACY) of Daniel 7:25:

"AND THINK TO CHANGE TIMES AND LAWS."

In a publication of the Roman Catholic Church called *A New Catechism of Christian Doctrine and Practice,* we read the following:

QUESTION — "WHAT DAY WAS THE SABBATH?"
ANSWER — "THE SEVENTH DAY, OUR SATURDAY."

QUESTION — "DO YOU KEEP THE SABBATH?"
ANSWER — "NO: WE KEEP THE LORD'S DAY."

QUESTION — "WHICH IS THAT?"
ANSWER — "THE FIRST DAY: SUNDAY."

QUESTION — "WHO CHANGED IT?"
ANSWER — "THE CATHOLIC CHURCH."

A New Catechism of Christian Doctrine and Practice, by James Bellord, pp. 86,87.

In *An Abridgement of the Christian Doctrine*, we read the following:

"Q — How prove you that the church hath power to command feasts and Holy Days?

"A — By the very act of changing the Sabbath into Sunday, which Protestants allow of; and therefore they fondly contradict themselves by keeping Sunday strictly, and breaking most other feasts commanded by the same church.

"Q — How prove you that?

"A — Because by keeping Sunday they acknowledge the church's power to ordain feasts, and to command them under sin." *An Abridgment of the Christian Doctrine*, by Henry Tuberville, p. 58.

From *The Faith of Our Fathers*, we read the following:

"You may read the Bible from Genesis to Revelation, and you will not find a single line authorizing the sanctification of Sunday. The scriptures enforce the religious observance of Saturday, a day which we never sanctify." Cardinal Gibbons, *The Faith of Our Father*, p. 111.

The papacy is right in saying there is no Scriptural authority for her changing the original day of worship (Saturday) to Sunday, but they do err when they say all modern religionists agree with her. Here in *A Doctrinal Catechism* is this statement:

"Q — Have you any other way of proving that the church has power to institute festivals of precept?

"A — Had she not such power, she could not have done that in which all modern religionists agree with her. She could not have substituted the observance of Sunday the first day of the week for the observance of Saturday the seventh day, change for which there is no scriptural authority." *A Doctrinal Catechism*, p. 174.

Again from the Catholic Church we read:

"The Catholic Church for over thousand years before the existence of a Protestant, by virtue of her divine mission changed the day from Saturday to Sunday." *Catholic Mirror,* Sept., 1893.

The Icelandic god Balder, was just another name that identified with Sun worship, and the papacy knowing this, states these startling words:

"She took pagan Sunday, dedicated to Balder, became the Christian Sunday, sacred to Jesus." *Catholic World,* 1894, p. 809.

The Catholic Church is right when she boasts about changing Sabbath, the day God commanded that all work be laid aside, to Sunday, which even carries the name, Lord's Day, now; but she is wrong when she says all modern religionists agree with her. For the Lord has reserved Him a Remnant that have not bowed their knee to Baal. But every week Christians both in the Americas and in the Old World keep the Fourth Commandment which says:

"REMEMBER THE SABBATH DAY, TO KEEP IT HOLY. SIX DAYS SHALT THOU LABOUR, AND DO ALL THY WORK: BUT THE SEVENTH DAY IS THE SABBATH OF THE LORD THY GOD: IN IT THOU SHALT NOT DO ANY WORK, THOU, NOR THY SON, NOR THY DAUGHTER, THY MANSERVANT, NOR THY MAIDSERVANT, NOR THY CATTLE, NOR THY STRANGER THAT IS WITHIN THY GATES:" Exodus 20:8-10.

Our Lord gives us six days to earn our living, and do our buying and our selling.

"BUT THE SEVENTH DAY IS THE SABBATH OF THE LORD THY GOD: IN IT THOU SHALT NOT DO ANY WORK." Exodus 20:10.

Some may question this commandment by asking how do we know that the Seventh day of the Bible is the same seventh day we keep today called Saturday? This can easily be answered by the Scriptures. In Luke 23:54-56 we read:

"And that day was the preparation, and the sabbath drew on. And the women also, which came with him from Galilee, followed after, and beheld the sepulchre, and how his body was laid. And they returned, and prepared spices and ointments; and rested the sabbath day according to the commandment."

This Scripture proves that the seventh day Sabbath is still the same day as it was in the time of Christ. Jesus died on Friday, which the Jews called the "PREPARATION DAY," and the women prepared spices and ointments on this same day, then observed the Sabbath according to the commandment.

"NOW UPON THE FIRST DAY OF THE WEEK, very early in the morning, they came unto the sepulchre, bringing the spices which they had prepared, and certain others with them." Luke 24:1.

This clearly shows Jesus arose from the dead on the "FIRST DAY" of the week (SUNDAY), and it's called by the pagan observance, Easter Sunday. It should also be remembered that Sunday worship is a fabrication of most Christians, and that the Jews never lost sight of which day was and is the seventh day. Except in their apostasy, the Jews always observed the Sabbath, it was the Christians who changed the Lord's Day to the first day of the week, not the Jews. The sun worshipping pagans kept Sunday sacred, and the Jews who were thrown out of their homeland for worshipping Baal, find it very hard to believe that Jesus is the real Messiah, when his followers exalt the day of the Sun god, and trample underfoot the Sabbath day.

By changing the Sabbath to Sunday, Satan tried to hide two very important truths of the Bible. First, he causes those who keep Sunday to break he Fourth commandment, and trample underfoot HIM that instituted it, JESUS CHRIST. It was Jesus who created the Heaven, the Earth and the Sea in six days and rested the seventh day. The seventh day Sabbath is a sign that Jesus is the Creator:

"WHO IS THE IMAGE OF THE INVISIBLE GOD, THE FIRSTBORN OF EVERY CREATURE FOR BY HIM WERE ALL THINGS CREATED, THAT ARE IN HEAVEN, AND THAT ARE IN EARTH, VISIBLE AND INVISIBLE, WHETHER THEY BE THRONES, OR DOMINIONS, OR PRINCIPALITIES, OR POWERS: ALL THINGS WERE CREATED BY HIM, AND FOR HIM:" Colossians 1:15,16.

"IN THE BEGINNING WAS THE WORD, AND THE WORD WAS WITH GOD, AND THE WORD WAS GOD. THE SAME WAS IN THE BEGINNING WITH GOD. ALL THINGS WERE MADE BY HIM; AND WITHOUT HIM WAS NOT ANY THING MADE THAT WAS MADE. AND THE WORD WAS MADE FLESH, AND DWELT AMONG US, (AND WE BEHELD HIS GLORY, THE GLORY AS OF THE ONLY BEGOTTEN OF THE FATHER), FULL OF GRACE AND TRUTH." John 1:1-3,14.

"THE SABBATH WAS MADE FOR MAN, AND NOT MAN FOR THE SABBATH: THEREFORE THE SON OF MAN IS LORD ALSO OF THE SABBATH." Mark 2:27,28.

It is Jesus who is the "LORD" of the Sabbath. The WORD OF GOD says:

"REMEMBER THE SABBATH DAY, TO KEEP IT HOLY. SIX DAYS SHALT THOU LABOUR, AND DO ALL THY WORK: BUT THE SEVENTH DAY IS THE SABBATH OF THE LORD THY GOD: IN IT THOU SHALT NOT DO ANY WORK, THOU, NOR THY SON, NOR THY DAUGHTER, THY MANSERVANT, NOR THY MAIDSERVANT, NOR THY CATTLE, NOR THY STRANGER THAT IS WITHIN THY GATES: FOR IN SIX DAYS THE LORD MADE HEAVEN AND EARTH, THE SEA, AND ALL THAT IN THEM IS, AND RESTED THE SEVENTH DAY: WHEREFORE THE LORD BLESSED THE SABBATH DAY AND HALLOWED IT." Exodus 20:8-11.

There are those who carry high titles in theological seminaries, and churches, who have been taught and teach that the Sabbath was only given to the Jews to observe and Christians are not under the law, so this gives them license to disregard the fourth commandment. Others say the Ten Commandments were nailed to the cross, so this makes them free from obeying it. Or, Jesus and His disciples changed it. Some teach that the apostle Paul kept the first day of the week. While others hold the reason for Sunday keeping is to keep in remembrance the resurrection of Jesus Christ. There might be other reasons, but these are the most popular among Christians. Lets examine each of these reasons separately, for keeping Sunday:

The ancient Seventh Day Sabbath is Jewish, not Christian.

Jesus said in Mark 2:27 that the Sabbath was made for man, not just for the Jews but for all men. The Sabbath was given over 2000 years before the Jews came into history. The Sabbath was given at "CREATION."

"THUS THE HEAVENS AND THE EARTH WERE FINISHED, AND ALL THE HOST OF THEM. AND ON THE SEVENTH DAY GOD ENDED HIS WORK WHICH HE HAD MADE; AND HE RESTED ON THE SEVENTH DAY FROM ALL HIS WORK WHICH HE HAD MADE. AND GOD BLESSED THE SEVENTH DAY, AND SANCTIFIED IT: BECAUSE THAT IN IT HE HAD RESTED FROM ALL HIS WORK WHICH GOD CREATED AND MADE." Genesis 2:1-3.

As the Bible reveals, it was God who created the Heavens and the Earth, and Adam was created on the sixth day (Genesis 1:27-31). Adam was the first man and Adam was the first to observe the Sabbath. And here is another truth. The Jews knew about the seventh day Sabbath before it was given to Moses at Mt. Sinai as one of the Ten Commandments. You can read this in Exodus, chapter 16. The Lord said He would prove the Israelites if they would keep his law or not. Six days the Lord would rain manna from Heaven but the seventh day there would be none (Exodus 16:4). But some didn't hearken to the law and went out on the seventh day to gather anyway. Exodus 16:25,26:

"AND THE LORD SAID UNTO MOSES, HOW LONG REFUSE YE TO KEEP MY COMMANDMENTS AND MY LAWS?" Exodus 16:28.

This test of loyalty was done in the wilderness of Sin, before they reached Mt. Sinai, (Exodus 16:1). Here is another truth. In the book of Revelation, which sums up the whole plan of Salvation, it is written in Revelation 21:1, the Lord will create a NEW HEAVEN AND A NEW EARTH:

"AND I SAW A NEW HEAVEN AND A NEW EARTH: FOR THE FIRST HEAVEN AND THE FIRST EARTH WERE PASSED AWAY; AND THERE WAS NO MORE SEA."

This present evil world will pass away, and a New Earth will be created without Satan and sin. Now, after the New Heaven and the New Earth are established, will there be confusion in the New Heaven and New Earth as well? Will the Jews and some Christians be observing the Sabbath, while other Christians keep Sunday to commemorate Christ's resurrection? Will there be religious confusion in the new world? The answer is NO. Isaiah the prophet, foretold also the New Heaven and the New Earth 750 years before the birth of Christ. Isaiah tells us what day will be observed throughout eternity:

"FOR AS THE NEW HEAVENS AND THE NEW EARTH, WHICH I WILL MAKE, SHALL REMAIN BEFORE ME, SAITH THE LORD, SO SHALL YOUR SEED AND YOUR NAME REMAIN. AND IT SHALL COME TO PASS, THAT FROM ONE NEW MOON TO ANOTHER, AND FROM ONE SABBATH TO ANOTHER, SHALL ALL FLESH COME TO WORSHIP BEFORE ME, SAITH THE LORD." Isaiah 66:22,23.

As the Scriptures say, the seventh day Sabbath will be restored in the New Earth. We now have seen the popular belief that the Sabbath is "for the Jew only" is False, now let's see if there is any truth in the next reason for Sunday observance:

Christians are saved by grace, therefore, they are not under the law.

But the Bible says:

"HE THAT SAITH I KNOW HIM, AND KEEPETH NOT HIS COMMANDMENTS, IS A LIAR, AND THE TRUTH IS NOT IN HIM. . . . BUT IF

THOU WILT ENTER INTO LIFE, KEEP THE COMMANDMENTS." I John 2:4; Matthew 19:17.

"WHOSOEVER THEREFORE SHALL BREAK ONE OF THESE LEAST COMMANDMENTS, AND TEACH MEN SO, HE SHALL BE CALLED THE LEAST IN THE KINGDOM OF HEAVEN: BUT WHOSOEVER SHALL DO AND TEACH THEM, THE SAME SHALL BE CALLED GREAT IN THE KINGDOM OF GOD." Matthew 5:19.

"FOR WHOSOEVER SHALL KEEP THE WHOLE LAW, AND YET OFFEND IN ONE POINT HE IS GUILTY OF ALL. FOR HE THAT SAID, DO NOT COMMIT ADULTERY, SAID ALSO, DO NOT KILL. NOW IF THOU COMMIT NO ADULTRY, YET IF THOU KILL, THOU ART BECOME A TRANSGRESSOR OF THE LAW." James 2:10,11.

"KNOW YE NOT THAT THE UNRIGHTEOUS SHALL NOT INHERIT THE KINGDOM OF GOD? BE NOT DECEIVED: NEITHER FORNICATORS, NOR IDOLATERS, NOR ADULTERERS, NOR EFFEMINATE, NOR ABUSERS OF THEMSELVES WITH MANKIND, NOR THIEVES, NOR COVETOUS, NOR DRUNKARDS, NOR REVILERS, NOR EXTORTIONERS, SHALL INHERIT THE KINGDOM OF GOD. AND SUCH WERE SOME OF YOU: BUT YE ARE WASHED, BUT YE ARE SANCTIFIED, BUT YE ARE JUSTIFIED IN THE NAME OF THE LORD JESUS, AND BY THE SPIRIT OF OUR GOD. HE THAT OVERCOMETH SHALL INHERIT ALL THINGS; AND I WILL BE HIS GOD, AND HE SHALL BE MY SON. BUT THE FEARFUL, AND THE UNBELIEVING, AND THE ABOMINABLE, AND MURDERERS, AND WHOREMONGERS, AND SORCERERS, AND IDOLATERS, AND ALL LIARS, SHALL HAVE THEIR PART IN THE LAKE WHICH BURNETH WITH FIRE AND BRIMSTONE: WHICH IS THE SECOND DEATH." I Corinthians 6:9-11; Revelation 21:7,8.

Only when a sinner realizes how deep his transgressions against God are, will he see his great need for Christ. There is not a man or woman in human history who has not sinned, save Jesus Christ.

"IF WE SAY THAT WE HAVE NOT SINNED, WE MAKE HIM A LIAR, AND HIS WORD IS NOT IN US." I John 1:10.

In Luke 13:3, Jesus said: "EXCEPT YE REPENT, YE SHALL ALL LIKEWISE PERISH."

The word repent means to feel self-reproach or contrition for past conduct and to turn from doing those things. What separated man from God? SIN! What is SIN?

"WHOSOEVER COMMITTETH SIN TRANSGRESSETH ALSO THE LAW: FOR SIN IS THE TRANSGRESSION OF THE LAW. WHAT SHALL WE SAY THEN? IS THE LAW SIN? GOD FORBID. NAY, I HAD NOT KNOWN SIN, BUT BY THE LAW: FOR I HAD NOT KNOWN LUST, EXCEPT THE LAW HAD SAID, THOU SHALT NOT COVET." I John 3:4; Romans 7:7.

Sin is breaking the Ten Commandments. This is the reason Christ died for each of us. There is no power in the Ten Commandments to save us. They just show us we are sinners:

"THEREFORE BY THE DEEDS OF THE LAW THERE SHALL NO FLESH BE JUSTIFIED IN HIS SIGHT: FOR BY THE LAW IS THE KNOWLEDGE OF SIN." Romans 3:20.

However, when a sinner sees his shame and humbles himself before the Lord, and acknowledges that he is a sinner and seeks forgiveness through the sacrifice of Christ, there comes this promise:

"FOR BY GRACE ARE YE SAVED THROUGH FAITH: AND THAT NOT OF YOURSELVES: IT IS THE GIFT OF GOD: NOT BY WORKS, LEST ANY MAN SHOULD BOAST." Ephesians 2:8,9.

Now, once a sinner has confessed his sins and accepted Christ's Atonement for him, does that give him a right, now that he is a Christian, to go out and kill his neighbor? To steal? To commit adultery? To lie? To use the name of the Lord in vain? To worship other Gods? To make graven images? A little child would answer, "NO." Neither does it give a Christian the right to trample underfoot the Fourth Commandment. The Fourth Commandment commands us to keep Holy the seventh day, not the first day of the week. Sin is breaking the Ten Commandments. Not just nine of them, but all of them. Jesus did not change the law:

"THINK NOT THAT I AM COME TO DESTROY THE LAW, OR THE PROPHETS: I AM NOT COME TO DESTROY, BUT TO FULFILL. FOR VERILY I SAY UNTO YOU, TILL HEAVEN AND EARTH PASS, ONE JOT OR ONE TITTLE SHALL IN NO WISE PASS FROM THE LAW, TILL ALL BE FULFILLED." Matthew 5:17,18.

Jesus kept the law including the FOURTH COMMANDMENT:

"IF YE KEEP MY COMMANDMENTS, YE SHALL ABIDE IN MY LOVE; EVEN AS I HAVE KEPT MY FATHER'S COMMANDMENTS AND ABIDE IN HIS LOVE." John 15:10.

If we are Christians we are to follow in Christ's footsteps. He is our pattern.

"HE THAT SAITH HE ABIDETH IN HIM OUGHT HIMSELF ALSO SO TO WALK, EVEN AS HE WALKED." I John 2:6.

"AND HE CAME TO NAZARETH, WHERE HE HAD BEEN BROUGHT UP: AND, AS HIS CUSTOM WAS, HE WENT INTO THE SYNAGOGUE ON THE SABBATH DAY, AND STOOD UP FOR TO READ." Luke 4:16.

Jesus kept the Sabbath. If he hadn't, he would have been a transgressor of the Law. But Jesus throughout his whole life never once sinned.

Now, another way most Christians deceive themselves is found in the popular belief of Colossians 2:16, of Paul's writings. They say that Paul said the Sabbath was nailed to the cross. Here is the Scripture used:

"Let no man therefore judge you in meat, or drink, or in respect of an holyday, or of the new moon, or of the sabbath days:" Colossians 2:16.

This passage of Scripture has nothing whatsoever to do with the Ten Commandments. Paul was speaking of the Ceremonial Law of the Jews. There were other Sabbath Days beside the seventh day Sabbath. One of these Sabbaths even fell on a Sunday during the Passover Festival. Turn in your Bibles to Leviticus 23. Verses 4-7 say the 14th day of the first month (Abib, Exodus 13:4), they were not to do any work. It was a sabbath. This is the Passover Feast that was held on a Friday, the 14th of Abib. The 15th to the 21st was the Feast of the Unleavened Bread, which leaven is a symbol of hypocrisy.

Verses 10-21, was the Wave Sheaf Offering. There were meat offerings and drink offerings held on Sunday after the seventh day Sabbath. This Sunday was a "sabbath." This first day of the week, "sabbath" foreshadowed Christ's first resurrection. Verse 24 says that the first day of the seventh month was a sabbath. Verse 25 also says not to work therein. Verses 27-32 say the 10th day of the seventh month was a sabbath which was a foreshadow of Judgment Day. Verses 31-39 say on the 15th day of the seventh month was a sabbath, also the eighth day. Verse 38 plainly states that these sabbath days were besides the other sabbaths the Jews were to keep as the Fourth Commandment states. None of the sacrificial sabbaths were to fall on the weekly seventh day Sabbath.

The very day of the Jewish Passover, was the very day Jesus the real Lamb of God, was crucified as a sacrifice for mankind. The minute Christ gave up his breath, the veil of the temple was rent in twain from the top to the bottom. (Matthew 27:51). This showed the earthly temple ceremonial services ended at Christ's death, because all of the ceremonial services were just a shadow of the real sacrifice Jesus made for man. When the real sacrifice was made, there was no more need for priests, meat and drink offerings, and the sabbaths that were just a type of the real events to happen in the life of Christ. All the sacredness of the ceremonial services in the temple at Jerusalem ended at the cross but not the SEVENTH DAY SABBATH. If the reader will read verse 17 of Colossians, 2nd chapter, it says these other sabbath days were "A SHADOW OF THINGS TO COME; BUT THE BODY IS OF CHRIST."

It was the SACRIFICIAL CEREMONIAL LAW that was nailed to the cross, not the moral law, THE TEN COMMANDMENTS. This doctrine makes Paul to look like he teaches contrary to what Jesus taught. For as we have seen, Jesus said in a most striking manner:

"BUT IF THOU WILT ENTER INTO LIFE, KEEP THE COMMANDMENTS." Matthew 19:17.

Another way the Protestant Sunday-keepers err from the word of God is their interpretation of Acts 20:7:

"And upon the first day of the week, when the disciples came together to break bread, Paul preached unto them, ready to depart on the morrow; and continued his speech until midnight."

Protestants claim that Paul held Sunday services for the disciples, and they use this to justify the observance of Sunday. However, like the authority of the pope, there are not five word of truth in it. Now let's study this passage of Scripture more deeply. First, in Biblical times a day was measured from sundown to sundown, not from midnight to midnight. The seventh day Sabbath was to start on what is called today, Friday, at sunset and end on Saturday at sunset. (Leviticus 23:32; Luke 23:54-56).

When the disciples came together to break bread, it was Saturday night which, in Bible times, began the first day of the week. Paul preached after the Sabbath day was over, when the first day of the week began (Saturday night), preached until midnight (Saturday night), and left on the morrow (Sunday morning). He did not hold church services Sunday morning!

Paul himself said:

"BUT THIS I CONFESS UNTO THEE, THAT AFTER THE WAY WHICH THEY CALL HERESY, SO WORSHIP I THE GOD OF MY FATHERS, BELIEVING ALL THINGS WHICH ARE WRITTEN IN THE LAW AND IN THE PROPHETS." Acts 24:14.

Paul kept the Sabbath:

"AND PAUL, AS HIS MANNER WAS, WENT IN UNTO THEM, AND THREE SABBATH DAYS REASONED WITH THEM OUT OF THE SCRIPTURES." Acts 17:2.

The Ten Commandments will be the standard by which all will be judged. (James 2:8-12).

THE TEN COMMANDMENTS

AS ORIGINALLY GIVEN BY GOD

(Exodus 20 : 3-17)

I

Thou shalt have no other gods before Me.

II

Thou shalt not make unto thee any graven image, or any likeness of any thing that is in heaven above, or that is in the earth beneath, or that is in the water under the earth : thou shalt not bow down thyself to them, nor serve them : for I the Lord thy God am a jealous God, visiting the iniquity of the fathers upon the children unto the third and fourth generation of them that hate Me; and showing mercy unto thousands of them that love Me, and keep My commandments.

III

Thou shalt not take the name of the Lord thy God in vain; for the Lord will not hold him guiltless that taketh His name in vain.

IV

Remember the Sabbath day, to keep it holy. Six days shalt thou labour, and do all thy work: but the seventh day is the Sabbath of the Lord thy God : in it thou shalt not do any work, thou, nor thy son, nor thy daughter, thy manservant, nor thy maidservant, nor thy cattle, nor thy stranger that is within thy gates: for in six days the Lord made heaven and earth, the sea, and all that in them is, and rested the seventh day : wherefore the Lord blessed the Sabbath day, and hallowed it.

V

Honour thy father and thy mother: that thy days may be long upon the land which the Lord thy God giveth thee.

VI

Thou shalt not kill.

VII

Thou shalt not commit adultery.

VIII

Thou shalt not steal.

IX

Thou shalt not bear false witness against thy neighbour.

X

Thou shalt not covet thy neighbour's house, thou shalt not covet thy neighbour's wife, nor his manservant, nor his maidservant, nor his ox, nor his ass, nor anything that is thy neighbour's.

If the Ten Commandments were done away with, or nailed to the cross, as some ministers teach, there would NOT be any SIN in the world today.

If there were no speed limit laws you could not be arrested or fined for speeding while driving your car.

Without the Holy Law of God, there would not be a law to break, therefore, there would be no sin.

"Sin is the transgression of the law." I John 3:4.

Every king, every dictator, every democracy has laws that the citizens must obey. If one of these civil laws is broken, the guilty one must pay a fine, or go to jail.

"Add thou not unto his words, lest he reprove thee, and thou be found a liar." Proverbs 30:6.

THE TEN COMMANDMENTS

*AS COMMONLY ABBREVIATED IN ROMAN CATHOLIC CATECHISMS

"He shall think himself able to change times and laws."
Daniel 7:25 (Douay Version.)

I

I am the Lord thy God. Thou shalt not have strange gods before Me.

II

Thou shalt not take the name of the Lord thy God in vain.

III

Remember thou keep holy the Sabbath day.

IV

Honour thy father and thy mother.

V

Thou shalt not kill.

VI

Thou shalt not commit adultery.

VII

Thou shalt not steal.

VIII

Thou shalt not bear false witness against thy neighbour.

IX

Thou shalt not covet thy neighbour's wife.

X

Thou shalt not covet thy neighbour's goods.

*Such as Keenan's and Geiermann's in English. The two vernacular catechisms here quoted and many more like them, bear the imprimatur of bishops of the Church and are used for teaching the laity.

"And he gave unto Moses, when he had made an end of communing with him upon Mount Sinai, two tables of testimony, tables of stone, written with the FINGER of God." Exodus 31:18.

"For verily I say unto you, Till heaven and earth pass, one jot or one tittle shall in no wise pass from the law, till all be fulfilled." Matthew 5:18.

"My little children, these things write I unto you, that ye sin not. And if any man sin, we have an advocate with the Father, Jesus Christ the righteous." I John 2:1.

"And he is the propitiation for our sins: and not for ours only, but also for the sins of the whole world." I John 2:2.

"And he reasoned in the synagogue every sabbath, and persuaded the Jews and the Greeks." Acts 18:4.

"FOR IF JESUS HAD GIVEN THEM REST, (SABBATH) THEN WOULD HE NOT AFTERWARD HAVE SPOKEN OF ANOTHER DAY. THERE REMAINETH THEREFORE A REST TO THE PEOPLE OF GOD. FOR HE THAT IS ENTERED INTO HIS REST, HE ALSO HATH CEASED FROM HIS OWN WORKS, AS GOD DID FROM HIS." Hebrews 4:8-10.

Jesus is calling for a reformation throughout the Churches, to restore the ancient Sabbath back to its rightful position. This message and its warning is for the people of the world just before Christ's second coming. WE ARE SOME OF THESE PEOPLE AND HERE IS THE PROMISE FROM THE SAVIOUR WHO WILL JOIN THIS EFFORT:

"IF THOU TURN AWAY THY FOOT FROM THE SABBATH, FROM DOING THY PLEASURE ON MY HOLY DAY; AND CALL THE SABBATH A DELIGHT, THE HOLY OF THE LORD, HONOURABLE; AND SHALT HONOUR HIM, NOT DOING THINE OWN WAYS, NOR FINDING THINE OWN PLEASURE, NOR SPEAKING THINE OWN WORDS: THEN SHALT THOU DELIGHT THYSELF IN THE LORD; AND I WILL CAUSE THEE TO RIDE UPON THE HIGH PLACES OF THE EARTH, AND FEED THEE WITH THE HERITAGE OF JACOB THY FATHER: FOR THE MOUTH OF THE LORD HATH SPOKEN IT." Isaiah 58:13,14.

"AND HALLOW MY SABBATHS: AND THEY SHALL BE A SIGN BETWEEN ME AND YOU, THAT YE MAY KNOW THAT I AM THE LORD YOUR GOD." Ezekiel 20:20.

What the Lord commanded His people to do on the seventh day Sabbath, Satan, using people in high positions in the governments and Churches, will attempt to do on SUNDAY by enforcing LAWS that will forbid buying and selling on that day. This will cause persecution of Sabbath keepers, and this IS THE MARK OF THE BEAST!

The SECOND BEAST of Revelation 13:11-17, will cause the whole world to:

"AND THEY WORSHIPPED THE DRAGON (DEVIL, Rev. 12:9) WHICH GAVE POWER UNTO THE BEAST (PAPACY): AND THEY WORSHIPPED THE BEAST, (PAPACY) SAYING, WHO IS LIKE UNTO THE BEAST? WHO IS ABLE TO MAKE WAR WITH HIM?" Revelation 13:4.

"AND I BEHELD ANOTHER BEAST (NATION) COMING UP OUT OF THE EARTH; AND HE HAD TWO HORNS LIKE A LAMB, AND HE

SPOKE AS A DRAGON (DEVIL). AND HE EXERCISETH ALL THE POWER OF THE FIRST BEAST (PAPACY) BEFORE HIM, AND CAUSETH THE EARTH AND THEM WHICH DWELL THEREIN TO WORSHIP THE FIRST BEAST, WHOSE DEADLY WOUND WAS HEALED. AND HE CAUSETH ALL, BOTH SMALL AND GREAT, RICH AND POOR, FREE AND BOND, TO RECEIVE A MARK IN THEIR RIGHT HAND, OR IN THEIR FOREHEADS: AND THAT NO MAN MIGHT BUY OR SELL, SAVE HE THAT HAD THE MARK, OR THE NAME OF THE BEAST. (PAPACY) OR THE NUMBER OF HIS NAME (666)." Revelation 13:11,12,16,17.

We will study who this SECOND BEAST of Revelation 13:11-17 is in the last chapter of this book. But before the reader can understand who this beast is he must understand the last part of Daniel 7:25:

". . . AND THEY SHALL BE GIVEN INTO HIS HAND UNTIL A TIME AND TIMES AND THE DIVIDING OF TIME." Daniel 7:25.

We will study this last part of Daniel about the LITTLE HORN (PAPACY) in a moment. The power Satan will use to enforce no buying or selling on Sunday is already legislated. These LAWS are called by the name of the color of paper they were written on, BLUE LAWS.

Nobody has received the MARK OF THE BEAST as yet and our Lord has accepted the worship of those who have observed Sunday in the past and have worshipped God with all the light they have been shown. But in our time, the Sabbath will be brought out in the open and all will be made to see its importance. The Sabbath will be the great test as to who serveth the Lord and who serveth Him not. Jesus will separate the pretenders, the hypocrites, the unbelieving, and the ungrateful Christians from the remnant shown to be God's true people, as given in Revelation 12:17 and Revelation 14:12:

"HERE IS THE PATIENCE OF THE SAINTS: HERE ARE THEY THAT KEEP THE COMMANDMENTS OF GOD, AND THE FAITH OF JESUS." Revelation 14:12.

There will be just two bands of people in the near future. Those who exalt the papal sabbath and those who try to restore the original Sabbath of the Bible. There are conditions we are to meet if we want to enter into the gates of the city. We must do the will of God. Just believing in Jesus is not enough, we must do his bidding:

"NOT EVERY ONE THAT SAITH UNTO ME, LORD, LORD, SHALL ENTER INTO THE KINGDOM OF HEAVEN; BUT HE THAT DOETH THE WILL OF MY FATHER WHICH IS IN HEAVEN. MANY WILL SAY TO

ME IN THAT DAY, LORD, LORD, HAVE WE NOT PROPHESIED IN THY NAME? AND IN THY NAME HAVE CAST OUT DEVILS? AND IN THY NAME DONE MANY WONDERFUL WORKS? AND THEN WILL I PROFESS UNTO THEM, I NEVER KNEW YOU: DEPART FROM ME, YE THAT WORK INIQUITY." Matthew 7:21-23.

The doctrine of once saved always saved is as false as Sunday sacredness and this doctrine strengthens the hands of the wicked that he turn not from his evil ways. If a man can be saved even if he continues to live a sinful life, what need is there for repentance? This is nothing less than a doctrine of the devil.

"FOR NOT THE HEARERS OF THE LAW ARE JUST BEFORE GOD, BUT THE DOERS OF THE LAW SHALL BE JUSTIFIED." Romans 2:13.

"TAKE HEED UNTO THYSELF, AND UNTO THE DOCTRINE; CONTINUE IN THEM: FOR IN DOING THIS THOU SHALT BOTH SAVE THYSELF, AND THEM THAT HEAR THEE." I Timothy 4:16.

Paul himself said if he did not continue in the faith that he had preached to others; "I MYSELF SHOULD BE A CASTAWAY." I Corinthians 9:27. There is still another class who seek not to know the truth, because they think that if they stay ignorant of it they won't have to turn from their evil ways, and they think they will not be judged. But to this class the Lord has said:

"HE THAT TURNETH AWAY HIS EAR FROM HEARING THE LAW, EVEN HIS PRAYER SHALL BE ABOMINATION." Proverbs 28:9.

Others will not want to take their stand for the Sabbath because they are afraid of the ridicule they might receive from family and friends. To this class the Lord has said:

"ALSO I SAY UNTO YOU, WHOSOEVER SHALL CONFESS ME BEFORE MEN, HIM SHALL THE SON OF MAN ALSO CONFESS BEFORE THE ANGELS OF GOD: BUT HE THAT DENIETH ME BEFORE MEN SHALL BE DENIED BEFORE THE ANGELS OF GOD." Luke 12:8, 9.

The Roman Catholic Church boasts about their changing the Fourth Commandment from Sabbath to Sunday, the day of Baal. Those who call themselves Protestants are not keeping the LAW of the Lord but are following in the footsteps of the BEAST (PAPACY) of Revelation 13:1-8, and not after the footsteps of Christ. One of the very few statements by the papacy that Christian Sabbath keepers will agree with is found in the following words from *The American Catholic Quarterly Review:*

"For ages all Christian nations looked to the Catholic Church and, as we have seen, the various states enforce by law her ordinances as to worship and cessation of labor on Sunday. Protestantism, in discarding the authority of the Church, has no good reason for its Sunday theory and ought logically to keep Saturday as the Sabbath. The state, in passing laws for the due sanctification of Sunday, is unwittingly acknowledging the authority of the Catholic Church and carrying out more or less faithfully its prescriptions. The Sunday, as a day of the week set apart for the obligatory public worship of Almighty God, to be sanctified by a suspension of all servile labor, trade, and worldly avocations and by exercises of devotion, is purely a creation of the Catholic Church." *The American Catholic Quarterly Review,* Jan. 1883, pp. 132-139.

"MYSTERY, BABYLON THE GREAT, THE MOTHER OF HARLOTS AND ABOMINATIONS OF THE EARTH," of Revelation 17:5, is not only the Roman Catholic Church, but all Churches that unite with her and teach her false doctrines. When she reaches the fullness of her iniquity she shall be destroyed. Her doom is foretold in Revelation, the 18th chapter. However, it is also very clear that the Lord still has His people within Babylon the Great, and is sending this message throughout the world:

"AND I HEARD ANOTHER VOICE FROM HEAVEN, SAYING, COME OUT OF HER, MY PEOPLE, THAT YE BE NOT PARTAKERS OF HER SINS, AND THAT YE RECEIVE NOT OF HER PLAGUES. FOR HER SINS HAVE REACHED UNTO HEAVEN, AND GOD HATH REMEMBERED HER INIQUITIES. REWARD HER EVEN AS SHE REWARDED YOU, AND DOUBLE UNTO HER DOUBLE ACCORDING TO HER WORKS: IN THE CUP WHICH SHE HATH FILLED FILL TO HER DOUBLE. HOW MUCH SHE HATH GLORIFIED HERSELF, AND LIVED DELICIOUSLY, SO MUCH TORMENT AND SORROW GIVE HER: FOR SHE SAITH IN HER HEART I SIT A QUEEN, AND AM NO WIDOW, AND SHALL SEE NO SORROW. THEREFORE SHALL HER PLAGUES COME IN ONE DAY, DEATH, AND MOURNING, AND FAMINE; AND SHE SHALL BE UTTERLY BURNED WITH FIRE: FOR STRONG IS THE LORD GOD WHO JUDGETH HER." Revelation 18:4-8.

"COME NOW, AND LET US REASON TOGETHER, SAITH THE LORD: THOUGH YOUR SINS BE AS SCARLET, THEY SHALL BE AS WHITE AS SNOW; THOUGH THEY BE RED LIKE CRIMSON, THEY SHALL BE AS WOOL. LET THE WICKED FORSAKE HIS WAY, AND THE UNRIGHTEOUS MAN HIS THOUGHTS: AND LET HIM RETURN UNTO THE LORD, AND HE WILL HAVE MERCY UPON HIM; AND TO OUR GOD, FOR HE WILL ABUNDANTLY PARDON. HAVE I ANY

PLEASURE AT ALL THAT THE WICKED SHOULD DIE? SAITH THE LORD GOD: AND NOT THAT HE SHOULD RETURN FROM HIS WAYS, AND LIVE? I CALL HEAVEN AND EARTH TO RECORD THIS DAY AGAINST YOU, THAT I HAVE SET BEFORE YOU LIFE AND DEATH, BLESSING AND CURSING: THEREFORE CHOOSE LIFE, THAT BOTH THOU AND THY SEED MAY LIVE:" Isaiah 1:18; 55:7; Ezekiel 18:23, Deuteronomy 30:19.

"THUS SAITH THE LORD, KEEP YE JUDGMENT, AND DO JUSTICE: FOR MY SALVATION IS NEAR TO COME, AND MY RIGHTEOUSNESS TO BE REVEALED. BLESSED IS THE MAN THAT DOETH THIS, AND THE SON OF MAN THAT LAYETH HOLD ON IT: THAT KEEPETH THE SABBATH FROM POLLUTING IT, AND KEEPETH HIS HAND FROM DOING ANY EVIL. NEITHER LET THE SON OF THE STRANGER, THAT HATH JOINED HIMSELF TO THE LORD, SPEAK SAYING, THE LORD HATH UTTERLY SEPARATED ME FROM HIS PEOPLE: NEITHER LET THE EUNUCH SAY, BEHOLD, I AM A DRY TREE. FOR THUS SAITH THE LORD UNTO THE EUNUCHS THAT KEEP MY SABBATHS, AND CHOOSE THE THINGS THAT PLEASE ME, AND TAKE HOLD OF MY COVENANT; EVEN UNTO THEM WILL I GIVE IN MINE HOUSE AND WITHIN MY WALLS A PLACE AND A NAME BETTER THAN OF SONS AND OF DAUGHTERS: I WILL GIVE THEM AN EVERLASTING NAME, THAT SHALL NOT BE CUT OFF. ALSO THE SON OF THE STRANGER, THAT JOIN THEMSELVES TO THE LORD, TO SERVE HIM, AND TO LOVE THE NAME OF THE LORD, TO BE HIS SERVANTS, EVERY ONE THAT KEEPETH THE SABBATH FROM POLLUTING IT, AND TAKETH HOLD OF MY COVENANT; EVEN THEM WILL I BRING TO MY HOLY MOUNTAIN, AND MAKE THEM JOYFUL IN MY HOUSE OF PRAYER: THEIR BURNT OFFERINGS AND THEIR SACRIFICES SHALL BE ACCEPTED UPON MINE ALTAR; FOR MINE HOUSE SHALL BE CALLED AN HOUSE OF PRAYER FOR ALL PEOPLE." Isaiah 56:1-7.

We have seen that it was the Roman Catholic Church as foretold, who changed the Sabbath of the Lord to the pagan day of Sunday. We have also seen a call from Jesus to restore it. Now let us review and compare the doctrines of Baal worship and compare them with the Doctrines of the Roman Catholic Church:

BAALIM	CATHOLICISM
1. THE NATIVITY OF THE SUN THE BIRTH OF TAMMUZ, December 25.	1. THE NATIVITY OF JESUS, CHRISTMAS, December 25.

2. THE MIDSUMMER FESTIVAL HELD June 24th.	2. THE NATIVITY OF ST. JOHN HELD June 24th.
3. THE ASSUMPTION OF SEMIRAMIS WHO BECAME THE MOTHER GODDESS.	3. THE ASSUMPTION OF MARY WHO BECAME THE MOTHER OF GOD.
4. THE MOTHER GODDESS WORSHIPPED AS THE QUEEN OF HEAVEN, Jer. 7:18.	4. THE VIRGIN MARY WORSHIPPED AS THE QUEEN OF HEAVEN.
5. CAKES DEDICATED TO THE GODDESS WITH A "T" DRAWN ON IT, Jer. 44:17, 19.	5. HOT CROSS BUNS WITH A CROSS DRAWN ON IT.
6. 40 DAYS FASTING FOR TAMMUZ, Ezekiel 8:14.	6. 40 DAYS OF LENT.
7. THE FESTIVAL OF EASTER, Ezekiel 8:16.	7. THE FESTIVAL OF EASTER.
8. THE RESURRECTION OF TAMMUZ AT EASTER AND THE PROCESSION OF GRAVEN IMAGES DURING HOLY WEEK.	8. THE PROCESSION OF GRAVEN IMAGES OF JESUS, MARY AND PETER DURING HOLY WEEK.
9. VENERATION OF GRAVEN IMAGES OF BAAL, ISHTAR, TAMMUZ AND LESSER GODS IN THE HEAVENS.	9. VENERATION OF GRAVEN IMAGES OF JESUS, MARY, PETER, AND OF THE SAINTS.
10. THE BELIEF IN IMMORTALITY OF THE SOUL AND BURNING PLACE OF TORMENT.	10. THE BELIEF IN IMMORTALITY OF THE SOUL AND BURNING PLACE OF TORMENT.
11. THE DOCTRINE OF PURGATORY.	11. THE DOCTRINE OF PURGATORY.
12. THE BELIEF OF THE DEAD VISITING THE LIVING. FEAST HELD FOR, IN NOVEMBER. (ALL SOULS DAY)	12. THE FESTIVAL OF ALL SOULS DAY HELD November 2nd, ALL SAINTS DAY HELD November 1st.
13. BURNING OF INCENSE. Isaish 1:13; Jer. 11:17; Ezekiel 8:11.	13. THE BURNING OF INCENSE AND CANDLES.
14. CHANTS AND REPETITIOUS PRAYERS. Matthew 6:6.	14. THE ROSARY, HAIL MARY.

15. THE SYMBOL OF THE CROSS AS SYMBOL OF SUN WORSHIP.	15. THE CRUCIFIX.
16. AMULETS AND IDOLS TO SCARE AWAY EVIL SPIRITS.	16. THE WEARING OF CRUCIFIXES AND IMAGES DISPLAYED FOR PROTECTION.
17. THE ROUND DISK WAFER IHS SYMBOL OF ISIS, HORUS, SEB, EATEN AS FOOD FOR THE SOUL.	17. THE WAFER USED IN THE EUCHARIST IS ROUND WITH IHS ENGRAVED ON IT.
18. PAINTING OF THE CHILD AND MOTHER, WITH THE GLORY OF THE SUN AROUND THEIR HEADS.	18. PAINTINGS OF THE CHILD JESUS AND MARY WITH HALOS OR A GLORY OF THE SUN AROUND THEIR HEADS.
19. INFANT BAPTISM, SPRINKLING HOLY WATER.	19. INFANT BAPTISM, SPRINKLING HOLY WATER.
20. NECROMANCY.	20. MYSTICISM.
21. THE FIRST DAY OF THE WEEK SUNDAY, KEPT SACRED TO HONOUR BAAL.	21. THE CHANGE OF SABBATH TO SUNDAY.
22. PONTIFEX MAXIMUS NAME FOR CHIEF HEAD OF THE PAGAN BABYLONIAN SYSTEM OF IDOLATRY.	22. PONTIFEX MAXIMUS, ONE OF THE FIRST NAMES FOR THE POPE.
23. JANUS AND CYBELE, HOLDERS OF THE KEYS TO HEAVEN AND HELL.	23. THE POPE CLAIMS TO HAVE THE KEYS OF PETER.
24. THE HIGH PRIEST KINGS CARRIED ON A THRONE TO THE TEMPLE OF HIS GOD.	24. THE POPE CARRIED ON A PORTABLE THRONE TO THE BASILICA OF ST. PETER. (SEDIA GESTATORIA)
25. THE PAGAN HIGH PRIEST KING BELIEVED TO BE THE INCARNATE OF THE SUN GOD.	25. THE POPE PRETENDS TO BE CHRIST'S VICAR HERE ON EARTH.
26. OFFERINGS TO APPEASE THE GODS.	26. PENANCE, INDULGENCES, SALVATION BY WORKS.

27. HOUSES FOR THE VIRGIN PRIESTESSES, TO BE EMPLOYED AT PAGAN TEMPLES.	27. NUNS.
28. HUMAN SACRIFICES BURNED BY FIRE AS OFFERING TO APPEASE THE SUN GOD.	28. OPPOSERS OF THE DOCTRINES OF THE ROMAN CATHOLIC CHURCH, BURNED AT THE STAKE.

There is not a nation under Heaven that has not been influenced by Nimrod's system of SUN WORSHIP:

"FOR ALL NATIONS HAVE DRUNK OF THE WRATH OF HER FORNICATION, AND THE KINGS OF THE EARTH HAVE COMMITTED FORNICATION WITH HER, AND THE MERCHANTS OF THE EARTH ARE WAXED RICH THROUGH THE ABUNDANCE OF HER DELICACIES." Revelation 18:3.

The WRATH OF HER FORNICATION in symbolic language means her false doctrines. Just as in ancient times Israel was called an HARLOT for mixing paganism with the true worship of God (Isaiah 1:21; Ezekiel 16:26-63), so is BABYLON THE GREAT called THE MOTHER OF HARLOTS today.

"AND ALL THAT DWELL UPON THE EARTH SHALL WORSHIP HIM, (PAPACY) WHOSE NAMES ARE NOT WRITTEN IN THE BOOK OF LIFE OF THE LAMB (JESUS) SLAIN FROM THE FOUNDATION OF THE WORLD. IF ANY MAN HEAR, LET HIM HEAR." Revelation 13:8, 9.

The doctrines of the Bible have been tampered with, a great breach in the Law of God prevails. The Lord is calling His people, no matter what positions they fill, or to what church they belong, to turn from their evil ways, and listen to His council as given in the Bible:

"I AM THE LORD, I CHANGE NOT; YE SHALL NOT ADD UNTO THE WORD WHICH I COMMAND YOU, NEITHER SHALL YE DIMINISH OUGHT FROM IT, THAT YE MAY KEEP THE COMMANDMENTS OF THE LORD YOUR GOD WHICH I COMMAND YOU. MY COVENANT WILL I NOT BREAK, NOR ALTER THE THING THAT IS GONE OUT OF MY LIPS. JESUS CHRIST THE SAME YESTERDAY, AND TODAY AND FOREVER." Malachi 3:6; Deuteronomy 4:2; Psalm 89:34; Hebrews 13:8.

Ironically enough, the very symbol the book of Revelation uses to describe "MYSTERY, BABYLON THE GREAT, THE MOTHER OF HARLOTS AND ABOMINATIONS OF THE EARTH . . . , having a golden cup in her hand. . ." (Revelation 17:4, 5); can be found on a medal Pope Leo XII struck in 1825. As shown above, one side bears the image of Pope Leo XII, while on the opposite side is a woman pictured with a cup in her hand sitting on the world. The woman is a symbol of the papacy. The world as her seat, represents the papacy being supported and uplifted in the world by the kingdoms of the world. Such is the meaning of the symbolic language describing the Mother of Harlots sitting on a Scarlet Colored Beast, (Revelation 17:3-5, 18.) Courtesy of Loizeaux Brothers, Neptune, N.J.

"I KNOW THAT, WHATSOEVER GOD DOETH, IT SHALL BE FOREVER: NOTHING CAN BE PUT TO IT, NOR ANYTHING TAKEN FROM IT: AND GOD DOETH IT, THAT MEN SHOULD FEAR BEFORE HIM." Ecclesiastes 3:14.

Those who in these last days make their stand to restore the Sabbath, and turn also from pagan superstitions and teach men so, shall be called "THE REPAIRER OF THE BREACH, THE RESTORER OF PATHS TO DWELL IN." Isaiah 58:12. We have seen three of the four acts the Antichrist will perform in the first phase found in Daniel 7:25, and how the Roman Catholic Church fulfilled each of them perfectly. Here is the last of Daniel's vision:

". . . AND THEY SHALL BE GIVEN INTO HIS HAND UNTIL A TIME AND TIMES AND THE DIVIDING OF TIME." Daniel 7:25.

This is a prophetic time period during which the LITTLE HORN (PAPACY) would commit blasphemy, persecution, change the Law of God and follow after the dragon who gave it its power. The reader will see that there are TWO periods of time in earth's history when the papacy

The Mother of Harlots, symbolizing the false religions of the World. She is riding on a scarlet colored Beast, which suggests she is exalted by earthly powers.

will rule as a religious dictatorship. The first was during the Dark Ages, and the second is still in the near future, called the GREAT TRIBULATION:

"FOR THEN SHALL BE GREAT TRIBULATION, SUCH AS WAS NOT SINCE THE BEGINNING OF THE WORLD TO THIS TIME, NO, NOR EVER SHALL BE. AND EXCEPT THOSE DAYS SHOULD BE SHORTENED, THERE SHOULD NO FLESH BE SAVED: BUT FOR THE ELECT'S SAKE THOSE DAYS SHALL BE SHORTENED." Matthew 24:21,22.

To understand what TIME, TIMES AND THE DIVIDING OF THE TIME means, the reader must understand the Jewish calendar. The ancient Jewish year has 360 days of 12 months with 30 days each.[1] In Bible prophecy a "TIME" is equal to ONE YEAR of 360 days. As in Daniel 4:25, where King Nebuchadnezzar of Babylon became like a beast of the field, TILL SEVEN TIMES pass over him, which was seven years. Daniel 4:16.

Now in Bible prophecy, a day can be a symbol for one year. When Moses was in the wilderness with the Israelites, he foretold that they would wander in the wilderness for FORTY DAYS, however, each day was actually one year. For Numbers 14:34 says:

"AFTER THE NUMBER OF THE DAYS IN WHICH YE SEARCHED THE LAND, EVEN FORTY DAYS, EACH DAY FOR A YEAR, SHALL YE BEAR YOUR INIQUITIES, EVEN FORTY YEARS, AND YE SHALL KNOW MY BREACH OF PROMISE."

In Ezekiel 4:6 we find days as symbols of years:

"AND WHEN THOU HAST ACCOMPLISHED THEM, LIE AGAIN ON THY RIGHT SIDE, AND THOU SHALT BEAR THE INIQUITY OF THE HOUSE OF JUDAH FORTY DAYS: I HAVE APPOINTED THEE EACH DAY FOR A YEAR."

To understand the meaning of TIME, TIMES AND A DIVIDING OF TIME and get the true length of this prophetic period, let us count the number of the days in TIME, TIMES AND A DIVIDING OF TIME. Here is the equation of this time period:

TIME	=	ONE YEAR	=	360 DAYS
TIMES	=	TWO YEARS	=	720 DAYS
½ TIME	=	HALF YEAR	=	180 DAYS
TOTAL 3½ TIMES	=	3½ YEARS	=	1260 DAYS

[1] See *Daniel and the Revelation*, by Uriah Smith, pp. 143,144.

The observance of the pagan Holy Week by Roman Catholics during Easter. Notice the graven images of Jesus, Peter, and the Virgin Mary. These photographs were taken in Guatemala, in the spring of 1979.

Now taking 1260 days which is equal to TIME, TIMES AND ONE-HALF TIME, and take each day for a year like Moses and Ezekiel did in Numbers 14:34 and Ezekiel 4:6, we have a time period of 1260 years.

John in the book of Revelation foretold the papacy by the symbol of a Beast. The same prophetic time period is given also in Revelation 13:5, but in months:

"AND THERE WAS GIVEN UNTO HIM A MOUTH SPEAKING GREAT THINGS AND BLASPHEMIES; AND POWER WAS GIVEN UNTO HIM TO CONTINUE FORTY AND TWO MONTHS." Reader, forty-two months equals 1260 days:

42 MONTHS
× 30 DAYS
1260 YEARS (IN PROPHECY)

In history, as pointed out earlier, it was the Roman Catholic Church which destroyed the Ostrogoths, the last opposing Arian nation in 538 A.D. This date began the 1260 years the papacy would:

1. AND HE SHALL SPEAK GREAT WORDS AGAINST THE MOST HIGH (BLASPHEMY).
2. AND SHALL WEAR OUT THE SAINTS OF THE MOST HIGH.
3. AND THINK TO CHANGE TIMES AND LAWS:
4. AND THEY SHALL BE GIVEN INTO HIS HAND UNTIL A TIME AND TIMES AND THE DIVIDING OF TIME. (DANIEL 7:25).

Although the papacy tried to hide the testimony of the real Gospel by forbidding its study, the Lord preserved Him a people that would keep the true Gospel of the Bible unmixed with paganism, throughout the 1260 years of papal supremacy. While Satan was transforming the Roman Catholic Church into Baalim in the name of Christianity, the Lord always had a small remnant who held the Bible as the only rule of life, who believed Christ to be the only Mediator between God and man, that man is saved by faith only and not by human merit, that the right to read the Bible is a God-given choice, and the Lord's day is the Seventh Day. Because the papacy taught just the opposite, a clash was brought between Bible believing people, and the people who believed in the authority of the papacy. The papacy sent learned men who went among those who held to the belief that the Bible only, was the guide of life. The papacy too, tried to confuse the Protestant doctrines. However, the learned men were easily shown the errors of the papacy, according to Scripture; and these faithful believing Christians would not change their convictions. The Roman Catholic Church commanded the governments of the land to exterminate the Protestants as heretics.

The persecuting power of the papal supremacy did not extend through the entire 1260 years; it was cut short. Due to the corruption within the papacy and the influence of the Reformation, the papacy lost its hold on the world. The death blow to papal supremacy started in 1789 in France, when the French Revolutionists stormed the fortress of the Bastille in Paris, murdered the mayor, and set up another government. A period in history called the Reign of Terror began in 1793. The worship of God was abolished by the French National Assembly. Bibles were collected and publicly burned. All religious worship was prohibited, and all Bible Institutions were closed and abolished. The blood of many papists ran where once the blood of the Protestants had run on the night of St. Bartholomew Day. The Papacy was outlawed by the French National Assembly and atheism took its place. From June 1793 until July 1794, at least 300,000 who opposed the new atheistic government were arrested, and 17,000 were officially executed. Napoleon entered into history in 1795, and in 1796 he was sent to command an army of 30,000 in Italy. In 1798 the papacy reached its last year of the 1260 years predicted by Daniel. France sent General Berthier to Vatican City and General Berthier dethroned Pope Pius VI (Giovanni Braschi),[1] and sent him into exile. This death blow to papal supremacy was also foretold in Revelation 13:3:

"AND I SAW ONE OF HIS HEADS AS IT WERE WOUNDED TO DEATH; AND HIS DEADLY WOUND WAS HEALED: AND ALL THE WORLD WONDERED AFTER THE BEAST."

Here is a diagram of the Time, Times, and Dividing of Time:

1260 years

538 A.D. Papacy Destroys Ostrogoths	1798 A.D. Pope Pius VI Dethroned by Berthier

DANIEL 7:25
TIME, TIMES, AND THE DIVIDING OF
TIME, THE FORTY TWO MONTHS OF
Revelation 13:5

The Reformation of the 16th century did not end at Luther's death. It was only a beginning. There is a call from Heaven to return to the

[1] See *The Vatican and Its role in World Affairs,* by Charles Pichon, p. 88.

doctrines of the Bible, and to restore their truths. The papacy lost her power to control individual lives by force, at the end of the 1260 years. However, if the reader will notice in Revelation 13:3, THE DEADLY WOUND WAS HEALED. The papacy as the Beast of Revelation, will again regain her dictatorial power. It will be done by the influence of the second Beast (nation) of Revelation 13:11-17.

Who is this SECOND BEAST (Nation), that causeth the earth and them which dwell therein to worship the first beast whose deadly wound was healed? We will study this in the last chapter.

But before we end this chapter, we would like to expose another major avenue where Satan uses man to destroy man. Our Adversary works 24 hours a day for the destruction of the human race. He has created a plastic and toxic world. Satan has diligently studied the weaknesses of the human being since the Garden of Eden. He knows the quickest and most efficient method to destroy each of us. One may be assured that he uses every power, every strategy to weaken the body temple, thereby making it an unfit dwelling for the Spirit of God. The average American diet is toxic and disease producing. As it stands now, it will lead us only in one direction, to rapid degeneration of all functions. The time of our high calling is here. Let us restore the paths to healthful living as well. We have too long lived with the world of chemicals, attempting to force our bodies to adapt to chemicals, trying to prove that we are smarter than God. We have filled our bodies and our live plants and animals with chemicals, poisons, and drugs and have created in ourselves a filthiness.

How does one return to the diet that was intended for man in the beginning? It is encountered through searching, by anointing the eyes with spiritual eyesalve to discern, and finally, by changing our course of living. We must educate ourselves. Too much money and power is behind the chemical and drug world. They will not be the ones to educate us. However there are concerned individuals and groups who have written very factual and shocking books about the effect additives and preservatives have on the body. A highly recommended source for this is *Consumer Beware!* by Beatrice Trum Hunter. It abounds in factual information about the horror stories of what we ingest every day of our lives. Take for instance a T-bone steak browned, sizzling hot and smothered in mushrooms. Looks good, doesn't it? Let us open our eyes a bit to see the story about the meats we consume from our super markets. To further increase production, cattle are injected with various chemicals, amongst them tranquilizers, enzymes and hormones. Stilbestrol is a hormone used for fattening beef. The beef becomes fatter, although yielding poorer meat due to water fat produced instead of protein, which is not only undesirable, but an economic fraud. Experiments show that in human beings Stilbestrol has produced breast cancer, fibroid tumors, and excessive menstrual bleeding in women, sterility and impotence in men, and arrested growth in children.[1]

The consumer has been conditioned to accept the white flesh of milk-fed veal as a sign of superiority. In reality, it represents a shocking practice. The milk-fed veal is an animal fed on an imbalanced, malnourishing diet of milk or milk substitute, and purposely kept in a state of induced anemia to keep the flesh white.[2] Perhaps one of the most devastating and effective works of the evil one to destroy the body temple has been the introduction of sugar. Virtually all modern day societies are at the mercy of this horrendous chemical. It has wiled its way into nearly all processed food, including ketchup, beans, baby food, canned food, — even toothpaste contains sugar! Refined sugar is lethal when ingested by humans because it provides only that which nutritionists describe as empty or naked calories. In addition, sugar is worse than nothing because it drains and leeches the body of precious vitamins and minerals, because of the demand, its digestion, detoxification and elimination make on one's entire system.[3] Satan is very astute because especially pertinent to our spiritual lives is the fact that the leeching of vitamins especially affects the nervous system and the brain. This contributes to the shocking number of nervous breakdowns, insanity, suicides and general bizarre behavior of our sugar-addicted society. Sugar is addicting. Ingestion of a piece of pastry for instance, raises the blood sugar. Then as the blood sugar soon falls, an uncontrollable need for something sweet results in perhaps coffee and a candy bar. The coffee lift again raises the blood sugar, but it soon plummets to an even lower level than before. This is the path many alcoholics have first trod. Millions of dollars a year are spent on advertising to perpetuate the sugar addition and other harmful products. Look how cute television commercials are about promoting their products. They use children, dogs, cats, animals, men and women to try to win their viewers attention. While a little innocent child is used to show other children how good a certain cereal is, people who go out to buy this product have no idea that this certain cereal could contain up to 40% sugar. In how many glittering, appetizing forms do you see this manifested in other areas for the consumer to behold? The council of the Lord for His people who have ears to hear is:

"GET WISDOM, GET UNDERSTANDING." Proverbs 4:5.

---

[1] See *Consumer Beware!* by Beatrice Trum Hunter, p. 116.
[2] Ibid. p. 125.
[3] See *Sugar Blues*, by William Dufty, p. 137.

We have only touched the surface of this most important subject. Seek knowledge that can be found in health books, and many other written materials on the subject. However, prove all things. For like Christianity, there are those who are too fanatical and could lead you to suffer malnutrition. We have seen what Satan has done in the past to deceive the very elect of God, if possible. Now it's time to see how Satan is working in our present day, and what will happen in the near future.

CHAPTER V

The Ecumenical Movement and the Second Phase Of The Antichrist

From the beginning of Nimrod's Babel (Babylon) to our present day, God's people have been subjected to earthly powers and oppressed by them. Except for very short periods of time, most of the history of the people of God has been written in much sorrow. But the worst is still to come, for the Originator of all sorrow and pain will appear in the world as Jesus Christ, and this will be thought of as the Kingdom of God. But those who know and have seen the great apostasy from God's Word in these last days and become doers of the law and not just hearers, shall be delivered from Satan's almost overwhelming deception. All nations of the world, according to Revelation 13:8, shall worship Satan through the Beast (Papacy), whose names are not written in the Lamb's Book of Life. Jesus said in Matthew 24:14:

"AND THIS GOSPEL OF THE KINGDOM SHALL BE PREACHED IN ALL THE WORLD FOR A WITNESS UNTO ALL NATIONS; AND THEN SHALL THE END COME."

Jesus said this Gospel shall be preached to all nations as a witness. But He didn't say all nations would believe. Most will not believe the Gospel in the Bible and will not obey its counsels. It shall be as the days of Noah, when the unbelieving were swept away by the flood. Jesus foretold in a twofold prophecy in Matthew 24:21,22, that His coming would be at the time of the great tribulation period. Many erring teachers have placed this great tribulation period as being the last week of Daniel 9:24-27. They claim that this great tribulation period is upon the Jews; and that the Christians will not have to go through this period of Satan's reign upon earth, because they will secretly be raptured out of the world.

But instead of following the speculations of men, let us search the Scriptures and history to find out what this wonderful prophetic time of 70 Weeks really means. Here from Daniel 9:24-27, is the prophecy:

"SEVENTY WEEKS ARE DETERMINED UPON THY PEOPLE AND UPON THY HOLY CITY, TO FINISH THE TRANSGRESSION, AND TO

MAKE AN END OF SINS, AND TO MAKE RECONCILIATION FOR INIQUITY, AND TO BRING IN EVERLASTING RIGHTEOUSNESS, AND TO SEAL UP THE VISION AND PROPHECY, AND TO ANOINT THE MOST HOLY. KNOW THEREFORE AND UNDERSTAND, THAT FROM THE GOING FORTH OF THE COMMANDMENT TO RESTORE AND TO BUILD JERUSALEM UNTO THE MESSIAH THE PRINCE SHALL BE SEVEN WEEKS, AND THREESCORE AND TWO WEEKS: THE STREET SHALL BE BUILT AGAIN, AND THE WALL, EVEN IN TROUBLOUS TIMES. AND AFTER THREESCORE AND TWO WEEKS SHALL MESSIAH BE CUT OFF, BUT NOT FOR HIMSELF: AND THE PEOPLE OF THE PRINCE THAT SHALL COME SHALL DESTROY THE CITY AND THE SANCTUARY; AND THE END THEREOF SHALL BE WITH A FLOOD, AND UNTO THE END OF THE WAR DESOLATIONS ARE DETERMINED. AND HE SHALL CONFIRM THE COVENANT WITH MANY FOR ONE WEEK: AND IN THE MIDST OF THE WEEK HE SHALL CAUSE THE SACRIFICE AND THE OBLATION TO CEASE, AND FOR THE OVERSPREADING OF ABOMINATIONS HE SHALL MAKE IT DESOLATE, EVEN UNTIL THE CONSUMMATION, AND THAT DETERMINED SHALL BE POURED UPON THE DESOLATE."

AS WE SAW EARLIER, a day in prophetic time means "ONE YEAR," Numbers 14:34 and Ezekiel 4:6. To get the number of years this prophetic 70 weeks has, we need to simply multiply 7 days × 70 weeks, for there are 7 days to one week. Seven days × 70 weeks = 490 prophetic days which are counted as years. Thus:

ONE WEEK = SEVEN DAYS = SEVEN YEARS (PROPHETIC TIME).
SEVENTY WEEKS = FOUR HUNDRED NINETY DAYS = 490 years (PROPHETIC TIME).

Now let us study carefully the Scriptures relating to the Seventy weeks again. In verse 24, 70 weeks are determined upon the people, and to anoint the Most Holy. In verse 25 this time period of 70 weeks would start at the commandment to restore and build Jerusalem, and to the "Messiah," it would be 7 weeks + 60 weeks + 2 weeks = 69 weeks. This prophecy of the Seventy weeks of years reveals God's redemption for man and Jesus Christ's first advent, not the Antichrist. This is a wonderful time period between the commandment to restore Jerusalem which Nebuchadnezzar destroyed, and Jesus to be anointed by the Holy Spirit. Verse 24 and verse 25 say it would be 69 weeks from the commandment to restore Jerusalem to the anointing of the Most Holy. Satan is not the Most Holy. This is not a time period of Satan the Antichrist, taught by some, but is a prophetic time period of Jesus Christ of Nazareth, and will prove without a doubt to the Jew first, then the unbeliever that Jesus is the real Messiah. Daniel the Jewish prophet was a captive still, but under the Persian kingdom, when he had this prophecy, Daniel 9:2. Jerusalem was destroyed by the forces of Nebuchadnezzar of Babylon as we saw earlier. Daniel's vision was in the first year of Darius, King of Persia, who was made king over the realm of the Chaldeans, Daniel 9:1.

This time period of "70 weeks" did start at the commandment to restore and build Jerusalem that had been desolate for 70 years, foretold by Jeremiah the prophet before King Nebuchadnezzar's armies destroyed Jerusalem. Jeremiah 25:11 says:

"AND THIS WHOLE LAND SHALL BE A DESOLATION, AND AN ASTONISHMENT; AND THESE NATIONS SHALL SERVE THE KING OF BABYLON SEVENTY YEARS."

And Jeremiah 29:10 says:

"For thus saith the Lord, that after seventy years be accomplished at Babylon I will visit you, and perform my good word toward you, in causing you to return to this place."

Daniel understood the prophecy of Jeremiah, that for 70 years Israel was to be captive of Babylon, then the Lord would let the Israelites return to Jerusalem. Daniel knew that the promises of God were sure, but didn't quite understand the meaning of another vision he had earlier in Daniel 8:13,14.

After Daniel prayed to the Lord for forgiveness of sin, for his people and himself, the angel Gabriel opened his understanding in Daniel 9:20-22.

The angel Gabriel told Daniel that the commandment to restore Jerusalem is when the 70 weeks would start its prophetic time and this would fulfill the Lord's promise to bring the Israelites back to Jerusalem after 70 years captivity in Babylon. Was there such a decree? Was a commandment to restore and to build Jerusalem pronounced? As sure as there is a Holy Temple in Heaven, so was there a commandment to restore Jerusalem and it is found in the book of Ezra 1:1-4:

"NOW IN THE FIRST YEAR OF CYRUS KING OF PERSIA, THAT THE WORD OF THE LORD BY THE MOUTH OF JEREMIAH MIGHT BE FULFILLED, THE LORD STIRRED UP THE SPIRIT OF CYRUS KING OF PERSIA, THAT HE MADE A PROCLAMATION THROUGHOUT ALL HIS KINGDOM, AND PUT IT ALSO IN WRITING, SAYING, THUS SAITH CYRUS KING OF PERSIA, THE LORD GOD OF HEAVEN HATH GIVEN ME ALL THE KINGDOMS OF THE EARTH; AND HE HATH CHARGED ME TO BUILD HIM A HOUSE AT JERUSALEM, WHICH IS IN JUDAH. WHO IS THERE AMONG YOU OF ALL HIS PEOPLE? HIS GOD BE WITH

HIM, AND LET HIM GO UP TO JERUSALEM, WHICH IS IN JUDAH, AND BUILD THE HOUSE OF THE LORD GOD OF ISRAEL, (HE IS THE GOD), WHICH IS IN JERUSALEM. AND WHOSOEVER REMAINETH IN ANY PLACE WHERE HE SOJOURNETH, LET THE MEN OF HIS PLACE HELP HIM WITH SILVER, AND WITH GOLD, AND WITH GOODS, AND WITH BEASTS, BESIDE THE FREEWILL OFFERING FOR THE HOUSE OF GOD THAT IS JERUSALEM."

We have read earlier, how Cyrus was chosen. But this was only part of the decree, for Cyrus said the house of the Lord was to be built. The commandment to rebuild the temple and Jerusalem was to be given. Not only the house of the Lord, but the street and wall of Jerusalem, Daniel 9:25. There was a halt to the building of the temple and two different Kings of Persia arose up in the meantime. Ezra 4:4-6:

"THEN THE PEOPLE OF THE LAND WEAKENED THE HANDS OF THE PEOPLE OF JUDAH, AND TROUBLED THEM IN BUILDING, AND HIRED COUNSELLORS AGAINST THEM, TO FRUSTRATE THEIR PURPOSE, ALL THE DAYS OF CYRUS KING OF PERSIA, EVEN UNTIL THE REIGN OF DARIUS KING OF PERSIA. AND IN THE REIGN OF AHASUERUS, IN THE BEGINNING OF HIS REIGN, WROTE THEY UNTO HIM AN ACCUSATION AGAINST THE INHABITANTS OF JUDAH AND JERUSALEM."

But after Darius, King of Persia found the decree of Cyrus the first King of Persia, who commanded the house of the Lord be built in Jerusalem; Darius also made a decree. Ezra 6:7:

"LET THE WORK OF THIS HOUSE OF GOD ALONE; LET THE GOVERNOR OF THE JEWS AND THE ELDERS OF THE JEWS BUILD THIS HOUSE OF GOD IN HIS PLACE."

The house of the Lord was finally finished in the sixth year of Darius the King, which would be in the year 515 B.C. Ezra 6:14,15:

"AND THE ELDERS OF THE JEWS BUILDED, AND THEY PROSPERED THROUGH THE PROPHESYING OF HAGGAI THE PROPHET AND ZECHARIAH THE SON OF IDDO. AND THEY BUILDED, AND FINISHED IT, ACCORDING TO THE COMMANDMENT OF GOD OF ISRAEL, AND ACCORDING TO THE COMMANDMENT OF CYRUS, AND DARIUS, AND ARTAXERXES KING OF PERSIA. AND THIS HOUSE WAS FINISHED ON THE THIRD DAY OF THE MONTH ADAR, WHICH WAS IN THE SIXTH YEAR OF THE REIGN OF DARIUS THE KING."

It took not one but three decrees from three Kings of Persia to finally let the work of restoring Jerusalem and the temple to continue. But it was not until 457 B.C. that the authorization was given for the complete restoration of the city.[1] This decree was in the seventh year of Artaxerxes, Ezra 7:16-25. Here again the three decrees:

1. Ezra 1:1-4 (536 B.C.) of Cyrus.
2. Ezra 6:7,8 (519 B.C.) of Darius.
3. Ezra 7:7-25 (457 B.C.) of Artaxerxes.

So the starting time of the Seventy weeks (490 years), would commence in the fall of 457 B.C. Daniel divides the 70 weeks into three parts:

Part 1

7 weeks
7 days × 7 weeks = 49 (PROPHETIC YEARS)

Part 2

Threescore and two weeks, (62 weeks)
7 days × 62 weeks = 434 (YEARS)

Part 3

One week
7 × 1 = 7 (YEARS)   49 + 434 + 7 = 490 (YEARS)

The first seven weeks from 457 B.C. to 408 B.C., was the period of the 49 years to build and restore Jerusalem. From 408 B.C. to 27 A.D., was the period of 434 years unto the anointing of Christ with the Holy Spirit. (Matthew 3:15-17). This is a total of 69 weeks of the "SEVENTY WEEKS." Daniel 9:25 says "AFTER" the 69 weeks the Messiah would be cut off. This would happen in the midst of this prophetic one week, Daniel 9:27. Half of one week is three and one half years. From 27 A.D. to 31 A.D. equals 3½ years, AND ALSO THE VERY YEAR JESUS CHRIST WAS CRUCIFIED! The remaining 3½ years of the last week was the 3½ years the disciples preached unto the Jews until the first martyr who was Stephen, Acts 7:56-60, Acts 13:46-48.

See the diagram of the 70 weeks of Daniel 9:24-27 on the next page.

Jesus, of whom the prophet Isaiah said:

"FOR UNTO US A CHILD IS BORN, UNTO US A SON IS GIVEN: AND THE GOVERNMENT SHALL BE UPON HIS SHOULDER: AND HIS NAME SHALL BE CALLED WONDERFUL, COUNSELLOR, THE MIGHTY GOD, THE EVERLASTING FATHER, THE PRINCE OF PEACE." Isaiah 9:6.

---

[1] See *Daniel and the Revelation,* by Uriah Smith, p. 209.

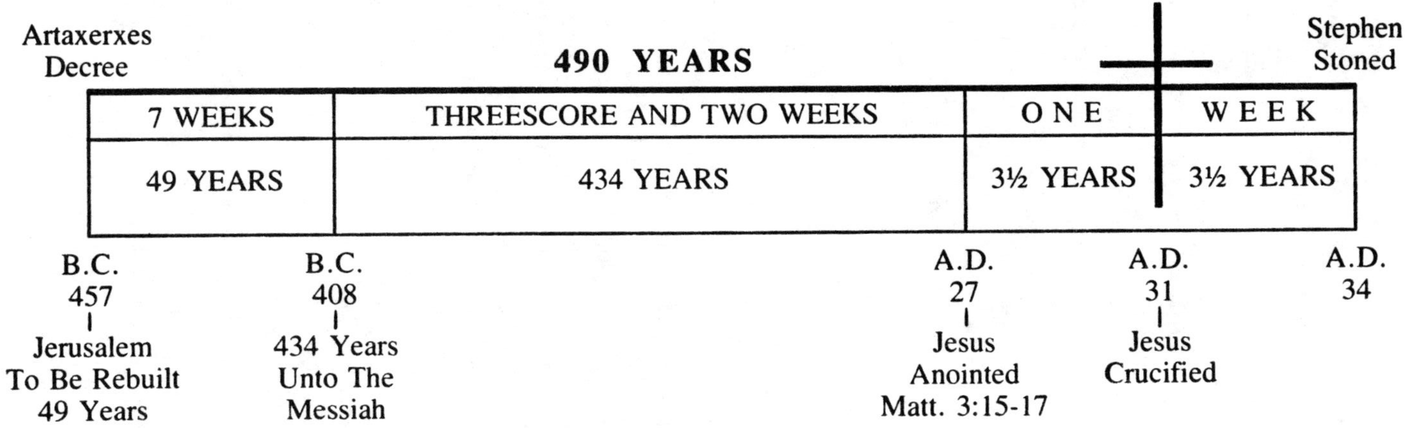

Know therefore and understand, that from the going forth of the commandment to restore and build Jerusalem unto the Messiah the prince shall be seven weeks, and threescore and two weeks: the street shall be built again, and the wall even in troublous times. And after threescore and two weeks shall Messiah be cut off. . . . And He shall confirm the covenant with many for one week: and in the midst of the week He shall cause the sacrifice and the oblation to cease. . . . Daniel 9:24-27.

"THEREFORE WILL I DIVIDE HIM A PORTION WITH THE GREAT, AND HE SHALL DIVIDE THE SPOIL WITH THE STRONG; BECAUSE HE HATH POURED OUT HIS SOUL UNTO DEATH: AND HE WAS NUMBERED WITH THE TRANSGRESSORS; AND HE BARE THE SIN OF MANY, AND MADE INTERCESSION FOR THE TRANSGRESSORS." Isaiah 53:12.

Here is an outline of prophecies about Christ from the Old Testament, and how these prophecies have or will be fulfilled:

PROPHECIES	FORETOLD OLD TESTAMENT	NEW TESTAMENT FULFILLMENT
Satan's destruction foretold by the promised seed.	Genesis 3:14, 15	(Still Future) Revelation 20:7-10 Malachi 4:1
A star to signal the birth of Christ.	Numbers 24:17	Matthew 2:2, 7, 9, 10
The promised seed to be born of a virgin.	Isaiah 7:14; 9:6	Luke 1:26-35
Foretold to be born at Bethlehem (Ephratah).	Micah 5:2	Luke 2:4, 11-16
The attempt to destroy the promised child.	Jeremiah 31:15	Matthew 2:16-18
The promised child foretold to flee to Egypt.	Hosea 11:1	Matthew 2:13-15
John the Baptist foretold to prepare the way for Christ's ministry.	Isaiah 40:3 Malachi 3:1	Matthew 3:1-3
Christ foretold to receive the baptism of the Holy Spirit.	Isaiah 11:2	Matthew 3:16
Christ foretold to teach in parables.	Psalm 78:2	Matthew 13:3, 34
Christ foretold to heal the blind, deaf, lame and sick.	Isaiah 35:4-6	Matthew 11:5; 15:30 Luke 4:18
Christ foretold to be hated by the Jews and rejected as the Messiah.	Psalm 69:4 Isaiah 49:7 Psalm 118:22, 23	John 15:24, 25 John 8:37-45 Matthew 21:42
Christ's Betrayal by Judas foretold.	Psalm 41:9 Zechariah 11:12, 13	John 13:18-27 Matthew 27:1-10
The Messiah's ministry would last 3½ years, then He would be put to death.	Daniel 9:26	Matthew 27:50

PROPHECIES	FORETOLD OLD TESTAMENT	NEW TESTAMENT FULFILLMENT
Christ's crucifixion foretold to be between two transgressors.	Isaiah 53:12	Mark 15:27, 28
Christ foretold to be given vinegar and gall to drink at His crucifixion.	Psalm 69:21	Matthew 27:34
Christ foretold to be laughed at and mocked on the cross.	Psalm 22:6-8	Mark 15:29-32
The Passover Lamb was a shadow of the sacrifice of Jesus' own life.	Exodus 12:2, 3, 6; 9:6	John 19:4 I Cor. 5:7
The Wave Sheaf Offering of the first fruits of barley on the first day of the week, was a shadow of Christ's resurrection, and believers.	Leviticus 23:10, 11, 21, 22 Numbers 16:17-31	Mark 16:1, 2, 9 I Cor. 15:23
Christ's resurrection foretold.	Psalm 16:10	John 20:1, 19
The Gentiles shall seek the promises of Christ foretold.	Isaiah 42:1, 6	Acts 13:46
A false religious spirit among God's people. A form of Godliness, but denying the power of God.	Isaiah 5:24; 24:5 Isaiah 30:1 Hosea 8:12 Jeremiah 23:17, 18, 20	II Timothy 3:1-7; 4:3 II Peter 3:14-18 I John 4:1-3
False teachers prophesying Baalim, in the name of the Lord.	Jeremiah 2:8; 23:13	Matthew 24:5, 11, 24
Satan foretold to come as Christ, the Prince and King of Israel.	Zechariah 11:16 Ezekiel 21:25 Isaiah 30:33	John 5:43 II Thessalonians 2:1-12 Mark 13:14
Christ foretold to destroy the living wicked and the world at His second coming.	Zephaniah 1:3, 14-16 Isaiah 13:6, 9-13 Jeremiah 25:31-35 Jeremiah 30:23, 24	Matthew 25:31-46 Luke 17:26-30 Revelation 14:9, 10 Revelation 21:8
The wicked slain by fire and brimstone at Christ's second coming.	Psalm 50:3 Isaiah 5:24 Isaiah 66:15-17	Matthew 13:39-41 II Thessalonians 1:7-9 II Peter 3:9, 10
At Christ's second coming the earth will be emptied of its inhabitants, there will be no man. The wicked will be food for the fowls.	Isaiah 24:1, 3 Jeremiah 4:23-28 Ezekiel 39:17-20	Matthew 24:37-39 Revelation 20:17-19

PROPHECIES	FORETOLD OLD TESTAMENT	NEW TESTAMENT FULFILLMENT
The resurrection of the believers from Adam to Christ's second coming foretold.	Daniel 12:1, 2, 14 Job 19:26 Ezekiel 37:12-14	I Corinthians 15:51-56 I Thessalonains 4:16, 17 John 5:24-29
The righteous living will be kept from Christ's wrath and will be translated to heaven for 1000 years.	Isaiah 56:1-7	John 14:1-3 I Thessalonians 4:16, 17 Revelation 20:4, 6

AFTER THE 1000 YEAR REIGN IN HEAVEN, CHRIST AND THE SAVED SHALL RETURN TO EARTH WITH NEW JERUSALEM (Revelation 21:9-27); and all the wicked from Adam's time to Christ's Second Coming will be resurrected. This is known in the Old Testament (Isaiah 28:21), as the Lord's STRANGE ACT. In the book of Revelation, it is described as the SECOND RESURRECTION AND THE SECOND DEATH:

"BLESSED AND HOLY IS HE THAT HATH PART IN THE FIRST RESURRECTION: ON SUCH THE SECOND DEATH HATH NO POWER, BUT THEY SHALL BE PRIESTS OF GOD AND OF CHRIST, AND SHALL REIGN WITH HIM A THOUSAND YEARS." Revelation 20:6.

Satan and all the wicked that ever lived, will finally be destroyed forever. Just as the waters in Noah's days covered the whole earth, so will fire cover the whole earth to purify it of its pollutions. This fallen planet will, one day in the near future, be exalted above all the planets of the Universe, for the Earth will become the Capital of the Universe; for the Creator Himself, will make His Home here and the saved will be His priests and kings:

"THE WOLF ALSO SHALL DWELL WITH THE LAMB, AND THE LEOPARD SHALL LIE DOWN WITH THE KID; AND THE CALF AND THE YOUNG LION AND THE FATLING TOGETHER; AND A LITTLE CHILD SHALL LEAD THEM. AND THE COW AND THE BEAR SHALL FEED; THEIR YOUNG ONES SHALL LIE DOWN TOGETHER: AND THE LION SHALL EAT STRAW LIKE THE OX. AND THE SUCKING CHILD SHALL PLAY ON THE HOLE OF THE ASP, AND THE WEANED CHILD SHALL PUT HIS HAND ON THE COCKTRICE' DEN. THEY SHALL NOT HURT NOR DESTROY IN ALL MY HOLY MOUNTAIN: FOR THE EARTH SHALL BE FULL OF THE KNOWLEDGE OF THE LORD, AS THE WATERS COVER THE SEA. AND I HEARD A GREAT VOICE OUT OF HEAVEN SAYING, BEHOLD, THE TABERNACLE OF GOD IS WITH MEN, AND HE WILL DWELL WITH THEM, AND THEY SHALL BE HIS

PEOPLE, AND GOD HIMSELF SHALL BE WITH THEM, AND BE THEIR GOD. AND GOD SHALL WIPE AWAY ALL TEARS FROM THEIR EYES; AND THERE SHALL BE NO MORE DEATH, NEITHER SORROW, NOR CRYING, NEITHER SHALL THERE BE ANY MORE PAIN: FOR THE FORMER THINGS ARE PASSED AWAY. AND HE THAT SAT UPON THE THRONE SAID, BEHOLD, I MAKE ALL THINGS NEW. AND HE SAID UNTO ME, WRITE: FOR THESE WORDS ARE TRUE AND FAITHFUL. AND HE SAID UNTO ME, IT IS DONE. I AM ALPHA AND OMEGA, THE BEGINNING AND THE END. I WILL GIVE UNTO HIM THAT IS ATHRIST OF THE FOUNTAIN OF THE WATER OF LIFE FREELY. HE THAT OVERCOMETH SHALL INHERIT ALL THINGS; AND I WILL BE HIS GOD, AND HE SHALL BE MY SON. BUT THE FEARFUL, AND UNBELIEVING, AND THE ABOMINABLE, AND MURDERERS, AND WHOREMONGERS, AND SORCERERS, AND IDOLATERS, AND ALL LIARS, SHALL HAVE THEIR PART IN THE LAKE WHICH BURNETH WITH FIRE AND BRIMSTONE: WHICH IS THE SECOND DEATH." Isaiah 11:6-9; Revelation 21:3-8.

"TURN, O BACKSLIDING CHILDREN, SAITH THE LORD: FOR I AM MARRIED UNTO YOU: AND I WILL TAKE YOU ONE OF A CITY, AND TWO OF A FAMILY, AND I WILL BRING YOU TO ZION. WHY SHOULD YE BE STRICKEN ANY MORE? YE WILL REVOLT MORE AND MORE: THE WHOLE HEAD IS SICK, AND THE WHOLE HEART FAINT. WASH YOU, MAKE YOU CLEAN; PUT AWAY THE EVIL OF YOUR DOINGS FROM BEFORE MINE EYES; CEASE TO DO EVIL; LEARN TO DO WELL; SEEK JUDGMENT, RELIEVE THE OPPRESSED, JUDGE THE FATHERLESS, PLEAD FOR THE WIDOW. COME NOW, AND LET US REASON TOGETHER, SAITH THE LORD: THOUGH YOUR SINS BE AS SCARLET, THEY SHALL BE AS WHITE AS SNOW; THOUGH THEY BE RED LIKE CRIMSON, THEY SHALL BE AS WOOL. SAY UNTO THEM, AS I LIVE, SAITH THE LORD GOD, I HAVE NO PLEASURE IN THE DEATH OF THE WICKED: BUT THAT THE WICKED TURN FROM HIS WAY AND LIVE: TURN YE, TURN YE FROM YOUR EVIL WAYS; FOR WHY WILL YE DIE, O HOUSE OF ISRAEL?" Jeremiah 3:14; Isaiah 1:5, 16-18; Ezekiel 33:11.

The Holy Scriptures.

The Second Beast of Revelation 13:11-17.

CHAPTER VI

Ecumenical Movement and the Second Phase of the Antichrist – Part Two

"AND I BEHELD ANOTHER BEAST COMING UP OUT OF THE EARTH; AND HE HAD TWO HORNS LIKE A LAMB, AND HE SPAKE AS A DRAGON. AND HE EXERCISETH ALL THE POWER OF THE FIRST BEAST BEFORE HIM, AND CAUSETH THE EARTH AND THEM WHICH DWELL THEREIN TO WORSHIP THE FIRST BEAST, WHOSE DEADLY WOUND WAS HEALED." Revelation 13:11,12.

Now it's time to study who this second Beast is, who shall cause the world to worship the first Beast (Papacy), whose deadly wound was healed. To help understand who this second Beast could possibly be, let us compare it with the first Beast (PAPACY).

1. The first Beast (PAPACY) came out of the sea. Sea in prophecy is a symbol of peoples, multitudes, nations and tongues. (Revelation 17:15). The large numbers of people were in the Old World, not from the New World at that time.

2. Notice in Rev. 13:11, the SECOND BEAST CAME OUT OF THE EARTH, not from the sea. The SECOND BEAST would rise out of a place that was not heavily populated.

3. Notice the SECOND BEAST has two horns like a lamb. This lamb-like nation shall speak as a dragon (SATAN).

What nation arose in the world where it was not filled with people, multitudes, and nations and tongues? What nation arose around the ending of the prophetic time period of 1260 years which ended in 1798? Everyone should know that America was born as a nation shortly before the death blow the papacy received from France. The United States of America, we are sad to say, is the SECOND BEAST of Revelation 13:11. There is no mistake about it. The United States was founded by our forefathers on the basic theme of civil and religious freedom. The Constitution of the United States was drawn up because of the religious dictatorship that we saw earlier. Our forefathers founded our country to be free from all religious and civil dictatorships that have blackened the history of the human race and the name of Jesus Christ.

In the Amendments to the Constitution, Art. I, we read:

"CONGRESS SHALL MAKE NO LAW RESPECTING AN ESTABLISHMENT OF RELIGION, OR PROHIBITING THE FREE EXERCISE THEREOF."[1]

In Art. VI of the Constitution of the United States we read:

"NO RELIGIOUS TEST SHALL EVER BE REQUIRED AS A QUALIFICATION TO ANY OFFICE OF PUBLIC TRUST UNDER THE UNITED STATES."[2]

The Constitution of the United States was designed by our forefathers to keep religious tyranny out of this country. The Constitution forbids the government of the United States to legislate religious laws, that the worship of God should be left to each individual's conscience, not by forcing him or her as a citizen, to obey the dictates of any religious movement. The church is to be kept out of politics!

In reply to a communication from the United Baptist Churches of Virginia, in which they gave expression to the fear entertained by many that liberty of conscience was not sufficiently secured under the Constitution, George Washington wrote, Aug. 8th, 1789:

"If I could have entertained the slightest apprehension that the Constitution framed by the convention where I had the honor to preside might possibly endanger the religious rights of any Ecclesiastical society, certainly I would never have placed my signature to it; and if I could now conceive that the general government might ever be so administered as to render the liberty of conscience insecure, I beg you will be persuaded that no one would be more zealous than myself to establish effectual barriers against the horrors of spiritual tyranny and every species of religious persecution. For, you doubtless remember, I have often expressed my sentiments that any man, conducting himself as a good citizen and being accountable to God alone for his religious opinions, ought to be protected in worshipping the Deity according to the dictates of his own conscience." *History of the Baptists,* by Thomas Armitage, D.D., pp. 806,807.

George Washington, Thomas Jefferson, Patrick Henry, James Madison, Benjamin Franklin, and many more we could name who helped set up the constitution, were most expressly opposed to any legislation that

[1] See *World Book Encyclopedia,* Vol. 18, p. 141.
[2] *Ibid.,* p. 139.

would endanger the freedom to worship God according to the dictates of one's conscience. These famous men were loyal and sincere Americans, and what they attempted to do for the people of America was righteous and upright. And God has truly favored our country. But little did these men know that the Lord who knows the end from the beginning foretold that this lamb-like country would grow up to speak as the Great Red Dragon. The United States of America will become as the "FIRST BEAST" (Papal Rome). It will happen within the United States. The people themselves within America will let down the shield that protects everyone from religious oppression and will join hands with the "MOTHER OF HARLOTS" and the United States will lead the world into the worship of the great "RED DRAGON" who gave power unto the BEAST (papacy).

"AND HE DOETH GREAT WONDERS, SO THAT HE MAKETH FIRE COME DOWN FROM HEAVEN ON THE EARTH IN THE SIGHT OF MEN." Revelation 13:13.

You might say, what organization in the United States could even attempt to change the Constitution of the United States, much less bring Church and State into politics with the papacy. It will be those who call themselves Protestants, those who call themselves Pro-test-ants against the Roman Catholic Church. They will be the ones that will cause the United States to become the same image to the world as papal Rome. The United States is the "IMAGE TO THE BEAST" (papacy). Who are these Protestant Churches that will cause this? It is they who teach the great whore's doctrines that sitteth upon Seven Mountains. The two biggest doctrines of error within both the Catholic and Protestant Churches is the doctrine of the Sunday Sabbath (the day of Baal) and the doctrine of immortality of the soul, which is (Spiritism). These two doctrines will the great Red Dragon use to unite the daughters of Babylon the Great, to their Mother Church, the papacy. There will be an attempt to have one world church. Even strong Protestant churches that are most strongly opposed to the doctrines of the Roman Catholic Church will give up their doctrines that have kept them separate, and will join the papacy in these last days. The Lord has warned His people to join no confederacy (union) whether political, civil, or religious. Isaiah 8:12:

"SAY YE NOT, A CONFEDERACY, TO ALL THEM TO WHOM THIS PEOPLE SHALL SAY, A CONFEDERACY; NEITHER FEAR YE THEIR FEAR, NOR BE AFRAID."

The Lord's people are not to raise up a multitude and march against the governments:

"THOU SHALL NOT FOLLOW A MULTITUDE TO DO EVIL; NEITHER SHALT THOU SPEAK IN A CAUSE TO DECLINE AFTER MANY TO WREST JUDGMENT:" Exodus 23:2.

According to the *Encyclopedia Americana,* 1972 ed., p. 52, the Roman Catholic Church is now the largest single religious denomination in the United States. Its listed membership in 1966 was 46,246,175, or 23.7 per cent of the total population. Its hierarchy, headed in rank by seven cardinals is second in number only to that of Italy. One way that the United States will be molded into the same image as the papacy, will occur through the movement called today the "ECUMENICAL MOVEMENT." The Ecumenical Movement is actually a movement to unite the Protestants with the Catholic Church.

From Vatican II we read the following about the Roman Catholic Church's efforts to unite all Christian churches into her fold:

"Today, in many parts of the world, under the influence of the grace of the Holy Spirit, many efforts are being made in prayer, word and action to attain that fullness of unity which Jesus Christ desires. The sacred Council exhorts, therefore, all the Catholic faithful to recognize the signs of the times and to take an active and intelligent part in the work of ecumenism.

"The term 'ecumenical movement' indicates the initiatives and activities encouraged and organized according to the various needs of the Church and as opportunities offer, to promote Christian unity."[3]

There are many well known and not so well known religious writers, who have studied the prophecies in the Bible relating to the work and kingdom of the Antichrist; who have written about the papacy and the United States, as the Beast and his Image. There are also many writers in many Protestant denominations who haven't completely understood the warning from Christ about the Mark of the Beast and the Number of his Name; but are beginning to see these things foretold, come to pass before their very eyes. When the Mark of the Beast, which is the FALSE SABBATH SUNDAY is brought before the public eye, this will also cause a genuine revival and a reformation among the people of God. As stated before, no one has received the MARK OF THE BEAST today. Prophecy says that certain events must take place before this comes to pass. First, the papacy would receive its death blow at the end of the 1260 years which was predicted. Second, the deadly wound of the papacy would be healed (Revelation 13:3). Third, the SECOND BEAST (AMERICA), will cause the whole world therein to worship the first beast, whose deadly wound was healed (Revelation 13:12).

---

[3] See *Vatican II,* General Editor Austin Flannery, O.P., pp. 456,457.

All the faithful who have been observing Sunday as their day of worship, and have been worshipping God with what light they have, our Lord has accepted their worship. However, today our God is calling the faithful in ALL walks of life to restore the Seventh Day Sabbath to its rightful position. As there is a Mystery of Godliness and a Mystery of Iniquity, so is there a Seal of God, and a Mark of the Beast according to Revelation. We have seen the prophecies about the MARK of the Beast, now let's examine the prophecy of the SEAL OF GOD:

"AND AFTER THESE THINGS I SAW FOUR ANGELS STANDING ON THE FOUR CORNERS OF THE EARTH, HOLDING THE FOUR WINDS OF THE EARTH, THAT THE WIND SHOULD NOT BLOW ON THE EARTH, NOR ON THE SEA, NOR ON ANY TREE. AND I SAW ANOTHER ANGEL ASCENDING FROM THE EAST, HAVING THE SEAL OF THE LIVING GOD: AND HE CRIED WITH A LOUD VOICE TO THE FOUR ANGELS, TO WHOM IT WAS GIVEN TO HURT THE EARTH AND THE SEA, SAYING, HURT NOT THE EARTH, NEITHER THE SEA, NOR THE TREES, TILL WE HAVE SEALED THE SERVANTS OF OUR GOD IN THEIR FOREHEADS." Revelation 7:1-3.

What is the SEAL OF GOD? In ancient times as well as modern times nations, and kings used a seal to show the authority of a signature on legal documents. The seal makes the document forever binding. The SEAL OF GOD is sealed in the foreheads of the servants of the Lord to show they are the property of the Lord. Isaiah 8:16 says:

"BIND UP THE TESTIMONY, SEAL THE LAW AMONG MY DISCIPLES."

In Revelation 14:9,10, is found the warning from God to those who receive the MARK OF THE BEAST, and how they will be destroyed by fire and brimstone in the presence of the Holy angels and in the presence of the LAMB (WHO IS CHRIST); HOWEVER, IN VERSE 12 just after that, it shows who do not receive the MARK OF THE BEAST:

"HERE IS THE PATIENCE OF THE SAINTS: HERE ARE THEY THAT KEEP THE COMMANDMENTS OF GOD, AND THE FAITH OF JESUS." Revelation 14:12.

The Fourth Commandment shows God as the Creator, the World as His, and His right to Rule. No other commandment of the Ten Commandments shows Christ's authority than the Fourth Commandment. The Seventh Day Sabbath is the SEAL OF GOD. For it was God who created the Heaven and the Earth in six days and rested the Sabbath Day from all His work.

"MOREOVER ALSO I GAVE THEM MY SABBATHS, TO BE A SIGN BETWEEN ME AND THEM, THAT THEY MIGHT KNOW THAT I AM THE LORD THAT SANCTIFY THEM." Ezekiel 20:12.

When the sincere believers, in Christ, learn that the change of the Lord's Day, brought about by the Roman Catholic Church is an historical fact, and it is Antichrist, many will turn to their religious leaders and ask, "Why?" And if the Sabbath which is the Seventh Day is not restored, they will leave their denominations and join hands with those who keep the Commandments of God, and the Faith of Jesus. (Revelation 14:12). They will hear the call of Revelation 18:4,5:

"AND I HEARD ANOTHER VOICE FROM HEAVEN, SAYING, COME OUT OF HER, MY PEOPLE, THAT YE BE NOT PARTAKERS OF HER SINS, AND THAT YE RECEIVE NOT OF HER PLAGUES. FOR HER SINS HAVE REACHED UNTO HEAVEN, AND GOD HATH REMEMBERED HER INIQUITIES."

In the book, *Preparation for the Final Crisis,* the author compiled some quotations from Roman Catholic writers on the subject of the Ecumenical Movement that deserve our attention:

"If Catholicism drops . . . the dogma of her own exclusive function to mediate between God and man, . . . she certainly would be no longer Catholic. . . . He must ask the Protestant to be converted to Catholicism." Father Gustave Wiegal, S. J. Woodstock College, *An American Dialogue,* New York, Doubleday & Co., Inc., 1961, pp 218,220, Quoted in *Preparation for the Final Crisis,* by Fernando Chaij, p. 171, Pacific Press Publishing Association, Mountain View, California.

There are many, many Protestants who seem to have forgotten, or have no knowledge about the Roman Catholic Church's abominations, both past and present. There are multitudes of Protestants who even recognize the Pope as their chief shepherd over God's people. If the Roman Catholic Church was in power today as it was during the Dark Ages, it would again practice the same atrocities we saw earlier in Chapter Four. It shall come! Listen to the real hidden motives again from the mouth of the Beast of Revelation. Again, from the book, *Preparation for the Final Crisis,* we read the following:

"Protestantism is just as wrong now as it was in 1517. It is the duty incumbent on us as Catholics to 'spread the word' and make America Catholic . . . Father Isaac Hecker founded the Paulist Fathers for the express purpose of 'making America Catholic.' They are still at it and doing a fine job of it. It is the goal of every bishop, priest, and religous order in the country. No Catholic can settle, with good conscience, for a policy of appeasement, or even mere co-existence with a non-Catholic community." *Our Sunday Visitor,* July 31, 1960, — Quoted from *Preparation for the Final Crisis,* by Fernando Chaij, p. 177, 1966.

We have seen the written testimony of the Roman Catholic Church about their efforts to reunite the Protestants; but now let's explore the views of some well-known personalities within the Protestant Churches who "ARE NOT" for this Ecumenical Movement. Theodore H. Epp, who is the director of Back to the Bible broadcast, has written a booklet called, *Believers Unity, Organizational or Spiritual?* Speaking of the World Council of Churches, who employ every effort in Protestantism to unite all the churches under one roof, Theodore Epp says:

"The great emphasis on organizational unity can be illustrated from the Bible itself. In Genesis 11, there is a record of a similar movement, partly religious and partly political with an emphasis on unity. God's Word says, 'And the whole earth was of one language, and one speech. And it came to pass, as they journeyed from the east, that they found a plain in the land of Shinar; and they dwelt there. And they said one to another, Go to, let us make brick, and burn them thoroughly. And they had brick for stone, and slime had they for mortar. And they said, Go to, let us build us a city and a tower, whose top may reach unto heaven: and let us make us a name, lest we be scattered abroad upon the face of the whole earth.'

"Important background to Genesis 11 is given in verse 8-10 of the previous chapter: 'And Cush begat Nimrod: he began to be a mighty one in the earth. He was a mighty hunter before (literally against) the Lord. . . . And the beginning of his kingdom was Babel, and Erech, and Accad, and Calneh in the land of Shinar.' Nimrod's kingdom was so corrupt that in Genesis 11 there was an endeavor to establish a world state in opposition to divine rule. The people wanted to produce a unity so tightly knit that even God could not interfere.

"In Genesis 11:3 it is said that 'they had brick for stone, and slime had they for mortar.' From this we can get a significant application. Bricks are made according to one mold: thus, today's ecumenical movement wants every denomination, church and individual to conform to its mold.

"However, believers are living stones (I Peter 2:5) and do not fit into the form of the world. Also, there is much application to be drawn from the fact that at the tower of Babel they used slime instead of mortar — they used a substitute cohesive.

"The uniting force in true spiritual unity is the Holy Spirit. But He does not unite that which is made according to man's mold. Only those who have received Jesus Christ as Saviour are sealed by the Spirit and have this spiritual unity. The best that natural man can do is to attempt to produce a substitute unity. The results of the people's desire for unity are seen in Genesis 11:5-9:

" 'And the Lord came down to see the city and the tower, which the children of men builded, and the Lord said, Behold, the people is one, and they have all one language; and this they begin to do: and now nothing will be restrained from them, which they have imagined to do. Go to, let us go down, and there confound their language, that they may not understand one another's speech. So the Lord scattered them abroad from thence upon the face of all the earth.'

"God clearly saw what the people were attempting to do — bring about structural unity just as our ecumenical church is attempting to do. God knew that the result of such a unity would be defiance of Him. Therefore, He confounded their language and scattered them over the earth. Even in this God was merciful. Earlier, because man was continually evil, God brought a universal flood on the earth to destroy mankind. At Babel, He only confused their language and scattered them so they couldn't continue with their man-made united rebellion against Him." Quoted from *Believers Unity, Organizational or Spiritual?* by Theodore H. Epp, pp. 69, 70, 71. The Good News Broadcasting Association, Inc., 1971, (by permission).

Let us now take a look at some writings from another well known radio pastor who is also against any ecumenical movement to unite the Churches. Dr. Bruce Dunn of Grace Worship Hour, heard on radio, delivered a sermon in the Grace Presbyterian Church, Forrest Hill and Knoxville Ave., Peoria, Illinois, at a Sunday morning service, heard over a network of over 20 radio stations. The title of his sermon was *The Ecumenical Dream. One Big Church!* Dr. Dunn had his sermon printed in booklet form. Here is a portion of his sermon:

"Where is ecumenism going to lead us then? It's going to lead, as far as the Church is concerned, to a 'great hierarchial' religious machine in which there will be less and less religious freedom for the individual congregation and people and pastor. We have already been told that bishops are on the way and we are going to have to have bishops in the new merged church . . . the 20 million member Blake-Pike Church. Hear me, my friends, . . . I believe this with all my heart, and I think the facts back me up . . . the ecumenical movement has as its main impetus and drive, the desire to have a great monstrous ecclesiastical power-block in order to influence governments and legislate in an era of righteousness and it cannot be done.

"The ecumenical movement is not interested in the salvation of souls. They couldn't care less about the person of Christ, no matter how much pious holy talk you may seem to hear to the contrary." Quoted from *The*

Ecumenical Dream – One Big Church! by Dr. Bruce Dunn, pp. 10,11.

We totally agree with Mr. Theodore H. Epp and Dr. Bruce Dunn on their views about this almost overpowering deception. There is to be no unity of believers, that will control the world both in temporal and religious views. According to Christ Jesus, this present world does not have much time to exist. For the Lord will destroy the face of this earth. The unity of believers will not happen until Christ comes and takes us out of this world:

"THE GREAT DAY OF THE LORD IS NEAR, IT IS NEAR, AND HASTETH GREATLY, EVEN THE VOICE OF THE DAY OF THE LORD: THE MIGHTY MAN SHALL CRY THERE BITTERLY. THAT DAY IS A DAY OF WRATH, A DAY OF TROUBLE AND DISTRESS, A DAY OF WASTENESS AND DESOLATION, A DAY OF DARKNESS AND GLOOMINESS, A DAY OF CLOUDS AND THICK DARKNESS, A DAY OF THE TRUMPET AND ALARM AGAINST THE FENCED CITIES, AND AGAINST THE HIGH TOWERS." Zephaniah 1:14-16.

But those who believe there will be a kingdom of Christ in this present world, will be proclaiming "THERE WILL BE PEACE" among nations. But there will never be peace until Satan is gone. More than most who profess to be Christians will fall for this last and final effort of Satan's to keep man from receiving eternal life with the Lord. This false system of Christianity will darken the spiritual discernment of even the very elect of God if possible.

It is and has and will become more difficult to distinguish the genuine from the counterfeit, the real from the false, the Holy from the unholy. It was foretold 600 years before Christ that in the last days "many shall run to and fro, and knowledge shall be increased." Daniel 12:4. Even though we have reached the moon, man is still way behind the times. For a man who called himself Jesus over 1900 years ago traveled beyond the stars to God's throne and He didn't use a rocket ship in which to travel.

Now, it's time to take a look within the governing powers of the United States, and see how our country is fulfilling prophecy as it was foretold. As stated earlier, it will be the powers within the United States that will make it turn into a religious dictatorship. This lamb-like country will grow up and speak as a dragon. He who understands divine language will understand:

"AND HE EXERCISETH ALL THE POWER OF THE FIRST BEAST BEFORE HIM, (papacy) AND CAUSETH THE EARTH AND THEM WHICH DWELL THEREIN TO WORSHIP THE FIRST BEAST, WHOSE DEADLY WOUND WAS HEALED." Revelation 13:12.

When the pope was dethroned by the French, in 1798, this marked the papacy's loss of temporal power in the world. Thereafter the popes shut themselves up as prisoners in the Vatican until the signing of the concordat with Italy in 1929, which restored "his dominion" over the Vatican City, a small section of the city of Rome.[1] This date marks the time that the apostle John foretold the deadly wound of the Beast would be healed. From 1929, until our present day, the papacy has regained much of her influence throughout the world.[2] A good example of this was shown during Pope John Paul's visit to America.

"AND HE CAUSETH ALL, BOTH SMALL AND GREAT, RICH AND POOR, FREE AND BOND, TO RECEIVE A MARK IN THEIR RIGHT HAND, OR IN THEIR FOREHEADS: AND THAT NO MAN MIGHT BUY OR SELL, SAVE HE THAT HAD THE MARK, OR THE NAME OF THE BEAST, OR THE NUMBER OF HIS NAME." Revelation 13:16,17.

If the reader will notice carefully in Revelation 13:11-17, it is the "SECOND BEAST" (AMERICA) who causes both small and great, rich or poor to receive the MARK OF THE BEAST, or the number of his name. To help the reader see how close we are to Sunday legislation, and a confederacy with the Vatican, let us investigate how the office of the Presidency could be nothing less than a dictatorship. Liberty Lobby, composed of dedicated Americans, is an organization dedicated to American freedom. They sent a pamphlet from which we quote the following:

"The Federal Register is probably the most powerful document printed in the United States today. What appears in its columns as notification of official Presidential actions assumes the power of law. No congressional authorization is required. There is no review by the judiciary. Executive orders are laws made by one man — The President.

"Through certain Executive Orders it would be possible for one man to completely ignore the Constitution, the authority of Congress, and the will of the people. Through implementation of these Executive Orders a complete dictatorship can be imposed.

"There are already such Executive Orders. Eleven of the more significant of these existing Executive Orders were signed in February and September of 1962 by the late President Kennedy.

"At first glance, these orders seem to be steps needed to enable the United States to prepare for and strike back in the event of a nuclear attack. The propaganda surrounding them implies this. Unfortunately, this is not the whole truth."

---

[1] See *Daniel and the Revelation*, by Uriah Smith, pp. 146,147.
[2] See *Italy*, by Herbert Kubly, p. 52.

A communication on February 14, 1962, between David Bell, Director of the Bureau of the Budget and the then President John Kennedy, states:

"This need (for Executive Orders establishing dictatorial powers — Ed.) is underscored by the fact that emergency planning is needed with respect to (a) limited war situation (involving concern with such matters as economic stabilization, manpower and other major programs supporting military action.) . . ." Bell went on to list nuclear attack and post attack recovery as two other reasons for the need.

"The head of the Office of Emergency Planning states that the approval of Congress would be necessary to put these Orders into effect."

But the fact is, Executive Orders are never approved by Congress! They have the "force of the law" WITHOUT legislation!

"The president could declare a 'national emergency' on his own and then invoke these orders!

"LIBERTY LOBBY suggests that all Americans acquaint themselves with these eleven Executive Orders which establish the machinery to authorize the President and his advisors to take control of every significant factor of the private sector of our society.

"Executive Order No. 11051 details responsibilities of the Office of Emergency Planning and gives authorization to put all other Executive Orders into effect in times of increased international tension or economic or financial crisis.

"Executive Order No. 10995 provides for a take-over of communications media.

"Executive Order No. 10997 provides for a take-over of all electrical power, petroleum, gas fuels and minerals.

"Executive Order No. 10998 provides for a take-over of all food resources and farms.

"Executive Order No. 10999 provides for a take-over of all modes of transportation and control of highways, seaports, etc.

"Executive Order No. 11000 provides for mobilization of all civilians into work brigades under government supervision.

"Executive Order No. 11001 provides for government take-over of all health, education and welfare functions.

"Executive Order 11002 designates Postmaster General to operate a National registration of all persons.

"Executive Order No. 11003 provides for the government to take over airports and aircraft.

"Executive Order No. 11004 provides for the Housing and Finance Authority to RELOCATE COMMUNITIES, BUILD NEW HOUSING

WITH PUBLIC FUNDS, DESIGNATE AREAS TO BE ABANDONED AS UNSAFE, AND ESTABLISH NEW LOCATIONS FOR POPULATIONS.

"Executive Order No. 11005 provides for the government to take-over railroads, inland waterways and public storage facilities." Compiled by — Liberty Lobby, 300 Independence Ave., S.E., Washington, D.C.

Most Americans have not seen or been made aware of how their freedom has been taken away. Like all Satanic deceptions in the past, they did not come all at once, but crept in behind the public eye. The United States will become like the Beast before it. Behold, it's at the doors!

Before we close, we want to show you some writings from another religious writer who was seen earlier in our book, and many believed her to be inspired by God. Her book, *Desire of Ages,* is the most read religious book about Christ in the Library of Congress in Washington, D.C., and she wrote another multimillion seller called, *The Great Controversy,* and several other Bible related books. We will examine her statements about The Mark of the Beast, The Seal of God, Sunday legislation, and Satan appearing as Christ in the flesh in the last generation. Here from *Testimonies,* Vol. 8, p. 117, we read the following:

"The Sign, or Seal, of God is revealed in the observance of the Seventh Day Sabbath, the Lord's memorial of creation. 'The Lord spake unto Moses, saying, Speak thou also unto the children of Israel, saying, Verily my Sabbaths ye shall keep: for it is a sign between me and you throughout your generations; that ye may know that I am the Lord that doth sanctify you.' Exodus 31:12,13. Here the Sabbath is clearly designated as a Sign between God and His people."

From *Testimonies Treasures,* Vol. 3, p. 232, we read:

"The Mark of the Beast is the opposite of this — the observance of the first day of the week. The Mark distinguishes those who acknowledge the supremacy of the papal authority from those who acknowledge the authority of God."

From *The Great Controversy,* by Ellen G. White, pp. 530,531:

"The Sabbath will be the great test of loyalty, for it is the point of truth especially controverted. When the final test shall be brought to bear upon men, then the line of distinction will be drawn between those who serve God and those who serve Him not. While the observance of the false Sabbath in compliance with the law of the state, contrary to the fourth commandment, will be an avowal of allegiance to a power that is in opposition to God, the keeping of the true Sabbath, in obedience to God's law, is an evidence of loyalty to the Creator. While one class, by accepting the sign of submission to earthly powers, receive the Mark of the Beast, the other, choosing the token of allegiance of Divine Authority, receive the Seal of God."

Again, from *The Great Controversy,* pp. 588,589 we read:

"The line of distinction between professed Christians and the ungodly is now hardly distinguishable. Church members love what the world loves and are ready to join with them, and Satan determines to unite them in one body and thus strengthen his cause by sweeping all into the ranks of spiritualism. Papists who boast of miracles as a certain sign of the true church, will be readily deceived by this wonder-working power; and Protestants, having cast away the shield of truth, will also be deluded. Papists, Protestants, and worldlings will alike accept the form of Godliness without the power, and they will see in this union a grand movement for the conversion of the world and the ushering in of the long expected millennium.

"Through spiritualism, Satan appears as a benefactor of the race, healing the diseases of the people, and professing to present a new and more exalted system of religious faith; But at the same time he works as a destroyer. His temptations are leading multitudes to ruin. Intemperance dethrones reason; sensual indulgence, strife, and bloodshed follow. Satan delights in war, for it excites its victims steeped in vice and blood. It is the object to incite the nations to war against one another, for he can thus divert the minds of the people from the work of preparation to stand in the day of God."

Speaking about the SECOND BEAST of Revelation 13 in *The Great Controversy,* pp. 578,579 we read:

"The prophecy of Revelation 13 declares that the power represented by the beast with lamblike horns shall cause the earth and them which dwell therein to worship the papacy — there symbolized by the beast like unto a leopard. The beast with two horns is also to say to them that dwell on the earth, that they should make an image to the beast; and, furthermore, it is to command all, both small and great, rich and poor, free and bond, to receive the mark of the beast. Revelation 13:11-16. It has been shown that the United States is the power represented by the beast with lamblike horns, and that this prophecy will be fulfilled when the United States shall enforce Sunday observance, which Rome claims as the special acknowledgement of her supremacy."

From a Ellen G. White publication she and her husband published (*Review and Herald* May 2, 1893), we read:

"The people of the United States have been a favored people; but when they restrict religious liberty, surrender Protestantism and give countenance to popery, the measure of their guilt will be full, and National apostasy will be National ruin."

Again from the pages of *The Great Controversy,* p. 588, we read: "Through two great errors, the immortality of the soul and Sunday sacredness, Satan will bring the people under his deceptions. While the former lays the foundation of spiritualism, the latter creates a bond of sympathy with Rome. The Protestants of the United States will be foremost in stretching their hands across the gulf to grasp the hand of Spiritualism. They will reach over the abyss to clasp hands with the Roman power; and under the influence of this threefold union, this country will follow in the steps of Rome in trampling on the rights of conscience." *The Great Controversy,* by Ellen G. White, Pacific Press Association, Mountain View California, (by permission of the E. G. White Estate).

This three fold union to unite the world in one world-wide apostasy, Ellen White referred to, is in Revelation 16:12-13:

"AND THE SIXTH ANGEL POURED OUT HIS VIAL UPON THE GREAT RIVER EUPHRATES; AND THE WATER THEREOF WAS DRIED UP, THAT THE WAY OF THE KINGS OF THE EAST MIGHT BE PREPARED. AND I SAW THREE UNCLEAN SPIRITS LIKE FROGS COME OUT OF THE MOUTH OF THE DRAGON, AND OUT OF THE 'MOUTH' OF THE BEAST, AND OUT OF THE 'MOUTH' OF THE FALSE PROPHET."

1. The Dragon — Satanic Power (Spiritualism working miracles).
2. The Beast — The promotion of Popery throughout the world.
3. The False Prophet — The efforts of the Protestants to unite with the papacy through the Ecumenical Movement.

When Satan has spread Spiritualism throughout the world, that imitates the real gifts of the Spirit (I Corinthians 12:1-10), the papacy is again in control of both temporal and spiritual things, and when the papacy's False Sabbath (Sunday) has been exalted by the Protestants of the United States, then, Satan will come as Christ Himself.

Once more, under the inspiration of the Holy Spirit, the late Ellen G. White writes the following in *The Great Controversy,* pp. 547,548:

"As the crowning act in the great drama of deception, Satan himself will personate Christ. The church has long professed to look to the Saviour's Advent as the consummation of her hopes. Now the great deceiver will make it appear that Christ has come. In different parts of the earth, Satan will manifest himself among men as a majestic being of dazzling brightness, resembling the description of the Son of God given by John in Revelation 1:13-15. The glory that surrounds him is unsurpassed by anything that mortal eyes have yet beheld. The shout of triumph rings out upon the air: Christ Has Come! Christ Has Come! The people prostrate themselves in adoration before him while he lifts up his hands and pronounces a blessing upon them, as Christ blessed His disciples when He was upon the earth. His voice is soft and subdued, yet full of melody. In gentle, compassionate tones he presents some of the same gracious heavenly truths which the Saviour uttered. He heals the diseases of the people, and then, in his assumed character of Christ, he claims to have changed the Sabbath to Sunday, and commands all to hallow the day which he has blessed. He declares that those who persist in keeping holy the Seventh Day are blaspheming his name by refusing to listen to his angels sent to them with light and truth. This is the strong, almost overmastering delusion."

However, Ellen White says also, in her book, *The Great Controversy,* on p. 548:

"But the people of God will not be misled. The teachings of this false Christ are not in accordance with the Scriptures. His blessing is pronounced upon the worshippers of the beast and his image, the very class upon whom the Bible declares that God's unmingled wrath shall be poured out. . . . Only those who have been diligent students of the Scriptures and who have received the love of the truth will be shielded from the powerful delusion that takes the world captive." *The Great Controversy,* by Ellen G. White, Pacific Press Publishing Association, Mountain View, California, (by permission of the E. G. White Estate).

Satan will come as Christ. Bible scholars from the earliest Christian churches throughout the world have warned their members about Satan's crowning deception.

However, the Crowning Advent on man's BEHALF will come shortly afterwards. Jesus the REAL KING OF KINGS AND LORD OF LORDS will be seen in the Heavens:

"AND HE SHALL SEND HIS ANGELS WITH A GREAT SOUND OF A TRUMPET, AND THEY SHALL GATHER TOGETHER HIS ELECT FROM THE FOUR WINDS, FROM ONE END OF HEAVEN TO THE OTHER. BUT OF THAT DAY AND HOUR KNOWETH NO MAN, NO, NOT THE ANGELS OF HEAVEN, BUT MY FATHER ONLY. WATCH YE THEREFORE, AND PRAY ALWAYS, THAT YE MAY BE ACCOUNTED WORTHY TO ESCAPE ALL THESE THINGS THAT SHALL COME TO PASS, AND TO STAND BEFORE THE SON OF MAN." Matthew 24:31, 36; Luke 21:36.

Before We Close . . .

. . . We thought the following current events should be brought to the reader's attention. The most troublesome time ever in the Christian Era is at the door. Satan will use Christianity to destroy many. Using those who profess Christ as their Saviour, but who error greatly in the Doctrines of the Bible, Satan will lead the ignorant to their doom.

Protestant America was a haven for Bible believing people during part of the 1260 years that the papacy was foretold to cast the truth to the ground. Many Bible believing people escaped with their lives from the sword of the papal inquisitors by coming to the wilderness of a land that was to become a great country. The persecuting power of the Devil, through the papacy, and God's people fleeing to America was foretold almost 2,000 years ago in Revelation 12:14:

"AND TO THE WOMAN WERE GIVEN TWO WINGS OF A GREAT EAGLE, THAT SHE MIGHT FLY INTO THE WILDERNESS, INTO HER PLACE, WHERE SHE IS NOURISHED FOR A TIME, AND TIMES, AND HALF A TIME, FROM THE FACE OF THE SERPENT."

The United States has been greatly blessed because of its civil liberties and religious freedoms, to worship God according to one's conscience. What right would the leader of the Moslems in Iran have to force through international legislation, if it were possible, a law forcing all Christians and Jews to observe FRIDAY (The Moslem Sabbath), as a day of rest? The people of America wouldn't stand for it! Right? Then what right does a Sunday keeping Christian have to force through legislation Sunday BLUE LAWS forcing Sunday observance on Jews and Sabbath keeping Christians, who do not sanction the papal Sabbath, Sunday? NONE! Although this nation was set up to be free from certain religious groups forcing their religious opinions on others it is foretold that this lamblike country will eventually enforce Sunday observance. As the sure word of prophecy from the Bible will come to pass, so will the United States become like the FIRST BEAST (PAPACY), Revelation 13:11,12, by taking away the rights of Americans to worship God according to their own dictates.

One group in America, dedicated to making the papal Sabbath, (SUNDAY), by law sacred, with no buying or selling in the stores on Sunday, is the THE LORD'S DAY ALLIANCE. This Christian group is made up from both Catholic and Protestant denominations. Following are Churches represented on the board of managers of this organization:

African Methodist Episcopal Zion
American Baptist Convention
Assemblies of God
Associate Reformed Presbyterian Church
Christian Reformed Church
Church of God (Cleveland)
Evangelical Congregational Church
Lutheran Church
Pentecostal Holiness Church
Presbyterian Church in U.S.
Protestant Episcopal Church
Reformed Church in America
Reformed Episcopal Church
Roman Catholic Church
Southern Baptist Convention
United Brethren in Christ
United Methodist Church
United Presbyterian Church in the United States

The following organizations are affiliated with The Lord's Day Alliance:

Lord's Day League of New England
Georgia Save Sunday Association
Christian Civic League of Maine
Lord's Day Alliance of New Jersey
Lord's Day Alliance of Pennsylvania
Lord's Day Alliance of Lawrenceville, Georgia

In a magazine of The Lord's Day Alliance can be found a startling message showing readers, who have ears to hear and eyes to see, that the end of this present evil world is nearer than what we might think!

For sure, the Sunday Blue Laws will soon be enforced and become the Mark of the Beast. Here from, *Sunday—The Magazine For The Lord's Day,* we read the following from the article CHRISTIAN DEFENSE OF BLUE LAWS:

"On Sunday, October 1, the new Connecticut Sabbath closing law went into effect. For the first time since 1976, we have in operation an effective legislation that closes supermarkets and large department stores on one day a week.

"This new law is modeled upon the Massachusetts law, already tested and found constitutional. This new law was enacted by our legislature and signed by our Governor only after many employees and employee unions asked for one day a week for family unity and rest, and after more than 50,000 Connecticut Church-going people petitioned the legislature for relief from the incessant and competitive commercialism of our society and the desecration of Sunday.

"The saving of energy should be considerable. It will not be necessary to fully heat and cool the gigantic stores on one day of the week. Empty parking lots will mean more people staying home and a saving of gasoline." *Sunday—The Magazine For The Lord's Day,* p. 10, April-June, 1979, James P. Wesberry, Editor.

To show the readers how dangerous these Blue Laws will become for those who keep the Bible Sabbath (Seventh Day), here are some more startling words from the same issue of *Sunday—The Magazine For The Lord's Day,* from the article, POLICE NOTING VIOLATIONS OF BLUE LAW:

"Cheshire police are cracking down on suspected violators of Connecticut's new blue law, which became effective Sunday.

"Reports of 'suspected violation' were made out against IGA and Everybody's markets on Sunday by local police under direction of the State's Attorney. The new law says that any store with more than 5,000 square feet of display area or employing more than five people on duty at one time cannot remain open on Sunday. Such stores can stay open Sunday only if they close on some other day of the week. Police Lt. George Spyrie said the old blue laws had been challenged and ruled constitutional by a Connecticut Superior Court Judge because of vagueness. On June 6 a new blue law was enacted and had now become effective. it will be up to the Prosecutor's office to decide what to do with violators, Lt. Spyrie said." *The Cheshire Herald,* October 5th, 1978, Quoted in, *Sunday—The Magazine For The Lord's Day,* p. 17, April-June, 1979, James P. Wesberry, Editor.

These Sunday Blue Laws are only just a shadow of the persecution by professing Christians on those who do not recognize Sunday, the Day of Baal, as a sacred day. Just as Baal worship was not completely accepted all at once, by the entire nation of Israel in days of Old, but crept into the pure worship of God, little by little, so will Sunday Blue Laws creep in through the closed doors of the legislative halls throughout the United States. When religious groups gain power to use the state to force Church Doctrines as the Roman Catholic Church did in the past, then shall the United States Government be molded into the same IMAGE of that of the Roman Catholic Church. Combining Church with State to force religious obedience is from the throne of Satan himself. This is why multitudes of Christians were murdered in the name of Jesus, and why multitudes fled from Europe to come to America during the 15th, 16th, and 17th centuries. Bigotry became so terrible that all that was needed to suffer the pain of death, was just to be accused of heresy against the religious dictatorship of the Roman Catholic Church. Now, today, before our very eyes, this same false religious spirit has taken root in Protestantism.

When Sunday Blue Laws are put into force nation wide, then shall the United States fulfill what it was predicted to do in the Last Days: "AND HE SPAKE AS A DRAGON (SATAN). AND HE EXERCISETH ALL THE POWER OF THE FIRST BEAST (PAPACY) BEFORE HIM, AND CAUSETH THE EARTH AND THEM WHICH DWELL THEREIN TO WORSHIP THE FIRST BEAST (PAPACY), WHOSE DEADLY WOUND WAS HEALED." Revelation 13:11(Last Part),12.

We, who compiled this book, do humbly appeal to all religious groups who profess Jesus Christ to be God manifested in the flesh (I Timothy 3:16), who created the Heavens and the Earth (Genesis 1:1; John 1:1-3, 14; Ephesians 3:9; Colossians 1:3-17; Hebrews 1:1-2), but have not realized that it was God who said: "BUT THE SEVENTH DAY IS THE SABBATH OF THE LORD THY GOD," Exodus 20:10, to examine their position on enforcing Sunday Blue Laws, according to the Word of God.

Thirty-four years in the making! Perhaps the most up-to-date and fully-documented study within seven volumes about the three-fold union of the secret societies of the Illuminati, the Papacy, and the apostate Protestants that you have ever read in your entire life! Take a historical and prophetical journey through the ages from 2200 B.C. up to the year A.D. 2005 and view, with your own astonished eyes, the real and true-to-life battle between the forces of good and the forces of evil. Truly see for yourself how this terrible struggle is about to reach its climax!

$11.00

$11.00

$11.00

$12.00

$12.00

$10.00

(still under construction)

$12.00

TO ORDER, PLEASE CALL OUR TOLL-FREE NUMBER

1-866-899-1877

SUNDAY-THURSDAY 9-9
PLUS POSTAGE & HANDLING

Please allow 3 to 6 weeks delivery

Also visit our website

www.18441888.com

Sim & Sons' Publishing House
10624 S. Eastern Avenue
Suite A, #177
Henderson, NV 89052

INDEX